CAN DEMOCRACY SURVIVE IN WESTERN EUROPE?

James N. Cortada and
James W. Cortada

Westport, Connecticut

London

Library of Congress Cataloging-in-Publication Data

Cortada, James N.
    Can democracy survive in Western Europe? / James N. Cortada and
James W. Cortada.
        p.   cm.
    Includes bibliographical references and index.
    ISBN 0–275–95680–6 (alk. paper)
    1. Democracy—Europe, Western—History.   2. Democracy—Europe,
Western.   I. Cortada, James W.   II. Title.
JN94.A91C67   1996
321.8′094—dc20   96–2803

British Library Cataloguing in Publication Data is available.

Library of Congress Catalog Card Number: 96–2803
ISBN: 0–275–95680–6

First published in 1996

Praeger Publishers, 88 Post Road West, Westport, CT 06881
An imprint of Greenwood Publishing Group, Inc.

Printed in the United States of America

The paper used in this book complies with the
Permanent Paper Standard issued by the National
Information Standards Organization (Z39.48–1984).

10 9 8 7 6 5 4 3 2 1

To
the youngest in our family, who will decide
if democracy will continue.
Beth, Julia, and Allison

Contents

Figures and Tables

FIGURES

TABLES

Preface

We live in an age of democracy, or so it would seem. Throughout the Western world, the media salutes every democracy born out of some dictatorial relic. The Franco regime in Spain, which ended in 1975, is cited as the current democratic miracle, while U.S. government officials push hard to see democracy come to Haiti and elsewhere in the New World. Third World governments hold elections and claim they are moving toward democracy, while the republics of the ex-Soviet Union do the same. Even parts of war-torn Yugoslavia use the ballot box to determine if the United Nations should interfere in the local civil war.

That there has been an enormous expansion of governments which mimic the features of democracy there can be no doubt. Clearly, representational governments have enjoyed a Golden Age in the late twentieth century. But we also know, as we enter the twenty-first century, that ours was only one of twenty centuries; that the previous nineteen were rarely marked by democratic behavior. We know that the long arm of history rests heavily on the shoulders of all peoples.

We have only to look around us to realize how profound the role of history is on today's events. The warfare in Bosnia is a classic example of long-standing historical issues flaring up. Basque and Catalan regionalism in Spain is another. In Ireland, resentment of the British has a 700-year history. Ethnic rivalries, repressed for some seventy-five years during the dominance of communist rule in Eastern Europe, instantly manifested themselves with the demise of the Soviet Union. In Italy, where the fifty-fifth government since World War II was installed in April 1996, the new Prime Minister, Romano Prodi, had to call for calm, saying that his fellow citizens were looking for political "sympathy." In short, historical forces are real and inescapable. To ignore them is to misread how societies approach such issues as family structure and political behavior.

That is exactly what we have done, particularly in the West and in the United States. Political scientists, foreign-policy makers, and especially politicians have looked to the experiences of their lives and drawn conclusions governing their actions. The United States, for example, considers the promotion and expansion of democracies around the world to be central to its foreign policy, regardless of historical traditions that may or may not facilitate the process. Political scientists frequently write about democracy's features based only on late twentieth-century conditions.

Sociologists and cultural anthropologists have studied human behavior with a greater sense of historical perspective than political scientists because of the role of tradition. Attitudes of families toward basic cultural issues, such as the authority of the father, the role of children, and the approach toward public authority, have been better studied. But we believe there is a link missing between the study of familial patterns of behavior and attitudes toward authority on the one hand and their relationship to a nation's political behavior on the other. The ancient Greeks spoke about public and private lives; we believe, like them, that there is a connection between the two. We believe political scientists need to build on the good work they have done in the later decades of this century, along with the tools developed by sociologists and cultural anthropologists in the same period of time, to examine the possibilities of democracy through a longer historical perspective. In short, we need to understand *handed-down values* as they relate to political attitudes and patterns of behavior if we are to appreciate what might be possible in the decades to come.

The government of the United States is attempting to foster democracy for everyone. It would be nice to know if (1) that is realistic and (2) what can be done to make such a policy successful. The questions are the same for a European, Asian, or Latin American society determining whether democracy makes sense or struggling with how to bring about a peaceful evolution toward democracy.

Because democracy and its attendant patterns of representative government first emerged in Europe, we believe a brief look at the historical cases it presents gives us insight about the future possibilites for democracy. We will argue that a better appreciation of democracy's possibilities can be identified by looking at the political and historical baggage of a nation, coupled with an appreciation of how individuals and families view authority. While this project, if done properly, would require many books, our's is intended to suggest lines of inquiry. Because the source of much democratic behavior and inspiration for others seeking representative government institutions lies in a handful of European states, we have chosen to look at these. Specifically, we comment briefly on Great Britain, then spend more time looking at the cases of Germany, France, Italy, and, most extensively, Spain. With these five, you have the makings of a deep appreciation for the nature and future of European democratic institutions.

We have reached several tentative conclusions, however, that we believe serve as a challenge to the reader, public officials, and academicians.

First, in the case of Europe, there are several historical patterns at work which make it impossible to generalize about the future of democracy across the continent. Interestingly enough, for example, those portions of Europe that were under Roman rule for many centuries seem to have enormous difficulty in applying democratic principles. Those that did not experience significant Roman rule had a different history.

Second, the connection between private and public life is significant, and the influence of familial attitudes are linked to public attitudes. However, the research done by scholars to validate this point is crude at best. A great deal of work is yet required on this topic.

Third, we believe that the historical perspective presented in this book provides a method for policy makers in Europe and in the United States to formulate policies toward the expansion of democratic principles. Specifically, two issues are of concern: how to implement democratic institutions in the first place, and then how to sustain and strengthen them.

Fourth, while the arguments in this book will lead the reader to conclude that we think many parts of Europe cannot realistically expect to have thriving democracies for a long time, we are not convinced that any people are absolute prisoners of history. Representational forms of government have increased in number since the eighteenth century and will no doubt continue to function into the next. However, we believe that democracy is not an inevitable evolution in a nation's political destiny. It will come slowly, if at all, over time and with great effort, because it must fight upstream against many historical traditions running contrary to it.

Fifth, we believe culture has a profound influence on political behavior. If, for example, a country recognized for a thriving democracy—such as the United States—were to fill up quickly with immigrants from some society that cherishes authoritarian rule within the family, democracy could be at risk. After all, U.S. democratic behavior is rooted in Anglo-Saxon traditions which continue to dominate North American culture. But what would happen if a third of the nation were first- and second-generation Latin Americans who came from an area of the world that has a long-standing liberal intellectual heritage and a history of unstable and dictatorial governments? Life carries no guarantees, and historical experience would suggest that major changes in culture influence political behavior. Looked at another way, if a culture does not change profoundly, and is currently characterized by unstable democratic experiences (such as in the Balkans, Eastern Europe, Mediterranean states, and Central Europe), what does this say for the future of that culture? The secret may lie in handed-down values, which come primarily out of the home, but also from what happens in schools. Home life may be, to use a biological analogy, the political gene that, when collected together for a whole nation, sets the political life on a path of action.

Our short book cannot definitively answer all the questions or lay out a guaranteed-to-succeed cookbook solution to insure the continued expansion of democratic forms of government. But if democracy cannot succeed in Europe, how can anyone realistically expect it to thrive in Africa, Asia, or Latin America? That is why looking at the European experience is so instructive.

Chapter 1 lays out the argument about the influence of history on modern political behavior. It is short, and leaves out too much material and many centuries, but does so to make the point that history and political science must go hand-in-hand if we are to appreciate the possibilities of democracy. Chapters 2 and 3 look at two general models of historically different patterns of behavior in Western Europe to further suggest the historical features influencing modern politics.

In Chapter 4, we suggest the role of familial mores on modern political behavior in Europe, and address the case of recent experiences in Germany. Our objective is to illustrate how politics and sociological issues are linked and suggest some of the questions that must be answered. Chapter 5 expands on the concept that individualism, specific historical traditions, and modern events influence the pattern of democratic behavior. This is done by examining recent events in Italy and France. Contemporary events and circumstances also have their role to play, ranging from European-wide communications, brought about by radio, television, and computers, to specific events designed to link disparate heritages together, such as the Common Market.

Chapters 6 and 7 focus on what is currently considered by many as the most important contemporary positive experience with democracy: Spain's transition from authoritarian to democratic government. We agree that it is a very important case and therefore devote two chapters to the subject, exploring in greater detail the application of our views introduced in earlier chapters. In these two chapters, we recognize that two sets of parallel activities were going on: one based on cultural and societal attitudes, the other on more traditional issues concerning contemporary political life.

Chapters 8 and 9 comment on the future of democracy, how it is created and sustained, and suggest specific actions that European and American policy makers can take. Because we, on purpose, kept the book short, we encourage the reader to go through the first seven chapters before jumping to the punch line in Chapters 8 and 9.

This book evolved slowly and painfully over a decade. Careful discussions with numerous political scientists, historians, and cultural anthropologists made it certain that we were raising many of the right questions. What started out as an intellectual exercise in the form of an article grew into this book. One author, James W. Cortada, was trained as a European historian and felt the profound influence of history on events as simple as how today's cities are laid out, how government regulations and laws are administered, and what history has been like in the past century. He has lived in Italy and Spain. The other, James N. Cortada, was an American diplomat who spent close to thirty years living in Europe, the Caribbean, and the Middle East, and was exposed in depth to many cultures and the long arm of history at work. Both came to the conclusion that Roman aqueducts in southern Spain were not just relics of the past but metaphors for society's behavior; that ethnic cleansing in the Balkans in the 1990s was a return to local normalcy; that the French, as the great French historian Fernand Braudel would admit, were French; that the British were English, and thus different than the Italians, the Russians, or the Spanish. We have lived in the United States, Italy, Spain, Cuba, and several Arab countries, and visited extensively the Caribbean, Central America, France, Great Britain, and other parts of Europe. In an earlier book, *U.S. Foreign Policy in the Caribbean, Cuba, and Central America*, we had to struggle with the issue of how to expand democratic institutions throughout the Caribbean. We came to many of the conclusions argued in this book as much from personal experience and observations as from reliance on what political scientists and historians have had to say.

A number of individuals have been of important help to us as we worked our way through the questions we raised. Our challenge was to determine how to apply a variety of traditional disciplines, bringing them all together in a manner in which we could begin determining what made sense for the years to come; specifically, to begin answering the question which is the title of our book. Financial expert James McConnell and his wife, anthropologist Mary McConnell, stressed the world economy as an important factor in the picture and political sociology as a key ingredient. Anthropologist Karla Baer reviewed our comments on Germany and made many suggestions for improvements. Her husband, industrialist Albert Baer, during our moments of doubt about this project, urged us to complete it. Howard Sollenberger, former director of the U.S. Department of State's Foreign Service Institute (now retired), clarified the role of the Institute in holding seminars in cultural anthropology in the late 1940s which were attended by James N. Cortada. The late John Bowling, historian and political scientist at Troy State University, helped us conceptualize the project in the beginning. To insure our historical conclusions were on target, we are grateful for the advice given to us by Dr. Juan Vernet, professor emeritus of the University of Barcelona, and Dr. Stanley G. Payne of the University of Wisconsin. Our political science themes concerning democracy were reviewed by professor Giovanni Sartori of Columbia University, who endorsed our concepts concerning handed-down values and our observation that states, not "the people," create democratic institutions.

The libraries of the University of Virginia, the University of Wisconsin at Madison, and the University of Wisconsin at Milwaukee were homes for our research; their librarians were helpful and very responsive. In addition to access to published books, their collections of publications from the United Nations and European newspapers proved essential to our work, as did their strong collections on early European history.

We are particularly grateful to our publisher for showing faith in the book and its message, and to the staff for moving our manuscript through the production process.

The patience of our family is our greatest debt of gratitude, because all branches of the family tolerated our musings over the subject of democracy and made it possible for us to spend a decade working on this book. We dedicate this book to the youngest members of our family who, ultimately, as part of their generation, will play out the next chapters in the story of democracy.

—1—

The Influence of History and Handed-Down Values on Political Behavior

Fellow citizens, we cannot escape history.

—Abraham Lincoln

This chapter introduces our central ideas concerning political dispositions, the role of Romanization and democracy, the effects of democracy on U.S. foreign policy in Europe, and the importance of historical experience and handed-down values.

Measurements of economic, sociological, and political evolution are important in assessing the political future of any nation. Attitudinal factors are also crucial elements in any such analysis. Without looking at a variety of such approaches, it becomes anyone's guess how well democracy will do in Western Europe; everyone then becomes an expert, and with as much success as those informed individuals who did not forecast correctly the demise of the Soviet Union, the reunification of Germany under a democratic banner, the surge in democracy throughout the Iberian peninsula, or the political chaos in the Balkans. Yet, recent work by many scholars in connection with political developments in Europe more than reflect—indeed, they suggest—that acute awareness of sociopsychological considerations represents a fruitful line of research.[1] However, people are not only creatures of habit, they are also products of a past which conditions greatly their political behavior and future. Historians have documented many social and political events; however, linking their work to that of political scientists, cultural anthropologists, and sociologists makes good sense.

The notion that current political behavior has grown out of previous experience is a perspective that political scientists and politicians can use in determining possible changes in political structures. More specifically, we want to know which societies in Europe and elsewhere can be expected to nurture democratic political systems and which, realistically, cannot. Such an approach could, for instance, help one determine if any hope is warranted for democracy in the ex-Soviet Union. In that specific case, we wonder about the prospects, since historical preconditions for a smooth transition to representative institutions do not exist. You cannot buy a box of instant democracy, add good intentions, stir, and serve to an eager nation; it just does not work that way. On the other hand, those with a Scandinavian heritage have a greater probability of implementing democratic institutions and sustaining them for long periods of time.

A brief look at several contrasting sets of early historical experiences illustrates the kinds of possible analysis. While areas of Western Europe are presented as a collective case study, we did not review all regions, since those studied illustrate key preconditions worthy of further study by others interested in democratic processes. In particular, fruitful work is needed on Portugal, some of whose historical conditions are sufficiently different from Spain's, to warrant caution about using the Spanish experience as an analogy; Greece, whose experience does not lend itself to some Mediterranean model of generalizations; and there is, of course, all of vast Central and Balkan Europe to explore.

But, first, some basic definitions of what we mean by democratic institutions are in order. In any Western democratic political system, it must be possible to change elected wielders of power at all levels through a peaceful process and within a widely recognized and accepted framework. Whether a nation's political structure reflects monarchical (e.g., British and Spanish) or republican (e.g., Italian and French) characteristics is basically irrelevant. The willingness of contenders for power, via the electoral process, to accept majority responsibilities, but with appropriate respect for a losing minority which could in the next elections become a majority, is essential for the functioning of a democratic process. Whether through the election of representatives in large-scale democracies, or by direct vote for governing councils in ministates (e.g., Andorra), the principle is the same.

Furthermore, the process must be functional over many generations of time, not for sporadic periods, as has frequently been the case in many parts of the world over the past century. It is the quality of continuous use of elected leaders that forms the basic definition of democratic institutions. This notion is applied to the analysis of various cases in this book.

To assess possibilities, much work has been done in the post–World War II period by political scientists, sociologists, psychologists, historians, and economists—especially from the United States—that can be used to find comparisons and concepts, and for analyzing contemporary political cultures and their relation to liberal democracy.[2] Building on that body of research, our approach will draw together several perspectives which we believe are essential to any analysis of the prospects of democracy. First, we propose that historical preconditions exist and need to be understood in order to appreciate democracy's prospects. Second, imposing on the first perspective has to be an understanding of handed-down values acquired primarily in the home. These change slower than historical events would suggest and therefore have their own rhythm and effect on events. Third, there are particular national characteristics recognized as peculiar to a nation that citizens of a nation and observers of their behavior believe influence behavior. Of particular importance to this book is the role of individualism in places like France, Italy, and Spain. Capping all these layers of influence are the modern political behaviors so favored by political scientists to study. Figure 1.1 illustrates graphically our primary approach. We recommend it to anyone attempting to understand democracy's characteristics and prospects, and as a source of possible ideas about how to alter and sustain democratic institutions. Working from the bottom up, historical preconditions have an influence on societal patterns of behavior and finally on the course of political events. Responses to political conditions, in turn, incrementally influence immediate political conduct; the roles of people, families, and nations; and, ultimately, historical preconditions.

First, one must look at the historical realities of a nation and its state infrastructures; then, approach more contemporary circumstances. Second, in looking at modern conditions, a multidisciplinary approach is crucial, because nobody and no institution operates in a social or cultural vacuum. This is a

FIGURE 1.1
How a Nation State Evolves Its Form of Government

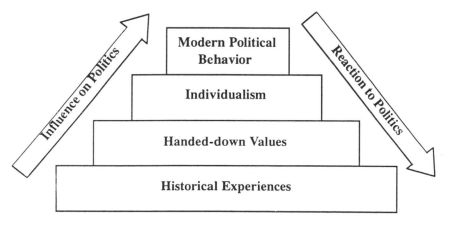

significant challenge, because we have to look at what is happening to the education of children, the rapidly changing role of women in the economic sphere in particular and in society in general, demographics (particularly the extensive migrations from rural to urban settings), economics, and political activities. These are five facets of a society's values and patterns of behavior. Looking at one or more, but not all, weakens any serious analysis of democracy's prospects.

QUESTIONS ABOUT POLITICAL PREDISPOSITIONS

When dealing with politics, most individuals want to start with a discussion of politics. Most studies published in the past forty years dealing with political cultures focus on the years after the two world wars. This approach is understandable given the profound worldwide upheavals stemming from those conflicts. One facet which warrants further attention, however, deals with the question of what influences historical and cultural events of many centuries ago had on contemporary political behavior. Looking at the cases below through a longer historical perspective adds to our appreciation of the patterns of political influence on modern affairs.

Related, if not separable from this issue, is the recent renewal of interest in the study of nation states and their behavior.[3] Colin Crouch took the next step by identifying variables that serve as preconditions of modern corporatism.[4] John Hall has recently called on scholars to appreciate the characteristics of states in historical context.[5] That call squares perfectly with the concerns of this book.

A second and very central, if more specific, issue deals with the question of why Anglo-Saxon and Scandinavian democracies, as well as those of Switzerland and the Netherlands (Holland), preserved the integrity of their democratic philosophies and structures and a high degree of political orderliness and stability during the post–World War I years and throughout the Great Depression of the 1930s. In contrast, why did the democratic regimes in other Western European countries either collapse (as in Spain, Italy, and Germany), or experience political instability (as in Belgium or France)? This line of questioning can be extended to other parts of the world as well. For example, in more recent times, the destruction of democracy in Uruguay raises the issue of what can happen to a Hispanic democracy under financial and social stress. If the United States were to become a heavily Hispanic-influenced society by the end of the next century, what would be the prospects for democracy in North America? In short, the subject is broad and significant.

Would democracy survive in Germany, Italy, and France should the world once again be immersed in acute economic deflation and dislocation, or rampant inflation destructive of the middle class? Could excessive taxation also lead to the ruination of this class—long heralded as the bulwark of democratic institutions? In short, under what conditions might "new" democracies fall apart and succumb to totalitarian or authoritarian regimes of some sort? These questions are important for Spain, as a recent member of Europe's democracies, and the ex-Soviet Union and Eastern Europe, also in the throes of change of immense historic proportions. What is there in the character of the Northern Europeans and their offspring elsewhere which permitted individual and collective political self-restraint in times of adversity, and why? Can this kind of discipline emerge in Spain and Italy, mature in France, and be introduced into the ex-Soviet Union and Eastern Europe (particularly into the four northern industrialized nations)? These concerns lie at the heart of our concern.

Alex Inkeles, in commenting on the relationship of national character and political systems, posed the following tantalizing question:

Are the societies which have a long history of democracy peopled by a majority of individuals who posses a personality conducive to democracy? Alternatively, are societies which have experienced recurrent or prolonged authoritarian, dictatorial, or totalitarian government inhabited by a proportionately large number of individuals with the personality traits we have seen to be associated with extremism? In other words, can we move from the individual and group level, to generalize about the relations of personality and political system at the societal level?[6]

With direct reference to those two points, Inkeles reminds us that, "Almost all the modern students of national character are convinced that the answer to this question is in the affirmative." However, "systematic evidence for this faith is unfortunately lacking."[7] Yet, Inkeles indicated acceptance of the definition of national character: "National character refers to relatively enduring personality characteristics and patterns that are model among the adult members of a society."[8] It is a reasonable and practical definition to apply in our study.

While the use of a concept like national characteristics has been criticized in recent decades by scholars, it remains a useful way to collect and communicate about patterns of behavior. For one thing, people rightly or wrongly characterize their nations that way, and either identify with these features or define their differences against some list of accepted national characteristics. Americans may speak about their penchant for changing homes and jobs frequently or being very informal and friendly; the French observer of America in the 1820s, Alexis de Tocqueville, generalized on these themes frequently. The Spanish talk about the value of strong leaders, but resist government attempts to regulate their personal behavior. Italians refer to their perceived acceptance of chronically ineffective national government, while the English see themselves as restrained. The point is, citizens identify with national characteristics and believe their governments and leaders act in accordance with these paradigms.

Historians, political scientists, and politicians long used the notion of national characteristics. In fact, the concept did not fall into ill repute until Adolph Hitler and his government extended the concept to many policies hostile toward Jews, Russians, and other ethnic groups and to programs designed to exploit perceived German national characteristics. Hence, the reluctance of scholars in particular to use the concept during the decades immediately following World War II. But that is changing as demonstrated by Inkeles's comments. We have, in effect, returned to the convenient use of the concept throughout this book, and employ it frequently, even though for each nation a local definition that is precise is not always possible to provide. It is a concept, however, that helps support any analysis of the future twists and turns democracy might take. For that reason, we encourage its return to the political language.

Inkeles flagged important considerations to keep in mind in this approach. For example, recall that accelerated evolution of the outward trappings and mechanics of representative democracy in Northern Europe—and, for that matter, in the United States—occurred only in the last 200 years or so, a short span in the long history of the European peoples. It seemed implausible that democratic structures and attitudes, among both elites and masses, permitting or causing such emergence would have evolved spontaneously and simultaneously. Basic attitudes and societal values are deeply rooted in the remote past of peoples and nations. They underpin existing political and social structures and offer intense resistance to grafting alien patterns of behavior and value systems. This tendency is increasingly manifesting itself in former European and American colonies as they move, or have moved, away from basic democratic philosophies inherited from the colonial powers. As younger leaders who never participated in the colonial regimes' administrations acquire power in the former colonies (for example, in Africa), there appears among them a tendency toward attitudes consistent with pre-colonial social or Northern European individual and collective behavior. Put less elegantly and more bluntly, tribal politics of a more ancient type are back. Rivalries and wars are more among tribes and less among African nations; they defy the elegant maps that were the product of European colonialism. Ethnic cleansing in the Balkans is done regardless of the state of Yugoslavia.

For the purposes of this book, we are assuming that modern peoples, regardless of race or physical climate, have a predisposition toward particular political systems as the result of attitudes and social values held individually and collectively from generation to generation. These concern basic views regarding law, custom, and traditions of local self-government. The accidents of history and geography through the centuries and the character or competence of rulers, when combined with technological, economic, and military development, tremendously influenced the eventual political lives and structures of nations in today's world. But the probability of underlying predispositions or tendencies should not be ignored in assessing any nation's political future.

If the assumption of predispositions is valid, can they be altered? Perhaps the answer is yes, but possibly only if there is full awareness of such "inherited" tendencies. In particular, this seems to be the case with senior political leaders in Germany concerned about the nation's Nazi experience and, to a lesser extent, Spain's political elites, now very conscious of their nation's migration from authoritarian to a pluralistic democracy. However, to increase the effectiveness of such a change in values, and to do so in more than one or two nations, requires coordination of school and family education, as well as affecting other circumstances that influence any modern polyarchy. The factor of predisposition is simply one of the important considerations when looking at the crystal ball of a nation's political future.

One could speculate that predisposition toward political compromise is also a factor deep in the psyche of a nation, the result of circumstances in the remote origins of a people with traits not completely eradicated by the blows of a historical experience. Nevertheless, the existence of such crucial inheritance is difficult to prove. Refinement of the methodology developed by such students of politics as Gabriel A. Almond and Sidney Verba, in their pioneering work, *Civic Culture*, would help to uncover solid evidence of this facet in certain national cultures.[9] Yet to be explored by sociologists are methods drawn from the society of animal life. The biological analogy of society functioning with many of the same "system-like" traits of living matter—replete with long- and short-term memory, neurological "feedback" systems, and subconscious direction of activity—offers a profoundly exciting avenue of research.[10]

But the point that is important right now is the concept of some crucial social inheritance. It is an important point because it can influence our ability to predict the prospects for liberal democracy or, to use Robert Dahl's term, "polyarchy" in such countries as Spain, which until recently was subjected to totalitarian rule. It would also help explain, in part, the historic, chronic instability of the political systems in countries which have tried or adopted Western democracy as a way of national life. In fact, if our suspicion proves valid, the argument could be made that *consociational democracy*—a term advanced by Arend Lijphart to denote the European "Grand Coalitions" characteristic of certain governments (e.g., Italy and France) in contrast to the basic Anglo-Saxon two-party system—may not survive in times of acute troubles.[11] Yet even his notion leads to tantilizing questions. For example, has any liberal democracy that has lasted for more than a generation ever reversed? The answer is, so far, "no"; although, as we will see with France, it is "no, but . . ." because of other extenuating predispositions and the actions of history (e.g., the collapse of France in 1940 in the face of German invasion).

Conquests of one people by another, and dissemination of ideas throughout the centuries, affected or transformed profoundly the behavior patterns of peoples and nations. This was especially the case if the incoming new invaders occupied the territory for hundreds of years, as often occurred with occupation by troops of the Roman Empire. But conversely, where total conquest failed, and with it escape from assimilation by the would-be conquerors, the fundamental spirit and values of free peoples survived through the ages with remarkable persistency. Even when political absorption occurred, if the national psyche remained intact, certain traits never vanished. One can point to the Welsh and to their persistence in preserving their local language and continued aspirations to disestablishment from Great Britain as one example. The French-speaking Cajuns of Louisiana, descendants of Acadians removed by the British from the former French colony in Canada ceded to Britain in 1713, represent another illustration of a people's tenacity to cling to language, behavior, and age-old customs. Jewish people have preserved their basic social, religious, and moral attitudes for over 2,000 years, despite brutal persecutions for centuries and under a wide variety of circumstances. In Spain, gypsies have maintained their identity and characteristics since time immemorial. This persistence seems to have surprised many recently, with the rapid reemergence of ethnic aspirations and ancient rivalries in Europe (e.g., from the Balkans to Eastern Europe)—just in the past ten years—reminiscent of pre–World War I circumstances. The lesson seems clear enough: Many long-held features of a society survive when suppressed, to reemerge on another day.

It would not be too risky, therefore, to assume that deep-seated attitudes governing interpersonal relations, derived from behavioral traits in the distant past, may be responsible for the kind of democracy which evolved in Scandinavian countries, Iceland, and the Anglo-Saxon world. Clearly, hidden strains of a psychosociological nature within a culture are difficult to detect, especially when identifying their effects on contemporary political attitudes, values, and behavior. Almond and Verba observed, in connection with the influence of education on political culture, that,

Later studies have overwhelmingly confirmed the importance of education as an explanatory variable for civic propensities. However, our study showed that education in a formal sense does not necessarily produce the affective and evaluative components of a civic culture, such as civic obligation and trust. These attitudes and values seem to be significantly affected by national and group historical and life experience.[12]

Their ideas, combined with fundamental historical experiences, suggest signs along a nation's path indicating relevant patterns of behavior.

ROMANIZATION AND DEMOCRACY

One source of political patterns for many Western European nations was Roman rule. The Anglo-Saxon type of democracy, as well as that evident in Scandinavian countries, evolved in areas of Europe never subjected to Romanization nor to Charlemagne's Holy Roman Empire. In the case of England, the Romans departed from the island in the fifth century. Vestiges of their culture were wiped out by successive invasions of Angles, Jutes, Saxons, and Danes, permitting us to lump these people in with Northern Europeans. European continental democracy, with its fragile coalitional characteristics, developed in those areas subjected mainly to Roman law and order, as enforced by long occupation. In Germany, Charlemagne's policies imitated Rome's and continued in the dream of a resurrected Holy Roman Empire. Political behavior here reflected similar effects. Furthermore, it was the policy of the Roman emperors to incorporate conquered barbarians (Goths, Alemanni, Franks, and Gauls) into Roman legions, a practice which contributed significantly to changes in the traits of enlisted Germans.[13]

This is a set of obvious links between Roman rule and modern democratic behavior worthy of more recognition. It is misleading to argue that Roman activities are a direct ancestor of modern behavior because many other influences crept into the culture of Western Europe between the end of the Roman Empire and the present, a period that exceeded the life of the Empire itself. However, that said, there is a strong link back to that earlier time that simply cannot be ignored. Research on Roman history in the past forty years has made it even clearer how close the link is to the present. It also makes obvious that Roman society and customs evolved substantially during the Roman era.[14]

As has already been suggested, emperors co-opted local leadership in the regions they conquered. Patronage, in other words, became a key strategy by which they ruled the empire. They chose not to use a large body of laws, complex regulations, or an army of Roman civil administrators. It remains a political strategy governing coalition governments to this day. Central administration was geared toward establishing policies, leaving actual implementation to the provinces. Key to the strategy was the Romanization of cities, not the countryside. Large urban centers were expected to provide the goods, taxes, and manpower required to sustain the empire and, therefore, these became the centers of Roman law, culture, and society. Roman intervention in local decision making centered in cities, and less so the further one moved into the countryside. That set a pattern of political power that has lasted to the present, in which the closer to an urban center one reaches, the greater the national or regional power. This was most true in the West and least true in the most eastern part of the Roman Empire.

The role of land became essential to the functioning of political and social processes of Western Europe. Since it was the source of much wealth—taxes, people, and food—possession of land led to power. Over time, Roman social stratification was reflected in the amount of property an individual had. The more they had, the the greater their role, position, and prestige in Roman society. In time, law reinforced a highly stratified social system of elites. In recent years, historians of the Roman Empire began arguing that there was social mobility among these classes, but that mobility does not in any way take away the fact that elites (nobility in particular) emerged and functioned. There is less evidence of a widespread freedman class (today we might call these people the middle class), and there was a large slave class.[15]

In short, what emerged was a social order essentially grounded in agrarian economics. To the extent that soldiers and other upwardly mobile residents of the Roman Empire cooperated in the administration and maintenance of law and order, they could expect to benefit from the patronage of the Emperor or, at a more local level, provincial authorities, such as governors. One authority on the period suggested the extent to which this social process was reinforced: "Inequalities, deriving from uneven property distribution that was confirmed or even accentuated by imperial policies, were underpinned by Roman law. In effect, the decisions of emperors . . . were the fount of law."[16] This was true all over the Empire and became a way of doing business. The introduction of Roman law and practices became so pervasive—because they favored Rome-backed local elites who gained sufficient wealth and political power to sustain many of themselves long after the demise of the Empire—as to make land-based political power a way of life complete with legal systems. These legal systems were further reinforced at the end of the Middle Ages, when another round of legal reforms in Western Europe, and in Italy in particular, led to the reintroduction of many Roman legal principles that had eroded over time.

The most articulated body of Roman legal principles involved highly developed laws concerning property rights, ranging from laws on entitlements to others on privileges involving social status. This body of legal thinking was more uniform than not in those sections of Western Europe that had been subjected to Roman rule.[17] Even the exploitation of the working poor by the rich—a well-recognized feature of Roman society—was for the wealthy and privileged; profits did not go to wage earners. They were channeled to the propertied classes and to their descendants for so many centuries that alternatives to that practice did not appear widespread until over a thousand years after the fall of the Empire.

The combined effect of land, wealth, law, and economic realities was the development of a society that from Roman times to the present proved very sensitive to social ranking. Everyone had their place; in Roman times there was even a dress code for each social rank, enforced by law. The key to social stability in Roman and subsequent times was the elaborate process by which new individuals could enter the ranks of the propertied classes. That process, which made it possible for residents of the Empire to move up the social scale in large numbers (sometimes more so than into the ranks of the nobility in the next thousand years), became atrophied during the Middle Ages, Renaissance, and Early Modern period. The one exception was the British nobility, where Roman rule, incidently, had been brief and superficial. Here, the upper classes renewed themselves more vigorously than on the continent.[18] If this description sounds vaguely familiar to European conditions long after the end of the Roman Empire, you begin to understand the echo of the past on modern affairs.

But that is public life. What about private life, the family, for example? Is there a Roman antecedent here, too? Two experts on the Romans had this to say about the question:

The family was the basic social unit through which wealth and status were transmitted. As such, the perpetuation of the aristocracy, the possibilities for social mobility, the distribution of landed wealth, and other matters depended fundamentally on patterns of family behavior. Beyond the social realities of the time, the image of the Roman family has had a continuing influence on western legal, political and social thought.[19]

All through that portion of Europe ruled by Rome, and down to the post–World War II period, for example, legal reforms concerning family matters embraced concepts of the patriarchy and attributed their inspiration to the Romans.[20] While this is not the place to discuss the power of the father over land and over the economic affairs of his wife and children, about which we will have more to say later, suffice it to point out that Roman precepts have remained central to and consistent with judicial practices evident in those areas once under Roman rule. The consistency also applied, it strongly appears, to all social classes, not merely to the elites of Europe.[21]

Central to our analysis about democracy is the changing role of women. What does Rome teach us about this topic? It turns out that a great deal has been unearthed about women during the Empire, which we can briefly summarize. The rights of women were defined in the context of families. While legal systems strongly reinforced the authority of the father and husband, practice changed over time within the Empire to make possible women inheriting property and having a say over assets and their role in regard to child rearing. Divorce laws varied during the course of the Empire's history, with many of the same issues evident as existed, for example, in Italy in the 1970s.

And what about men? Honor and status became a highly defined process in Roman times, to the point where one could not help another (i.e., exchange comparable benefits) unless they were of the same class. The Emperor, like European kings later, was the ultimate provider of patronage, usually to those closest to him in social class. Patronal networks extended down through the social order, with each class helping its fellow members and dolling out jobs, ranks, and other privileges to those beholding to them in lower classes. One's status was thus defined largely by the assets and patronage that one controlled. Tacitus considered this pattern of behavior crucial to the well-being of society.

Other features of Roman life still echo to this day. For example, in Roman times, as through most of Western Europe's history, religion and political power were formally merged together, or so closely linked that they constituted a common bond. We have the image of bishops in the Middle Ages controlling large tracts of land and leading armies into battle; but, in Roman times, religion was also woven into the fabric of the political state. Religion was another strategy for injecting social stability into various provinces. The cult of the Emperor is an obvious example; we hear about the "divine rights of kings" long after the end of the Empire. And, as late as the Franco era in Spain (1936–1975), the Spanish dictator cultivated the support of the Catholic Church, an institution born within the territory of the Roman Empire. While the Roman Empire had been tolerant of various religions in its early and middle years, it clearly was not by the later centuries. This is an important development, because it reinforced the notion that a single religion, closely aligned with the state, encouraged political and economic stability—an idea that remained a constant almost to the present, even during the centuries following the upheavals of the Reformation.

One final note on Roman influence concerns philosophy or world view. For most of the Roman period, the conventional body of philosophy emanated from the Stoics, who provided an ethical system. Stoicism championed the status quo, both in politics and in personal behavior. Over time, during the days of the Empire, it made possible the consolidation of many beliefs and practices that continued long after the end of Roman rule. It appealed to the nobility of the Roman Empire because it gave much advice to this class concerning political behavior. For example, it called on the wise and the virtuous to be statesmen. Emperors and literary figures wrote Stoic philosophy and about its application to politics. Beginning in the sixteenth century, a renewed interest occurred in this body of philosophy that had originated in Greek society, been co-opted and expanded by the Romans, and was renewed in waves all the way down to the twentieth century.[22]

So, a variety of Roman influences encouraged a status quo tied to the land and a social structure dominated by a hierarchy of elites. Property systems ensured that wealth passed through propertied families, while direct dependence of workers on them ensured a continued growth in that wealth. This pattern, coupled with Roman obsession with social position, did not disappear with the end of the Empire.

Implementation varied from region to region, taking into account the intended mix of local patterns of behavior with healthy doses of Romanization. But can it be argued, for example, that the emergence of feudalism in England and Scandinavia, as well as on the continent, would have destroyed these kinds of fundamental traits and produced a massively submissive population in ex-Roman regions? While one could argue the case for this important point, the fact remains that feudalism evolved differently in the various regions of Europe, in part precisely because of the persistence of what would today be called character traits in the affected people. Certainly, in Spain, feudalism took root in Catalonia (northeastern Iberia) differently than in Castile. The same could be said of practically every other European area. In short, the study of European democratic institutions of the twentieth and twenty-first centuries requires an appreciation of the Romanization process in the area under consideration. It is, to use a modern genetic term, a "marker" for any nation that the Romans ruled.

IMPLICATIONS FOR U.S. FOREIGN POLICY

Because of the profound influence the United States has had globally in this century on politics, it is possible that American foreign policy will also represent a marker on the affairs of subsequent decades and, possibly, centuries. Closer to our time, however, is the undeniable reality that the government of the United States has been very interested in promoting the expanded use of democratic forms of government. It has been a well-documented foreign policy obsession since the founding of the nation. The Constitution of the United States enshrines the dogma of American democracy. Indeed, the magnificent evolution of the United States into a large, powerful, wealthy nation has amply justified the vision of its forefathers and set a constant beacon before nations striving for similar economic and social success. It has equally been a role model for the preservation of individual and collective liberties.

Since World War II, political scientists, sociologists, economists, and historians, mainly American and European, but also Asian, Latin American, and some Africans, have examined essentials for the emergence and survival of democracies. American foreign policies and strategies for aid programs have been designed to encourage development and strengthening of democracies. These approaches have been basic to American international relations.

To this point, a Foreign Service Officer in the United States Information Agency wrote, in the house organ of the American Foreign Service Association (*Foreign Service Journal*), a confirmation of that approach as a key element in American foreign policy. Because of the source of the article, his views on democracy and American foreign policy are relevant to our argument. The author, Joe B. Johnson, refers to Secretary of State Warren Christopher's comments to the North Atlantic Council on February 26, 1993, in which the Secretary stated that "promoting democracy and free markets" is the third pillar "of the new administration's diplomacy" and that "it would be the height of folly to spend hundreds of billions of dollars to overcome communism and then refuse to invest in the survival of the new democracies that are emerging."[23]

Underlying the Secretary's position appears an assumption that, just as communism was and is hostile to a broad range of American interests, democracies would prove the opposite. They would enhance American security while promoting capitalism and free markets. Whether this viewpoint is justified will be dealt with later. What is important is the outline developed by Johnson, in which he describes efforts by the State Department, the Department of Defense (DOD), the Agency for International Development (AID), the United States Information Agency (USIA), and other organizations in pursuit of the objectives highlighted by the Secretary. To quote from Johnson, these approaches include the following:

Radio and television broadcasting, including "surrogate" news services like the Voice of America, Radio Marti, Radio Free Europe and Radio Liberty, promote the free flow of information by carrying objective news to populations living under censorship.

Training programs run by USIA and the Agency for International Development transfer American know-how to foreign lawyers, judges and other agents of social change.

International and non-governmental organizations, some supported by the U.S. government, monitor and assist elections in transitional countries.

Exchange and information programs, perhaps the oldest way of spreading American ideas about government, have built cadres of foreigners with direct exposure to the U.S. society.[24]

Johnson accurately observes that "activities like these have burgeoned in recent years with little scrutiny and even less coordination." Actually, these efforts emerged from the Cold War arena and were part of the more than forty years of dueling with the Soviet Union. They still have not been tailored to meet post–Cold War objectives, and it is not clear that these have, as yet, been clearly identified. However, the Secretary's remarks point to a probable general direction combined with altruistic concern for human rights. At some point, the latter will probably be tied specifically to survival of democracies and private enterprise as two sides of a coin.

Johnson throws in to high relief some key issues which should be dealt with in the development of new policies:

Can we judge which nations offer the brightest prospects to succeed as democracies? Shouldn't the tax payer's investments in political reform go to the best risks?

Can we agree on a methodology? For example, is it safe to say that the considerable resources devoted to monitoring the 1991 elections were to put it kindly, premature? Is a dollar spent on radio broadcasting to China more effective than a dollar toward exchange programs for Chinese students?

What if pro-democracy efforts might harm other U.S. foreign policy interests, for example, the stability of a military ally? Shouldn't that be considered, or at least factored into the allocation of resources?

Why should the American public support these efforts in the first place? Is it enough to say that democracies are rarely aggressors? For example, do we really believe that a free parliamentary system will make Ukraine more compliant with arms control agreements? In fact the reverse seems to be true.[25]

This same Foreign Service Officer noted publicly that "Democracy building has seemed exempt from critical scrutiny so far, but the programs are now big enough for a reality check: the National Endowment for Democracy at $30 million, Eastern Europe and former Soviet Union initiatives at about $50 million, and $30 million proposed to start up a Radio Free Asia on top of the already successful Voice of America China Service."[26]

Johnson's position is well taken, not only for the best interests of the United States, but because his observations are yet another testimony to the need to look at some basics when assessing a society's capability to deploy democracy. There should be a lucid understanding of why the United States should support the evolution of democracies in general or in some specific case. There should also be full awareness that while democracies are slower to engage in war, or draw on armed conflict as a foreign-policy measure, their existence by no means assures peace. A pre–World War I proto-democratic Germany did not hesitate with support of the Reichstag (Parliament) to vest war-making powers in the Kaiser nor to keep Germany from invading Belgium and France. A democratic France yearned for another go at the Germans to even the score of the 1870 defeat and to recover Alsace-Lorrain. In the case of the United States, the fact was ignored that, in 1897–1898, Spain had acquiesced to U.S. demands when President William McKinley, bowing to the war party, declared war on Spain with Congress's blessings. In short, when democratic nations perceive war as essential to their aspirations, they will seize aggressive initiatives. Such bellicose actions are different, of course, from armed defense, in which case the rallying of a democratic people is crucial and effective, as Great Britain demonstrated during the Nazi blitz in World War II. But even in desperate situations of survival, people will place national defense above even tyrannical regimes, as occurred, for example, with the Russian stand at Stalingrad during World War II.

In an earlier book, we argued the case in favor of establishing a clear understanding of why democracies should be supported. That understanding had to be framed in terms of national interest, not some idealism about what forms of government should exist.[27] Based on our examination of American foreign policy in the Caribbean, we focused on four issues that become even more urgent when looking at Europe's situation:

1. Democracies facilitate development of service trades, light industries, and productive farming. This economic flexibility creates employment, wealth, and higher standards of living.
2. Authoritarian regimes do not necessarily restrict economic growth to the extent evident in Marxist–Leninist political structures, yet authoritarian regimes do not allow for as open an economic system as evident in democracies. One repeatedly evident by-product is massive labor discontent that has the risk of destabilizing the government.
3. For democracies to survive, a literate population which votes and a substantial urban and rural middle class are required.
4. Lack of sufficient national income does sap the strength of a democracy.[28]

Economic benefits derived from genuine, truly rooted democracies contribute to the world economy, and either directly or indirectly to America's well-being through foreign trade and two-way international investments. Hence, the nexus between capitalism and democratic philosophies and practices is close.

The reaction of the United States to the values of democracy are thus often intertwined with its own sense of what constitutes self-interest, just like every other nation mixes its values with its policies. For example, the use of the issue of human rights, which has come to the fore in recent years as a major U.S. foreign-policy consideration. Nowhere in the Constitution or Declaration of Independence is there any statement implying that national security requires imposition of higher standards of behavior on the citizens of other nations. Yet, American policy makers find it necessary to try to impose their values on others. The easiest way to focus on national self-interest is to tie policies to the thoughts contained in the Preamble to the Constitution: "We, the people of the United States, in Order to form a more perfect union, establish Justice, insure domestic Tranquility, provide for the common defense, promote the General Welfare, and secure the Blessings of Liberty to ourselves and our Prosperity, do ordain and establish this Constitution for the United States of America."[29] In 1994, Henry Kissinger, an ex-U.S. Secretary of State and an expert on European diplomatic history, essentially argued the same case, citing national self-interest as the benchmark for action, not idealistic concepts about democracies.[30]

The uneasiness reflected in Johnson's thoughts about uncertainty in U.S. foreign policy, and our related suggestion of linking international initiatives to self-interest as described by the Preamble, were shared quietly by other highly placed U.S. diplomats. For example, retired Ambassador Carlton S. Coon, Jr., in an unpublished paper which he presented publicly in 1974 while Diplomat-in-Residence at Carlton College, argued, "After nearly a quarter of a century of employment in the U.S. Foreign Service, I am convinced that there is something basically wrong in the way Americans customarily go about their business of managing their country's relations with the rest of the world."[31]

Ambassador Coon felt uneasy about the U.S. foreign-policy process in 1974; we felt disquiet as reflected in our study in 1985; Johnson expressed similar concerns in 1993. Thus, during a span of nearly three decades, aspects of U.S. foreign policies are still subject to serious debate. American publishers have produced hundreds of books and thousands of articles critiquing American foreign-policy formulation, while the U.S. Congress has used a forest of trees to publish its proceedings on the same topics. The points are that a nation reflects its values in what it does and is slow to change those values. More to the point of action, without understanding what makes for a successful implementation of a democracy—even in Western Europe—how can we expect U.S. foreign policy concerning fostering of democracies to be grounded in the kind of reality that makes success possible?

THE VALUE OF HISTORICAL INQUIRY

A serious problem which affects how the United States conducts its foreign policy relates to American secondary school and college requirements for future policy makers and voting citizens. History, in general, is treated very lightly. In most U.S. colleges at the undergraduate level, except for history and some political science majors, history (if required at all) is normally a one-year superficial course. The future lawyer, business professional, scientist, engineer, or other educated American who, by middle age, has achieved outstanding success in his or her profession and then enters politics may be in line for a top foreign policy-making position, either at the White House (where policy is really set) or in some diplomatic position. That individual generally comes to the job with only a smattering of knowledge of the historical forces at work in the area of their responsibility. Advisors who are knowledgeable may be on hand, but decision making would still be the responsibility of the incumbent. Without fairly deep knowledge of the subject, intelligent selections of policy options become, at best, a gamble.

By contrast, statesmen in Western Europe usually come out of similar academic molds, which include wide exposure to the facts of historical developments. In the United States, the singular exception was Henry Kissinger, and he is credited with having made important contributions to the foreign policy of the United States. But Kissinger's background describes what is more normal among all key foreign-policy executives in Western Europe and across the major nations of Asia. Frequently, if not generally, a European incoming political appointee is just as aware of the historical background of an issue or country as career specialists. When they make mistakes, these are generally the result of misjudgment, not from ignorance. Henry McDonald explained clearly why knowing history is so important:

To know the past is to know, in a logical sense, the future. The past, present, and future are a whole cloth that is continuously woven; what is eternal are the weaves, the forms and patterns of temporality. Those forms are like rules read out of the data of experience, the logic of our expressions that permeates the constant flux of its applications. Eternity is carried along through history; we must submit to it.[32]

The implication of the stress we put on the necessity of policy makers, both in Europe and in the United States, knowing the history of their area of responsibility is to lessen the chances of error in development of national political or diplomatic policies. It is the same stress that needs to be placed on anyone wishing to understand the future course of democracy. At this particular junction in the history of the world, and because of the intense attention focused on democracy, it is probably more important than ever that policy leaders know their history. They should be aware, for example, of the fragility of democracy in most of the Western European countries. This awareness is particularly needed by U.S. policy makers, who show little or no evidence of appreciating how much democratic forms of government are at risk around the world, Europe included. The issue of democracy's fragility—and what may cause one's democratic government to be more or less fragile—is the focus of the subsequent seven chapters.

It would be difficult to exagerate the importance of the past in contemporary affairs. The distinguished political scientist, Barrington Moore, while discussing totalitarian elements in preindustrial societies, cut quickly to the heart of the matter:

Both the conservative and the radical critiques of modern society converge on one major thesis. They explain the rise of totalitarian regimes and of a totalitarian atmosphere in formerly democratic countries as the consequence of certain processes at work in industrial society. I believe that this indictment contains much that is sound.[33]

We are thus not the first nor alone in proposing the necessity to study the past in order to have a better understanding of the rise of totalitarianism in former democratic countries, since democracy is really a recent phenomenon. The task before American and European scholars is to develop an approach which will permit more accurate gauging of survival prospects for democracy in continental Western Europe, and what both Europeans and Americans can do to assure an optimistic prospect. If democracy cannot thrive in Western Europe, how confident can we be of its survival elsewhere in the world (with the exception of the United States)? Such findings by students of democracy would be of vital importance for the formulation, for example, of U.S. foreign policy. They would also lead to more realistic assessments of long-term prospects for democracies in Latin America, which, after all, is essentially an extension of Southern European culture (albeit with intense native Indian influence). There are, of course, also implications for the former Eastern European states, including Russia and the Ukraine, which are seeking a path toward some form of democracy and capitalist economy.

THE IMPORTANCE OF HANDED-DOWN VALUES

In focusing on the issue of democracy, it became apparent that, in addition to in-depth knowledge of history, handed-down values and their impact on the young in home atmosphere and in school, church, and community relationships (or lack thereof) are of vital importance. This observation applies not only to all nations, but also to subcultures within each, some of which perpetuate devisive and destructive handed-down familial values and behavior relative to democracy. The intensity of these differences, if sufficiently large numbers of people are involved, almost negates the prospect for survival of democracy in a national unit.

Discussion of how to undertake the study of handed-down values and what to look for is, for us, nonspecialists in sociology and cultural anthropology, a slippery slope. Some idea of the complexity of the problem can be gleaned from the work of T. W. Adorno, Else Frenkel-Brunswick, Daniel J. Levinson, and R. Nevitt Sanford, begun in the late 1940s. They studied the roots of fascism and, in the process, identified antidemocratic factors in the people they interviewed.[34] What they uncovered was described later by a British scholar, John Madge:

When Hitler seized power, world Jewish opinion was shocked at the number of ordinary Germans who fell in with the anti-Semitism of the Nazi regime. As the tide flowed toward the United States it was felt that some means should be found of identifying potential anti-Semites in the American population. Various inquiries were therefore sponsored, and of these the best known and the most profound was that entrusted to a mixed team of German social scientists and American psychologists jointly led by Adorno and Sanford.[35]

Madge commented on how their research was done: "In America for the first time the sophisticated psychoanalytic thinking, which derived from Central Europe, had been interwoven with the shell of American social psychology."[36] Research for that early study took place only in the United States, but from Madge's comments, the complexity involved in structuring theory, methodology, and assessment is readily apparent. As we will suggest in subsequent chapters, studies in Western Europe should make at least an equal effort in determining current handed-down values and how they affect democracy's future. There is good news: Sociologists in Europe have done research in recent years on children's attitudes, a start that now has to be linked to study of their potential political attitudes and behavior, because that research has not been done.

Sociologist Milton M. Gordon, in his book, *The Scope of Sociology*, touches on aspects which serve as a springboard in connection with the kinds of studies we propose. He throws in high relief a truism of the human condition: "Human beings do things because they want to and because they have to. They want to for two reasons: biological needs and urges and what they have been taught."[37] This last observation goes to the heart of our thinking, because "what they have been taught" essentially concerns handed-down values. By the time a child is about twelve to fourteen years old, attitudes toward authority, interpersonal cooperation, and general view of his or her place in the social milieu is pretty well formed.[38]

Gordon further states that "social control emphasizes the punishment factors and negative psychological sanctions, and socialization, which highlights the internalization of norms and values of the groups we belong to into our own psyches, so that we learn to want to behave in certain ways and to regard these ways as proper and right."[39] Precisely what these are affect the long-term survival of democracy in a particular country and the form it may take, probably very different from that of the United States. Gordon's observation is right on the button.

In the chapters ahead, we explore further the views of specialists concerning certain aspects of societal inheritance, and very brief histories of key Western European countries where democracy either collapsed under stress or survived. We will offer suggestions about what can be done to anchor democratic prospects more firmly in Western Europe. We take the position that the United States and Canada are extensions of Northern Europe, mostly Protestant, and the rest of North America and South America extensions of Southern Europe, mostly Catholic. Implications go well beyond Western European prospects, with broad possibilities for the development of realistic

American foreign policy where support for democratic principles is a factor, one based on the handed-down values of people and intrafamilial attitudes.

In Chapters 4 through 7, we highlight widely recognized national traits which affect or could influence the future of democracy in Germany, France, Italy, and Spain. We describe important societal changes that occurred in the years following the end of World War II and, particularly in the case of Spain, in the post-Franco period. What we failed to unearth in our research are inquiries into what goes on in the homes in these countries which, by osmosis, seeps into the psyche of today's children and could (in fact, probably would) affect their attitudes and behavior toward democracy and other "isms" when reaching adulthood. This lack requires study by sociologists, political scientists, and others, the results of which would be conclusions and recommendations to national leaders. They could bring about modified policies and strategies concerning the young and their parents, all aimed at strengthening commitments to democratic behavior in a political sense. At present, all four nations view democracy with favor, and formal legislative support exists. But what happens if a grave social or economic crisis should shake the body politic? Would democracy survive, or would some form of extremism take over? In a similar dilemma, what will be the attitude of the German, French, and Italian third generation since World War II, and that of Spain's fourth generation since the Civil War of 1936–1939? Finally, what would such a turn of events mean for the United States?[40]

NOTES

1. M. I. Finley, *Democracy, Ancient and Modern* (New Brunswick, N.J.: Rutgers University Press, 1973); Arend Lijphart, *Democracies* (New Haven: Yale University Press, 1984); Robert A. Dahl, *Democracy and Its Critics* (New Haven: Yale University Press, 1989); John R. Hall and I. C. Jarvie, eds., *Transition to Modernity: Essays on Power, Wealth and Belief* (Cambridge: Cambridge University Press, 1972). See also an important article by Colin Crouch, "Sharing Public Space: States and Organized Interests in Western Europe," in *States in History*, ed. John A. Hall (Oxford: Basil Blackwell, 1986), 177–210.

2. Gabriel A. Almond and Sidney Verba, "The Intellectual History of the Civic Culture Concept," in *The Civic Culture Revisited*, ed. Gabriel A. Almond and Sidney Verba (Boston: Brown, 1980), 1–36.

3. Hall, ed., "Introduction," in *States in History*, 6.

4. Crouch, "Sharing Public Spaces," 177–210.

5. Hall, *States in History*, 20.

6. Alex Inkeles, "National Character and Modern Political Systems," in *Psychological Anthropology: Approaches to Culture and Personality*, ed. Francis L. K. Hsu (Homewood, Ill.: Dorsey, 1961), 172, but see also 172–207.

7. Ibid., 173, 193–194.

8. Ibid., 173.

9. The authors applied modern methods of social research to various problems in comparative politics. They focused on the political culture of democracy in West Ger-

many, Italy, Mexico, the United States, and Great Britain. Their primary interest was on defining the relationship between the attitudes of a nation's citizens and the operations of modern democratic nations. See Gabriel Almond and Sidney Verba, *The Civic Culture: Political Attitudes and Democracy in Five Nations* (Princeton, N.J.: Princeton University Press, 1963). Also useful is G. Lehmbruch, "Consociational Democracy, Class Conflict and the New Corporatism," in *Trends toward Corporatist Intermediation*, ed. P. C. Schmitter and G. Lehmbruch (London: Sage, 1979).

10. For an up-to-date summary, see Paul M. Churchland, *The Engines of Reason, the Seat of the Soul* (Cambridge, Mass.: MIT Press, 1995).

11. Arend Lijphart, *Democracy in Plural Societies* (New Haven: Yale University Press, 1977), 25.

12. Almond and Verba, "Intellectual History," 24. William Strauss and Neil Howe, *Generations: The History of America's Future, 1584–2069* (New York: William Morrow, 1991) presents this observation in a brilliant illustration at work in the United States, where thirteen generations of people living in North America since the 1500s have been shown to carry generationally distinct patterns of behavior while simultaneously continuing core values and practices from earlier times.

13. Much work remains to be done on this theme. However, a good start is J. A. O. Lamsen, *Representative Government in Greek and Roman History* (Berkeley and Los Angeles: University of California Press, 1966), and Stewart C. Easton, *The Era of Charlemagne: Frankish State and Society* (Princeton, N.J.: Van Nostrand, 1961).

14. See, for instance, Peter Garnsey and Richard Saller, *The Roman Empire: Economy, Society and Culture* (London: Duckworth, 1987), and P. Brown, *The Making of Late Antiquity* (Cambridge, Mass.: Harvard University Press, 1978).

15. T. D. Barnes, "Who Were the Nobility in the Roman Empire?" *Phoenix* 28 (1974): 444–449; Peter Garnsey, ed., *Non-Slave Labour in the Greco-Roman World* (Cambridge: Cambridge University Press, 1980); M. I. Finley, ed., *Studies in Roman Property* (Cambridge: Cambridge University Press, 1976).

16. Garnsey and Saller, *The Roman Empire*, 110.

17. Ibid., 110–111.

18. For statistical studies on replacements of nobilities in various countries as compared to the Roman Empire, see K. Hopkins, *Death and Renewal* (Cambridge: Cambridge University Press, 1983), and M. Hammond, "Composition of the Senate, AD 68–235," *Journal of Roman Studies* 47 (1957): 74–81.

19. Garnsey and Saller, *The Roman Empire*, 126.

20. R. P. Saller, "Patria Potestas and the Stereotype of the Roman Family," *Continuity and Change* 1 (1986): 7–22.

21. For a useful overview of the family and Roman law, see Garnsey and Saller, *The Roman Empire*, 126–147.

22. B. D. Shaw, "The Divine Economy: Stoicism as Ideology," *Latomus* 44 (1985): 16–54; Garnsey and Saller, *The Roman Empire*, 178–186.

23. This organization is private, nonprofit, and completely independent from the U.S. Department of State. See Joe B. Johnson, "Make Room for Democracy," *Foreign Service Journal* 70 (4; 1993): 16–18.

24. Ibid., 16.

25. Ibid., 17.

26. Ibid.

27. James N. Cortada and James W. Cortada, *U.S. Foreign Policy in the Caribbean,*

Cuba, and Central America (New York: Praeger, 1985), 3–5.

28. Ibid., 5.

29. Ibid., 14.

30. Henry Kissinger, *Diplomacy* (New York: Simon and Schuster, 1994), 6–7.

31. Carlton S. Coon, Jr., unpublished paper, Carlton College, 1974, 1.

32. Henry McDonald, *The Normative Basis of Culture* (Baton Rouge: Louisiana State University Press, 1986), 232–233.

33. Barrington Moore, Jr., *Political Power and Social Theory* (Cambridge, Mass.: Harvard University Press, 1958), 30.

34. T. W. Adorno et al., *The Authoritarian Personality* (New York: Harper, 1950).

35. John Madge, *The Origins of Scientific Sociology* (New York: Free Press, 1967), 9, 377–423.

36. Ibid., 381, 377–423.

37. Milton M. Gordon, *The Scope of Sociology* (New York: Oxford University Press, 1988), 54.

38. R. N. Caine and G. Caine, *Making Connections: Teaching and the Human Brain* (Alexandria, Va.: Association for Supervision and Curriculum Development, 1991); L. A. Hart, *Human Brain and Human Learning* (New York: Longman, 1983).

39. Hart, 54.

40. Strauss and Howe, *Generations*.

—2—

The Northern European Experience: Germany, Great Britain, Scandinavia, Switzerland, and the Netherlands

I believe the British government forms the best model the world ever produced. . . . This government has for its object public strength and individual security.

—Alexander Hamilton

This chapter focuses on the origins of handed-down political values in Northern Europe, an area that did not come under Roman rule. To demonstrate common characteristics, all the major Western European regions outside the Roman Empire are discussed briefly.

To the north of the Roman Empire, people developed different cultural, linguistic, political, and legal traditions than occurred closer to the Mediterranean world. The historical evolution of government practices of the Northern Europeans, in which we include most Germans, the English, Scandinavians, Swiss, and Dutch, had many common elements still evident today. Political handed-down values were profoundly influenced by the role of political elites (e.g., kings and nobles), geographic realities (e.g., distance from Roman lands and islands), and military experiences (e.g., tribal military command and control, invasions, and wars). By looking at all these people together, we can demonstrate how democratic preconditions took root over many centuries.

GERMAN EXPERIENCE

Nowhere does the influence of specific historical experiences appear so obvious on modern events than in the case of those regions influenced by Charlemagne. In large part, it is why, after a thousand years, European historians still pay attention to this remarkable leader. Apart from the Latinization of Spain, Italy, France, and, for that matter, practically all territories bounded by the Danube and Rhine Rivers, the effects of Charlemagne's forty-six-year reign on Germany proper must be carefully understood, because this experience also influenced subsequent political behavior for centuries. Both as king of the (Latinized) Franks (768–814) and as emperor of the Holy Roman Empire (800–814), Charlemagne imposed on what are now modern France, western Germany, and Italy a thoroughly absolutist political regime and disciplined Christanization based on patterns familiar to the Latinized Franks. Despite the fact that his personal consolidation of power into one set of hands did not continue long after his death, what he did was to profoundly change politics and society, which endured long after his reign ended.

As most historians of the period assert today, Charlemagne's policies provided the basis for the feudalism of the Middle Ages and the eventual birth of nation states.[1] But the manner in which feudalism evolved in Germany served (to a greater extent than elsewhere) to elevate the nobility almost to the stateliness of kings, with a corresponding debasement of the original mass of free men. In time, the thoroughness of the system greatly weakened the basic German tribal trait of participation in decisions affecting their destiny. A by-product of this development was the evolution of a pattern of authoritarian behavior affecting all social classes to the exclusion of compromise as an attitude or habit. One cannot ignore the obvious observation that this sense of authoritarian behavior has perdured for many centuries, serving as additional evidence of the profound social changes effected during the late 700s and early 800s.

Other remote events caused the Germanic tribes to acquire attitudes which differentiated them from their ethnic kin in England and in Scandinavia—areas that Charlemagne and his successors did not control. A. J. P. Taylor, a long-time British student of Germany and European affairs, stated the case effectively:

The Germans are the peoples of the northern European plain, the people without a defined natural frontier. Without the sharp limit of mountain ranges, except for the Alps and the Bohemian mountains, the great plain is intersected by four great rivers (Rhine, Elbe, Oder, Vistula) dividing lines sharp enough to split the German people up among themselves, not rigid enough to confine them within settled frontiers. There is no determined geographic point for German contraction; and, in the course of a thousand years, geographic Germany has gone out and in like a concertina.[2]

A consequence of this geographic reality has been exposure, at times of a most violent nature, to extraneous physical presences characterized by different customs and values, usually the result of frequent invasions. For example, there was a great assault on Europe by Attila and his Huns, who swept through the Eastern Goths and into Gaul until stopped in northeastern France by a combined German and Roman army.

Another consideration to keep in mind in looking at the long history of the Germans and the Romans was their blending through intermarriage in many parts of the Empire, a process which aided the Latinization process in parts of what one might call German lands, a subject long drawing the attention of historians.[3]

With Latinized Franks to the west and Slavs to the east—a situation which left the Germanics in-between—the cultural and sociological outlooks of the latter were affected severely. On the one hand, even before Charlemagne's heavy hand fell on the Saxons and other tribes east of the Rhine, these people had long been exposed to Latin influences, either through conflict or accommodation. The inevitable result was the development of a German national character different from that of their kin in England and in Scandinavia. If, in addition to the veneer of Latinization imposed by Charlemagne and his immediate heirs, one considers the eventual adoption of Roman law in Germany proper, the difference in political direction and internal sociological development becomes clearer. Ernst Levy, a student of the process, observed this phenomenon of legal history:

Among the numerous receptions of Roman law one event stood out, to the extent that, at least in Central Europe, it almost monopolized the term. "Reception of Roman Law" used to designate that development in the fifteenth, sixteenth, and seventeenth centuries in the course of which Germany turned from her native customs to Justinian's Corpus Juris, from her popular courts to learned judges, from her own legal language to the esoteric Latin of the Roman sources.[4]

The linkage between law and government is generally well understood. But one may venture further and suggest that attitudes toward law help condition peoples toward their political systems.

Another earlier contributing factor in the assimilation of Roman ideas by barbarians in conquered areas or associated with Rome lies in the latter's continuity as an imperial state, regarding which Ronald Syme observes, "It [the imperial state] resides in the governing class. A Roman emperor explained the matter in an allocution to the Praetorian Guard: The Senate, ordained by Romulus in the beginning, was perpetual from the kings to the emperors, and immortal." Syme went on to explain that, "The primeral Senate was mixed in origin: Latin, Sabine, Etruscan. As the Roman State extended its dominion in Italy, it brought the other peoples into subjection or alliance, and frequently drew their leading families to Rome. Under the Caesars the first men from among the nations by birth and wealth enter the imperial Senate."[5]

The same policy explained by Syme opened the highest ranks in the armies to non-Romans, who embraced Roman citizenship when this privilege was broadly extended. To an important extent, Roman citizenship encompassed, in time, an ample range of races and peoples, much in the way that American citizenship is held by people descended from practically every part of the globe. The German barbarians were attracted to the image of Rome as an imperial power, and took advantage of the opportunity to become Roman citizens when it was offered to those within the Empire's confines. The Latinization of France in Gaul accelerated as a result of Rome's generous policy toward citizenship. The early patterns of behavior evident with the Germans as a consequence of Latinization can be contrasted with the different heritage of the Anglo-Saxon peoples.

Looked at in terms more familiar to political scientists, we see the decline of tribal political structures, giving way to more nation state organizations.[6] The political egalitarianism evident in tribal societies did not survive to the extent evident in earlier times in the face of the more structured governments of Rome and Charlemagne, despite long-standing attempts to retain some of its features. An exception to this pattern are the Arabs, since they dominated much of Iberia for 700 years, making the case of Spain a unique laboratory for the study of historical preconditions and about which we will have more to say in later chapters.

ANGLO-SAXON HERITAGE

Scandinavians and Anglo-Saxons, along with the Franks, Goths, Lombards, and others who spread throughout the remnants of the Roman Empire in the west, had kin-related Germanic tribes as common ancestors. Therefore, it is appropriate to examine certain traits of these early peoples which came to influence political structures over time.

It is customary when dealing with the topic of Germanic tribes in this period to refer to Roman writings on the subject. However, without downplaying the value of Julius Caesar's history of the conquest of Gaul, there is little in his narratives about attitudes of the Germanic tribes with which he fought near the Rhine.[7] He was impressed by their ferocity and warlike proclivities, but said little more about their attitudes. For a deeper initial comment on the character of these early Germans, we have no other alternative but to turn to the frequently cited Tacitus.[8]

What essentially comes through Tacitus's comments concerns the German penchant to hold assemblies, attended by all warriors, regarding matters of great importance. This pattern of behavior included decisions involving custom as the source of law, election of tribal chiefs and kings (a general practice), election on a temporary basis of leaders for particular military ventures based on ability and not blood lines, and recognition of a wife's role as partner, including the obligation to fight if necessary. He also noted the intense warlike propensities of these people. These five characteristics are perhaps not too different from those of other early, non-Germanic and nomadic societies. Hence, Tacitus's help is of limited value in the search for persistent traits. However, a connection may be considered between the nature of Germanic tribes later established in England and in subsequent developments in their history.

On this point, Goldwin Smith notes a consequence of the elimination of the Roman presence and influence in Britain: "As a result, English constitutional history has nothing to do with Roman Britain. It has a great deal to do with Angles, Jutes and Saxons."[9] The same reasoning may be applied to legal and government institutions in the Scandinavian countries. Implicit in the nature of law is the attitude of people themselves toward these rules of public conduct and the governments developed for their implementation. The most important point to call out is that there are distinctions of a profound nature between all these early peoples that set their societies on courses different from each other.

Without going into the details of preconquest Anglo-Saxon government, about which historians have written a great deal, there are some important points to consider. One concerns the freedom to select leaders. Rulers of post-Roman England brought practices common to all Germanic tribes. These included use of money power to control "the legal relations of men." Political life included equality within social class, a liberty reserved to the wealthy, and an element of sordid and vicious political behavior.[10]

Germanic tribal practices were designed to reduce the prospect of bloodshed caused by revenge as the only means of obtaining redress for violent injury. These survived through the Dark Ages of despotism which plagued Saxon and later Norman England. Commitment to the principle of equality and, for that matter, to custom as the primary source of law survived sacrosanct (at least among the wealthy nobility). It was then only a question of time before fortuitous circumstances prompted the flowering of those civic virtues at all levels of English society. These circumstances stemmed from the evolution of technology, military practices, and economic prowess. Indeed, over many centuries that process occurred, although at varying paces of evolution.

The concept was not at all far-fetched. As Goldwin Smith observed about the period, "At no time did Anglo-Saxon rulers obtain absolute authority. They were limited in scores of ways. . . . Above all they were limited by custom, the stream of life-habit."[11] Smith noted that, "Law was tribal custom or folkright. The king and all his subjects were subordinate to custom. With the advice and consent of the great and wise men of his kingdom the monarch might occasionally declare what the law was, but he never gave or made it."[12]

Along the same vein, historians John Thorn, Roger Lockyer, and David Smith, commenting about the condition of Britain at the time of the Norman Conquest, recognized that, "The status of the churl had by 1066 undoubtedly declined; many were having to work for their lords in order to keep their plots of land. The villagers were still responsible for law and order in their districts and had to attend a few times a year at the local hundreds courts where the king's sheriff or bailiff would preside."[13]

Despite the fact that William the Conqueror replaced most of the Anglo-Saxon aristocracy with Normans, the new monarch preserved the entire administrative structure of shires, hundreds, and boroughs developed by the Anglo-Saxon kings, the shire and hundreds courts, and a judicial system still based on law determined by custom—the very basis of common-law philosophy characteristic of Anglo-Saxon democracies. For military reasons, that is to say, the provision of heavy-armed cavalry by knights holding fiefs which could financially support this expensive weaponry, the Conqueror's policies led to Norman feudalism in England.

There are those who maintain that prior to William's mission, something similar to feudalism already existed in some de facto manner in Saxon England. Others, such as Carl Stephenson, held varying judgments. A key point made by Stephenson was that "When thanks to the economic changes of the twelfth century, the king was able to base his government on the employment of mercenary troops and professional ministers, England was already ceasing to be feudal."[14] This is in contrast with Germany and France, where feudalism was a long-lasting phenomenon. The situation was exacerbated in Germany by the existence of petty duchies and kingdoms ruled autocratically for hundreds of years without regard to any principles of local assembly. Such was the price paid by Germany to maintain the fiction of a Holy Roman Empire, despite the growth of towns, town leagues, and their diverse systems of urban law.

NORMAN TRADITIONS

William the Conqueror, who invaded England with a force of between six and seven thousand men, occupying a land with a population of approximately 1.5 million, did not tamper severely with the basic way of life of the vast mass of people. He was particularly careful to respect local customs. He also did not attempt mass replacements with Normans. William, thereby, avoided provoking a revolt of catastrophic dimensions for him and the relatively small number of adventurers who came to England. His elimination of the Saxon aristocracy, some of whom probably embraced the new order, appeared to be of small concern to the Anglo-Saxon churl. The Norman lord was difficult to deal with, but so had been his Saxon predecessors.

Language also contributed to the preservation of early Anglo-Saxon beliefs and attitudes. Three languages were spoken on the Isle. The dynasty and court spoke Norman French, the masses and lower clergy spoke English, and the upper clergy spoke Latin, French, and English. This situation of multiple languages isolated most Englishmen from contact with non-English speakers; and, in time, the Norman aristocracy, in order to rule effectively, became bilingual. This process gradually led to the unification of the two cultures and peoples. Significantly, where Anglo-Saxons were involved, language in the courts of law was English. Since Anglo-Saxons outnumbered invaders by an immense majority, it would have only been a question of time before the Normans melted into the basic ethnic stock. The Royal House led the way. Henry I, the Conqueror's youngest son, who followed his older brother, William II (Rufus, 1097–1100), married a princess of the Anglo-Saxon royal line.

The origin of the invading Normans, and William in particular, is relevant to any understanding of what, in time, occurred. The Normans were a kindred people of Germanic origin. The dynasty's founder, Hrolf (known as Duke Rollo), was a Viking raider. Rollo accepted baptism and, at least externally, became a Christian. He also moved to accommodate the French polities abutting his duchy. William Longsword, Rollo's son and successor, continued his father's inclinations and learned French and French ways, as well as how to meddle in French politics. Richard I (known as the Fearless) followed his father's and grandfather's policies, as did, in essence, the succeeding two Richards and Duke Robert.

Although the span between Rollo's grant and Duke William's accession extended about 120 years, not all of that period was substantially devoid of Viking contact. Danish immigration continued sporadically after Rollo's and Longsword's consolidation. Given the absence of schooling for the mass of the population and general immobility of the peasantry (due to economic constraints and the lack of adequate transportation), one could assume that much of the Saxon culture perdured in Norman outlook and behavior. It is doubtful that the high nobility escaped totally from their attitudinal roots. Certainly, the Normans gave no evidence that their Viking penchant for adventure and warfare had shown any abatement by 1066.[15]

At the time of Rollo and his son, the threat of invasion from Denmark or harassment from Normandy hung over England, particularly the possibility of Norman support for a Danish adventure. In a policy move designed to weaken or eliminate Norman blessings for Danish aspirations, the English king, Ethelred II (known as the Unready, reigned 978–1014), married, in 1022, Emma, daughter of Richard I, Duke of Normandy, and thus the great granddaughter of Rollo. From this marriage was born Edward, the first of this name, who later reigned as king of England between 1042 and 1065 (and was blessed by the Church with the designation of "Confessor").

Despite Ethelred's marital diplomacy, Sweyn (Swegen) the Dane conquered England in 1013. He was succeeded in 1016 or 1017 by his son Canute, who dreamed of forming a great northern empire consisting of Sweden, Norway, Denmark, and England. His death at about forty-one years of age cut short his aspirations; not long after, the empire tumbled like a deck of cards.

Following the Danish invasion, Ethelred II sent his wife Emma and then nine-year-old Prince Edward to Normandy, to put them out of Sweyn's reach. Consequently, Edward grew into manhood Norman in speech and outlook. During his long stay in Normandy, he established a close friendship with his second cousin, Duke Robert's son, William. Soon after Edward became King of England, William (already Duke of Normandy) visited him in England, continuing a practice of Norman–Saxon ties. Edward I (known to history as the Confessor), summoned from Normandy, reigned from 1042 to 1065. He brought with him a considerable number of his Norman friends, to whom he accorded high honors and positions, to the dismay of his Saxon subjects. In time, the English nobles imposed their will on Edward and forced a lessened dependence on his Norman retinue.

The purpose of this genealogical excursion is to throw in high relief the fact that Norman–Saxon interrelationships in England had long been a reality. Thus, when William came to the throne in 1066 he entered into a political, military, and social environment with which he and many of his followers, including exiled Anglo-Saxons, were familiar. William regarded himself as the legitimate heir to the throne and hence showed respect for existing customs as they had been supported by Edward the Confessor.

Significantly, when during his reign the Norman baronage challenged the crown, William summoned the "fyrd" (Saxon troops), and they responded to his support. The tolerance of the Conqueror for Saxon customs and law proved definitive in the eventual evolution of Common Law. With early Saxon approval, king and subjects lived under the Common Law, and thus their liberties rested "on immemorial slow-growing custom declared by juries of free men who gave their verdict case by case in open courts."[16] The key point is that early practices influenced behavior over long expanses of time. This observation is, for example, relevant to Spain, Italy, and France, whose legal systems were long based on the philosophy of Roman law—an extremely important reality which influenced individual attitudes toward law and government for centuries.

American readers would recognize, in the account just given of the English experience, commonalties with their own judicial and constitutional structure: rule of law and role of juries. Also evident would be the role of legal traditions. So now imagine a nation that had different legal traditions—such as Spain, Italy, and France, which grew up in the shadow of Roman legal tradition—and you begin to understand how the long arm of history can influence a society's behavior and a people's propensity for one form of government over another for many hundreds of years.

ORIGINS OF BRITISH DEMOCRACY

When one thinks of the origin and nature of democracy, particularly if a North American, the first thought that comes to mind is usually about England. It is, after all, the British model which became *de rigour* the definition of democracy. Included in that perspective is the give-and-take of compromise, representational government, and the profound influence of Common Law and juries in adjudicating disputes. Tied to all three features are respect for the dignity and civil rights of the individual, and the role of the rule of law overarching the behavior of citizens. Indeed, for Western Europeans, the British model for democracy was the theoretical operative one, modified only to account for local peculiarities. Therefore, no discussion of democracy can avoid continuing the focus on the origins and progression of the English experience.

Fundamental to the development of Anglo-Saxon democracy was the continuation throughout many centuries of the principle and concept of a national assembly, which, in England, flowered in time into a Parliament. Through hundreds of years, the role of Parliament dipped and soared, affected by the struggles of crown, nobility, clergy, and people in all walks of life jockeying for position and influence from one issue to another. The history of Parliament's role need not detain us here; suffice it to say that the constituencies, eventually comprising the House of Lords (upper house), evolved slowly, drawing members from the elites of Anglo-Saxon society. In time, national councils (witenagemots) became the House of Lords. The House of Commons (lower house) also evolved slowly, initially from local assemblies of Anglo-Saxons (moots).

Clearly, over the 600 years of Saxon rule, and the grafting from time to time of Danish political and military thought, the degree and extent of the systems of liberties varied enormously. They depended on the strengths and weaknesses, relative to each other, of monarchs and lords, and on the ever-changing relations of both to the mass of population. But the principles always survived, and even when buried under catastrophic civil war or national wars, they never became completely extinct. They simply lived to blossom another day, just like ethnic tensions in a country like Yugoslavia were sublimated for a generation or two, only to emerge again when an opportunity presented itself. Even after the Norman invasion and the imposition of feudalism, the germ of these institutions remained alive. In other words, the attitudes of Englishmen toward assemblies and to law were conditioned by centuries of experience, during which they were never ground out; nor was the spirit of individual liberty, which had lodged permanently in English psyche regardless of class. For that reason, the English could claim to be the source of modern democratic behavior in the Western world.

SCANDINAVIAN TRADITIONS

In Norway, Sweden, Denmark, Iceland, and Finland (the latter under Swedish control for some 600 to 650 years, and relatively autonomous while under Russian rule from 1809 to 1917), a combination of geographical factors contributed greatly to three historical traditions. The first was preservation of their national cultures; second, of early Germanic attitudes toward law based on custom; and third, recourse to elected local or national assemblies for various levels of expressions on key issues. Even in the case of Denmark, which, because of its proximity to Germany experienced feudalism and abuse by the nobility, these three basic characteristics were never extinguished totally. The ruggedness of the peasantry in North Jutland and the circumstance of a small nation which included almost 500 islands with settlements, throughout the centuries, in almost one-fifth of them helped perpetuate basic social views and behavior. As a consequence, isolation made it possible for a local culture to develop that was homogeneous and little influenced by alien concepts. The Baltic, like a moat, served to thwart the influx of experiences with Central Europe.[17] Scandinavian elites, however, did embrace continental culture and Christianity. But we also know that these adoptions were selective at best, and that, essentially, Swedes, Danes, and Norwegians "remained a people apart—uninvolved, unconquered and undiluted."[18] This appelation applied to the Finns as well, despite 650 years under Swedish control.

Although a substantial proportion of Finland's population is today of non-Swedish origin, the long association with Sweden led to its adoption of Sweden's legal system and characteristics. These, in turn, produced a nation with political predispositions and attitudes strikingly similar to those of the other four Nordic countries. In the case of Iceland, this nation has the longest existing Parliament in European history; it has been in existence for more than 1,000 years.[19]

SWISS DEMOCRACY

What about Switzerland? Here is a country that is, by reputation, stable and unchanging from one century to the next, equipped with some sort of federated democracy that makes it possible for the nation to remain neutral in wars and supply the Vatican with guards and the rest of the world with watches and chocolates. The Swiss have a representational form of government, the roots of which can be traced to four valley communities in the area approximately corresponding to the modern cantons of Uri, Schwyz, and Unterwalden, surrounding Lake Lucerne. In these communities, both Swiss democracy and the nation's independence were born.

Cutting through the haze of fable and fact, these people, in the thirteenth century, formed an alliance *in perpetuam* for their common defense. In time, this nucleus of valleys was occupied by descendants of the Alemanni (a miscellaneous conglomeration loosely known as "all men"), a large confederation of German tribes which, together with other barbarians such as the Vandals, Franks, Goths, Saxons, and Thuringians, exerted unremitting pressure on Rome's eastern and northern frontiers. In time, the Alemanni occupied northern Switzerland and southwestern Germany (Swabia). The much older linguistic boundary, determined largely by variations within Germanic settlements, defined much of the German–French speaking areas. The Burgundians, near Lake Geneva and outnumbered by the local Romanized Celtic inhabitants, adopted their tongue, much as the Franks had in France. In time, roughly 20 percent of all Swiss came to speak the French that evolved from Latin. Alemannians in the northeast did maintain cultural and linguistic contact with their homeland, controlled a larger area because of their greater number, and felt less Roman influence than did the Burgundians. Hence,

Germanic dialects prevailed along the modern linguistic frontiers of Switzerland. In short, areas controlled by Burgundians continue to speak French, and those occupied by Alemannians speak German (the latter forming about 7 percent of the modern population).[20]

It is important to note that the Alemanni in Switzerland were never Romanized. They permanently occupied the Alpine valleys after Roman Helvitia had ceased to exist, both in population and historic fact. The Merovingians and the Carolingians after them indeed cast their mantle over the areas held by the Swiss Alemanni. But the interests of these two dynasties were confined mainly to the passes which led to and from Italy. The poverty of Alpine pastoral agriculture and limited intervalley communications permitted little outside influence to infiltrate the relatively isolated communities. Thus, these preserved their early Germanic attitudes toward law based on custom and local assemblies. Not until the ambitious Austrian Habsburgs threatened the autonomy of their way of life did the areas—which eventually evolved into a powerful federation of cantons—resort successfully to arms. As a consequence of the impulse to safeguard their independence, the Swiss became interested in controlling the passes and ultramontane approaches to their homelands.[21]

Interestingly, even with the eventual adoption of the Napoleonic code for the Swiss legal system, the rights of the canton have always complicated the jurisprudence and political structure and practice of the nation in a *sui generis* manner. Furthermore, Swiss independence was established so long ago that direct internal effects of their early tenuous connection with the later versions of the Holy Roman Empire proved negligible. Their early predispositions were thus never destroyed by the actions of autocratic princes. They were only modified over time through their relations with surrounding states.

THE NETHERLANDS

The Netherlands is a designation commonly interchanged with that of Holland. Holland is used in this book only in connection with the Dutch province which bears this name. The distinction is important, because the three "sea provinces" of North and South Holland, Friesland, and Zealand were fundamental factors in the events which ultimately led to Dutch independence. They were also important depositories of characteristics shared to a greater or lesser extent with the other provinces of North Erabant, Guelderland, Drenthe, Groningen, Overyssel, Ultrecht, and Limburg to the south, which form the remarkable Dutch nation. Historically, the term "Low Countries" refers to both the Kingdom of the Netherlands and to that of Belgium, which were once united. However, our immediate concern is with the Netherlands, because it demonstrated the persistence of early traits involving the love of liberty, respect for law, and right of assembly (despite the area's incorporation into Charlemagne's empire); the disadvantage of small size; lack of natural resources; and isolation. That Dutch predisposition toward democracy derived from its early roots is a demonstrable fact.

The Dutch have claimed considerable attention from students of Spanish history because of the occupation of the general area by Spain. Yet, as with the Swiss, geographical factors proved far more determinative in the preservation of certain early Germanic attitudes toward customs as the sources of law and assembly in a primitive political sense than the occupation by Spaniards. More than the influence of Spain, in the Netherlands the sea and the relative isolation of the area played a somewhat similar role. Conversely, the heritage of the Dutch had no impact on the fundamental characteristics of the Spanish nation. As with the other areas surveyed throughout this book, the experience of the Dutch once again reinforces the concept that predispositions exist and continue to influence the political behavior of people.

In common with England and all of Scandinavia, the Netherlands escaped Romanization. One expert on the region, Ivo Schoffer, described the local encounter with the Romans this way: "When Caesar conquered the more densely populated Gallis, his legions invaded the Dutch territory along the banks of the Rhine." He qualified this invasion in the following way:

The area south of the Rhine could be considered to have belonged to the Roman empire from 57 B.C. and was thoroughly Romanized. But although the Romans did penetrate north of the Rhine, this did not result in a definite submission of the Frisians or other tribes in that region. The Rhine in fact remained the natural defense line for the Romans, and as a result Roman influence was regionally varied.[22]

Schoffer built a strong case for the argument that Roman influence was very limited:

Not until 200 A.D. did the defense line in the Netherlands (Low Countries) begin to crumble, as elsewhere, and as the Netherlands were the most far-flung post for the Romans, they were the first to be evacuated. Together with Romans the Eatavian tribes (Germanic allies of Rome) disappeared from history having probably moved south with their Roman allies. Complete evacuation, though, was very slow and in the south (of the Low Countries) it did not happen until the 4th century. There were no real battles in this area, but the Roman retreat coincided with the immigration of Saxons and Angles from the north, Franks in the south.[23]

In other words, the ancestral roots of the Dutch were somewhat similar to those of Anglo-Saxon England and kindred to those of Scandinavia, the Alemanni of Switzerland, and the Frisians, who were already established in the islands facing the Netherlands.

A key factor which contributed to the development of a spirit of cooperation among the Netherlands, affecting all levels of society, was the perennial fight against the sea's encroachment and the reclamation of swampy or inundated lands. Repeated flooding of catastrophic dimensions and stubborn determination to remain where they lived contributed greatly to this characteristic. As a consequence of Charlemagne's stern and persistent efforts, the Low Countries were incorporated into the Holy Roman Empire, flooded fields and all, and converted forcibly to Christianity. In line with the Emperor's policy for the entire realm, land in the Low Countries was divided into political and administrative entities under the control of dukes, counts, and prelates of the Church. From this arrangement emerged the dukedom of Brabant; the countships of Holland, Flanders, and Guelderland; and the bishopric of Utrecht. After the death of Charlemagne, these areas became independent in all but formality.

While there is very limited information about life in these areas during the early Middle Ages, existing evidence suggests that respect for local customs and traditions prevailed.[24] Isolation, a relatively small population, and absence of important natural resources shielded the area of present-day Netherlands from the rapacity of neighboring princes. For hundreds of years, the Dutch made their own laws, imposed river-dues (an imperial right), held a high court of justice, and pursued war or peace at will under the rule of their counts. The autonomy of self-rule of the cities was based on constitutions or charters extended by the Counts, who understood clearly the financial advantages to them of having prosperous urban centers in their territories.

The Counts of Holland governed their jurisdiction for some 400 years, beginning in the latter part of the ninth century and ending about 1300 with the death of Count John I. With the exception of Count John, in the long span of time during which this dynasty ruled, each succeeding Count proved to be of outstanding ability.[25] It was only when the Countship of Holland was inherited by Duke Philip the Good of Burgundy (circa 1436) that Dutch political liberties were severely curtailed. Even so, Dutch prosperity continued. When Duchess Mary, daughter of Duke Charles the Bold, inherited the Countship in March 1477, the authoritarianism of the Burgundian House in Holland came to an end with the granting of what Dutch history refers to as the "Great Privilege." With this development, cities and provinces regained the right to hold diets (assemblies); a high court of justice was established for Holland, Zealand, and Friesland; and Dutch became the official language.

Philip II of Spain, in 1556, after his father's abdication (Charles V of Germany, known as Charles I in Spain), inherited the dominions in the Low Countries, and in the struggle against the Protestant Reformation attempted to throttle Dutch liberties. A struggle for Dutch independence lasted eighty years, finally ending by the treaty signed with Spain at Munster in May 1648. By its terms, the Spanish evacuated the area, allowing the Dutch to rely once again on their own historical traditions to provide the framework of government. Thus, the spirit of authoritarian rule never took hold in the Netherlands as it did further south, where both the Roman and Carolingian traditions of government were more prevalent and for a far longer period of time than in Northern Europe.

CONCLUSION

One can conclude that Northern European historical experiences, handed-down values (particularly as concerning political behavior), and geographical conditions insured that, from early times, political traditions would vary from those in Southern Europe. Roman legal traditions, for example, did not take root. Political traditions evolved in forms different than in most of the countries studied in the rest of this book. Put another way, many of the necessary preconditions of historical and social realities necessary to encourage representational government were in place long before anybody understood the concept of democracy.

In addition, observers of contemporary political affairs in Europe have failed to take seriously the influence of Charlemagne's rule over the Holy Roman Empire which, over the centuries, left a legacy of political and legal traditions that still echo in modern life, especially in parts of Germany. Long reigns offer much opportunity for altered political behavior if the rule is consistent on practices. Just as will be shown in Chapters 6 and 7—how Francisco Franco's long rule (nearly four decades) created conditions that profoundly influenced post–Franco life—so too one can look at the Carolingian period in search of insights, to which we next turn our attention.

NOTES

1. For an introduction see, for example, Harold Lamb, *Charlemagne: The Legend and the Man* (Garden City, N.Y.: Doubleday, 1954), and Geoffrey Barraclough, *The Crucible of Europe: The Ninth and Tenth Centuries in European History* (London: Thames and Hudson, 1976).

2. A. J. P. Taylor, *The Course of German History* (New York: Capricorn Books, 1962), 13.

3. See, for example, Percy E. Corbett, *The Roman Law of Marriage* (Oxford: Clarendon Press, 1930), and more recent scholarship by Susan Treppiari, *Roman Marriage: Iusti Coniuges from the Time of Cicero to the Time of Ulpian* (Oxford: Clarendon Press, 1991).

4. Ernest Levy, "Reflections of the First 'Reception' of Roman Law in Germanic States," *American Historical Review* 48 (1; 1942): 20.

5. Ronald Syme, *Tacitus*, vol. 2 (Oxford: Oxford University Press, 1958), 585.

6. Patricia Crone, "The Tribe and the State," in *States in History*, ed. John A. Hall (Oxford: Basil Blackwell, 1986), 73.

7. Julius Caesar, *The Conquest of Gaul*, trans. S. A. Handford (New York: Penguin, 1982).

8. Tacitus, *The Agricola and the Germania*, trans. S. A. Handford and introduced by a noted historian on Spain, H. Mattingly (New York: Penguin, 1976).

9. Goldwin Smith, *A Constitutional and Legal History of England* (New York: Charles Scribner's Sons, 1952), 2.

10. Winston S. Churchill, *Birth of Britain*, vol. 1 of *A History of the English Speaking Peoples* (New York: Dodd, Mead, 1956), 66.

11. Smith, *A Constitutional History*, 7.

12. Ibid.

13. John Thorn, Roger Lockyer, and David Smith, *A History of England* (New York: Thomas Y. Crowell, 1961), 81.

14. Carl Sephenson, "Feudalism and Its Antecedents in England," *American Historical Review* 48 (2; 1943): 265.

15. George Duby, Dominique Barthelemy, and Charles de La Ronciere, "Portraits," in *Revelations of the Medieval World*, vol. 2 in *A History of Private Life*, ed. George Duby (Cambridge, Mass.: Harvard University Press, 1988), 102–103; Robert Delort, *Life in the Middle Ages* (New York: Universe Books, 1982); R. Allen Brown, *The Normans and the Norman Conquest* (London: Constable, 1969); Henry R. Loyn, *Anglo-Saxon England and the Norman Conquest* (Harlow, England: Longman, 1991).

16. Churchill, *Birth of Britain*, 225.

17. Donald S. Connery, *The Scandinavians* (London: Eyre & Spottiswoode, 1967), 4.

18. Ibid.

19. A number of scholars either concur with Connery's observations as they apply across the entire Northern European sociopolitical landscape or have taken a similar position. Among them are Palle Lauring, *A History of Denmark* (Copenhagen: Host & Son, 1981), 89–91; J. H. S. Birch, *Denmark in History* (London: John Murray, 1938); Knut Gjerset, *A History of the Norwegian People* (New York: AMS Press, 1968), 68–119, 433–434; and Vilhelm Moberg, *A History of the Swedish People* (New York: Pantheon Books, 1972), 8–47, 186–197.

20. E. Bonjour, H. S. Offler, and G. R. Potter, *A Short History of Switzerland* (Oxford: Clarendon Press, 1952), 17–18.

21. On legal history, see Pio Caroni, *"Privatrecht": sine sozialhistorische Eifuhrung* (Bassel: Helbing und Lichtenhahn, 1988); on the Hapsburgs, one of the best sources continues to be Frieda Gallati, *Die Eidgenossenschaft und der Kaiserhof zur Zeit Ferdinands II, und Ferdinands III, 1619–1657* (Zurich: A. G. gebr. Leemann, 1932).

22. Ivo Schoffer, *A Short History of the Netherlands* (Amsterdam: Albert de Lange, 1973), 16.

23. Ibid., 18.

24. Ibid., 49–53.

25. The nature of political leadership in this part of Europe still awaits serious study.

—3—

The Mediterranean Experience: France, Italy, and Spain

A form of government that is not the result of a long sequence of
shared experiences, efforts, and endeavors can never take root.
                                                    —Napoleon Bonaparte

*This chapter focuses on the political experiences of France, Italy,
and Spain in the nineteenth and early twentieth centuries to demonstrate their shared instability and fragility.*

The historical experiences of the southern half of Western Europe were significantly different than to the north. The long-standing historical traditions
were the product of a variety of factors: geography, extensive Latinization of
the area, and the ethnic composition of the populations of the region. All
came together in a body of historical experiences that influenced the nature
of government in the region. France, because of its enormous size and influence in subsequent centuries, is of particular interest. Italy—both the center
of the Roman Empire and a gateway for many non-Europeans into Europe—
is also important to any appreciation of the historical traditions of the West.
Spain is of vital concern, because of its Roman and Arab heritages and also
its extraordinary success with democracy in the brief period since the death
of General Franco. All three nations, as with Germany, will be discussed in
greater detail in future chapters; however, it is important to understand recent
historical forces from which both handed-down values emerged and, subse-

quently, political behavior. Here, we pick up the thread we left in Chapter 1 to continue our discussion of the influence of regional experiences as demonstrated in more modern times. Again, our search is for patterns of behavior that are instructive for the future of democracy in Europe.

THE FRENCH EXPERIENCE

French history and politics is very popular with students of European democracy. It was ruled by Rome and partially by Charlemagne, and therefore draws the attention of historians of early times. But, because Roman and Carolingian influences affected the eventual nature of modern political behavior, it is important to show the link between those earlier experiences and nineteenth- and twentieth-century politics. French territory has long served as a cultural bridge between the Mediterranean world and Northern Europe. Also, it became a powerful nation state that, until at least the middle years of the Cold War, profoundly influenced European political affairs.

As in the cases of Germany, Italy, and Spain, one can identify national patterns of behavior that do influence politics. Gabriel Le Bras, in studying the psychology of French people, focused attention on national characteristics which, because of their relevance to our purposes, is worth quoting at length:

[The Frenchman's] love of clarity results simultaneously from a certain laziness which turns him away from a deeper search and complications; from a desire never to be fooled and from the example set by an elite group which has been trained for two millennia by the exercises of composition and by dialectics: the Romans have imparted it to the Gauls, the lasting influence of the rhetors, the Justinian and Aristotelian renaissance, humanism, the Jesuit program, and later the [Napoleonic] University have reinforced ancient traditions. The qualities of the French mind are a precious gift. . . . The gift is that taken together, a certain superficiality neglecting the shadowy zones of thought simplifies decisions excessively or complicates them by an excess of abstract logic. It sometimes resolves a difficulty with an elegant sally.[1]

Any review of France's extremely complex and fascinating history leads one to the observation that this is a people imbued with a love of clarity, logic, and order, but who are also characterized by political instability as a permanent feature of their national lives.[2] Just from the time of the French Revolution to the present, there have been five republics, the reign of three kings during the Bourbon restoration, two empires, and sixteen constitutions. And, as recently as November 1991, the European press was reporting a serious intent by President François Mitterrand to seek an important constitutional change in 1992, one which would weaken the presidency for the benefit of parliament and that would shorten the chief executive's term in office. The consequences of these political gyrations—change in senior leadership, governments, and constitutions—has placed in some jeopardy France's position as a democracy in times of acute crisis. To repeat the central theme of this book, because of the political instability of French politics, when the times become very difficult, democracy in France is threatened.

Apart from intensive rivalry between monarchists and republicans—still a reality in French politics—there is also a deep cleavage between those who favor representative democracy and opponents who press for an authoritarian approach. This philosophical and ideological conflict leads to others who equate democracy with parliament and to those who look to a direct appeal to the public, bypassing positions and views of elected representatives. The roots of the plebiscitarian approach lies with Napoleon Bonaparte and his rise to power based on his appeal to the masses through plebiscites as a means of legitimating centralization of power. This tactic ended the prospect of long-enduring popular elections and true self-government, and led to the creation of the first empire.[3] A brief review of the main political events of the past two centuries illustrates currents of instability and their effect on democracy in France. Because we have touched on much earlier traditions in Chapter 2, and will again throughout the book, it is more important to focus on more recent political affairs because they illustrate uncertainties in national affairs in French democracy.

Restoration of the Bourbon Monarchy (1814–1830)

The restoration of the Bourbon Monarchy in the persons of Louis XVIII in 1814 and, after his death, his brother, Charles X (until his abdication in 1830), was initially based on the Charter of 1814. This charter had as its intention to create a regime somewhat like that of Great Britain. While not a return to the *ancien régime*, the Bourbon rule retained the bureaucratic reforms developed by Napoleon, particularly the legislative and judicial systems. These included the Great Codes, a complex fiscal system; the important Council of State, the civil service which, in time, came to personify much of how French political administration functioned; and the Bank of France.[4] But there was little that advanced the underpinning of democracy in France in any of these important government reforms. The electorate consisted of about 1 percent of the adult male population; power lay with the upper bourgeoisie and, to some extent, still with the nobility.

The utterly anachronistic character of Charles X's government, and attempts by his ultra-right-wing supporters and religious extremists to exercise total political control through four July ordinances in 1830, resulted in a violent public reaction in Paris. The ordinances called for severe press censorship, dissolution of a Chamber which had not met, reduction in the number of deputies, and electoral rules which would have further reduced the number of voters from 100,000 to about 25,000.[5] What modest gains had been achieved in the direction of constitutional government were mortally threatened by the appointment of Prince Polignac to lead the government. He represented all that most Frenchmen detested: a full return to the *ancien régime*.

The July Monarchy (1830–1848)

The crisis led to the "July Monarchy" of Louis Philippe, Duke of Orleans and distant relative of the Bourbons. The previously dissolved Chamber proclaimed the throne vacant after Charles's abdication and exile to Great Britain, and offered the crown to Louis Philippe. As Ernest John Knapton (long a student of French politics) observed, the July Monarchy was essentially a compromise, with Louis Philippe supported by "the bankers, property owners, industrialists, bondholders, and professional men who were equally distrustful of Ultras and of the Republicans."[6] But the compromise meant an advance in France's move toward a genuine democracy.

Under Louis Philippe (1830–1848), constitutional monarchy in France advanced to become a greater reality. A revision of the nation's Charter, acceptance of which by Louis Philippe constituted a condition to become King of the French, was important for the support of French liberties. The Charter which Charles X had wished to annul was modified. All crimes of the press and those political in nature were to be subject to trial by jury. Departmental and municipal institutions were to be based on an elective system, thus broadening the democratic base of the nation. Freedom of education was established. The Chambers, equally with the Monarch, could initiate introducing laws. Roman Catholicism was declared the religion of the majority of Frenchmen and not the official one of the state. Among other changes included the right to vote, which was extended to include some 200,000 people, primarily property owners. In short and on paper, it appeared that the French government was transforming itself into a substantial democratic institution.

Despite early efforts by the various political leaders to broaden the democratic base, the regime of Louis Philippe developed into a narrow and selfish plutocracy. Lackluster, splintered political groups, tensions between pro- and anticlerical elements, and profound political and social philosophical divisions among the Royalists, Republicans, and Bonapartists all contributed to a general malaise.[7]

The success of one political formula over another often is linked to the economic well-being of a nation. This old observation was true in France, where there were economic problems. In addition to ideological fractionalism, France did not progress economically in the early decades of the nineteenth century, most notably in the industrial sector, for she remained essentially an agricultural nation at a time when there was also a marked increase in population. People were moving in significant numbers to urban centers in search of work. Against this backdrop of political fractionalism, slow economic transformation, and demographic shifts, the multiple crosscurrents underlying the French body politic prevented the emergence of two major parties reflecting basic attitudes, such as occurred in Great Britain or in the United States. This lack of political evolution, combined with the opposite pulls of those leaning or committed to plebiscites as their approach to democratic government and opponents who favored representative democracy, has, down to the present, contributed much to the chronic political fluctuations that so characterize French national affairs.

More immediately in the period of the 1840s, these factors, plus memories of the recent glories of French arms under Napoleon, led to the inglorious demise of Louis Philippe's regime and to the "Second Revolution." This political instability has, at times, placed French democracy in peril, leading to its actual destruction, as occurred in Napoleon III's era, or even more recently, in 1958, when its future depended on the views of one man, Charles de Gaulle.

Second Revolution and the Second Republic (1848–1851)

Upon the abdication of Louis Philippe in February 1848, a provisional republican government came into being. A key and far-reaching plan developed by the temporary government was designed to rapidly provide a firm underpinning for democracy. It included plans for a constituent assembly and for universal suffrage. The latter was an enormous departure for the heretofore small number of property-owning voters. Overnight, the electorate of France increased to some 9 million. With respect to foreign affairs, a manifesto indicated that France "would regard itself as the ally of every people aspiring to determine its own fate."[8] Perhaps historian and President Woodrow Wilson, at the Peace Conference in Versailles following the end of World War I, found inspiration for his doctrine of self-determination in Foreign Minister Alphonse de Lamartine's manifests to the same effect in March 1848.

In the elections held in April 1848, 7.8 million out of an electorate of 9 million Frenchmen went to the polls. In the resulting Assembly of 876 members, Lamartine's moderate Republicans controlled about 500 seats, while Socialist Louis Blanc and his followers barely captured 100 seats. Another temporary form of government emerged from this election. The Assembly appointed an executive commission and a separate group of ministers to govern and carry out policy. In the interim, a constitution was drawn up by the moderate republicans and proclaimed in November.

Meanwhile, between June 23 and 26, extreme violence broke out in Paris, exceeding by far that of the First Revolution (1789). Some 1,500 rioters and 900 soldiers were killed, and 15,000 were arrested, with 4,000 subsequently sent to overseas prison colonies. General Louis Eugene Cavaignac assumed control of the executive commission pending the results of the general elections.

In the new constitution, the rights of free speech and assembly were guaranteed. It provided for the election of a president, the first in French history and the only instance of a direct election until that of General de Gaulle in 1958. A second republic came into being following these elections.

Louis Napoleon, Bonaparte's nephew (the son of Hortense de Beauharnais, Napoleon's brother), had long been attempting to enter French politics, including two unsuccessful coup attempts. In the December elections, Louis

Napoleon emerged with 5.4 million votes, nearly three times the combined totals of four opponents.[9] With these elections, the Second Republic emerged; Louis Napoleon became its President. The Republic lasted only from 1848 to 1851, when the erstwhile President emerged as Emperor Napoleon III.

Second Empire (1852–1870)

Louis Napoleon's problem was that according to the Constitution he could not succeed himself and elections were to take place in 1852. Also, early in his regime limits were set affecting free speech as well as measures curtailing other freedoms (e.g., republican clubs were forbidden). As a young man, Louis Napoleon had flirted with republican and socialist politics, even advocating self-determination for regions (especially in Italy). Therefore, he always suffered from a combination of contradictory impulses: On the one hand aspiring to be the great leader of a great nation and personally accepted as an equal to such other rulers as the tsar of Russia or the emperor of Austria, yet, on the other, harboring republican impulses.

The death knell for the Second Republic and the Constitution of 1848 sounded on December 2, 1851. A coup organized by the Duke de Morny, Louis Napoleon's half-brother, succeeded in dissolving the Chamber of Deputies. Universal suffrage was declared, which included 3 million persons who had been disenfranchised by the Chamber because of any royal or court condemnations. A new Constitution promised free speech, but all newspaper offices were seized. In short, de facto personal rule by Louis Napoleon was supported by a plebiscite which gave him a 92 percent majority. An approving plebiscite of 7.8 million votes in his favor resulted in a December 1852 proclamation confirming Napoleon III as emperor. The issue of government by plebiscite in matters of crucial importance to the nation, with Emperor as Head of State wielding the baton, placed democracy in France on a very shaky basis. In short, the pattern was based on the first Napoleon's conception of democracy.

It is interesting to note the penchant of modern dictators in Europe to rely on the practice of the plebiscite to justify or legitimize their undemocratic regimes (e.g., France, Hitler in Germany, Mussolini in Italy, and, periodically, Franco in Spain). Napoleon III's regime, like those of other future European dictators, was essentially authoritarian; although, toward the end of his reign, after the disastrous war with Germany in 1870, there was a discernible move toward a more liberal government and to a parliamentary system. The fact remains that despite economic and social achievements, the imperfect character of France's democracy, based on a regime legitimized by plebiscite but weak in parliamentary evolution, could not permit Napoleon's regime to weather the crisis stemming from the 1870 Franco–Prussian War.[10]

When dealing with French political history, therefore, we are often required to speak about the role of individuals, rather than merely of the state or of "the people." In fact, the French experience during the first half of the nineteenth century and at times during the twentieth century depended much on the character and ambitions of individual men. In the case of Napoleon, having failed as a personal leader meant that the public rejected both the man and the instruments of governance as they existed in his time. Henry Kissinger, more than simply an experienced diplomat, is also an authority on nineteenth-century European history. He may have captured the essence of Napoleon's problem best of all when he wrote,

The role of the leader is to assume the burden of acting on the basis of a confidence in his own assessment of the direction of events and how they can be influenced. Failing that, crises will multiply, which is another way of saying that a leader has lost control over events. Napoleon turned out to be the precursor of a strange modern phenomenon—the political figure who desperately seeks to determine what the public wants, yet ends up rejected and perhaps even despised by it.[11]

Because the French system so depended on the capabilities of the individual, rather than on the capabilities of a form of government that transcended the activities of one person, France suffered the problem of continued political instability. Once again, Kissinger saw the problem well: "Napoleon's tragedy was that his ambitions surpassed his capacities." Further, "The legacy Napoleon left France was strategic paralysis."[12] The nation continued to pay the political price.

Third Republic (1871–1940)

With the collapse of the Napoleonic government and the Emperor's departure for Great Britain after abdicating, another attempt was made to create a republic. This effort succeeded, in that it at least lasted for seventy years, longer than any of the other systems which followed the *ancien régime*. However, its existence and democratic base were at times vulnerable. For example, the creation of the Action Française in 1898, a monarchist Catholic organization, was for the purpose of destroying the republic. The League of Patriots, formed in 1882 with the aim of war with Germany to recover lost territories from the 1870 conflict and sparked also by the emotion of *revanche*, apparently was prepared to overthrow the republic. These groups, and the persistence of *Boulanguerisme* (another pro–war with Germany movement of those disaffected with the republic, led by General Georges Ernest Boulanger), were but some of the pitfalls which threatened the Third Republic and its democratic constitutional basis.[13] Knapton summarizes the situation well:

The kaleidoscopic pattern of change in French government and parties under the Third Republic can easily baffle an observer accustomed to the relative simplicity of the British or American two-party system. Although certain basic divisions were evident between adherents of the old monarchy, Bonapartists, moderate Republicans and radical Republicans, these groups did not coalesce into well disciplined and manageable entities. Certain issues such as that of clericalism and anticlericalism tended to cut across other allegiances. Some moderate Royalists gave a reluctant support to the Republic in default of any working alternative for, as Thiers had put it, it was the form "which divides us least."[14]

The French became accustomed to the existence of many political parties. That tolerance made possible a situation in which the only way a premier could succeed to office was to form a coalition giving him sufficient support from a wide band of political entities. At best, these parties might only be "generally sympathetic to his aims."[15] The process of having to rule with coalition support proved highly unstable. Between 1875 and 1912, France had thirty-seven premiers, as well as more than forty cabinets. That pattern mimicked the turnover rates evident in Italy. By comparison, there were only eleven ministries in Great Britain during the same years.

Fourth Republic (1946–1958)

In the face of the total military collapse of France in 1940, the French democratic structure disintegrated, to be replaced by the creation of the authoritarian and collaborationist Petain and Laval regime and government by decree. The situation was understandable; probably no nation's democracy could survive during a period of occupation and dominance by a foreign power. It was not until October 1945, when a Constituent Assembly was elected, that another start in the direction of a democratic France emerged once again with the Constitution of 1946. New political forces and philosophies, stemming from the resistance movement and changed circumstances during World War II, complicated the rarely stable traditional French political picture. One could argue that the restoration of a democratic form of government is proof of resilience or interest in democratic practices; republics had been in place since the end of the Franco–German War of 1870. But, nonetheless, the result of the latest rebirth of democratic institutions was a further multiplicity of parties and extreme difficulty in reaching the concensus required to meet grave problems arising from France's wartime defeat.

While the endless round of political coalitions and problems became monotonously familiar, one problem proved to be of unique importance in this period: Algeria. The problem of Algeria—torn between *colons*, local residents who wished Algeria to remain French, and the Algerian National Liberation Front, a native Arab movement which was created to seek total independence—marked the political conscience of a generation of French politicos. The inability of the French and Algerians to resolve the issue, replete with revolution and violence, led to the downfall of the Fourth Republic.[16] The problems with Algeria paved the way for a strong leader, General de Gaulle, to restore a sense of direction and actual discipline to France. Again, as so often in its history, France turned to an individual and not to its institutions to provide the way out of a grave crisis. With the return of de Gaulle to center stage, the French had sounded the death knell for the Fourth Republic.

Fifth Republic (1958–Present)

Immediately upon assuming power in June 1958, de Gaulle sought and obtained from the Assembly full authority for six months. During this time, yet another new Constitution would be drafted and submitted to public referendum. In September 1958, the new Charter was approved by 80 percent of the voters. The fact remains that the granting of full powers to de Gaulle in the interim period was tantamount to the suspension of democracy in France. This is a very important point because had de Gaulle sought to perpetuate himself in power, like Napoleon III did a century before, it is doubtful that the movement could have been prevented by legal means. In short, France's democratic future largely depended on the volition of one man. That such a disaster did not occur is a tribute to de Gaulle's political standards and not necessarily to French traditions or democratic institutions. However, with the new Constitution, de Gaulle was given greater presidential authority than had existed in the previous republic.

De Gaulle served a first term of seven years and was reelected for a second term, of which he served only four years. During both terms, there were only three premiers under his firm leadership. In 1969, he proposed an important constitutional change, one which would have reduced the number of senators elected to half of the Senate's body, and the other half appointed, with the Senate's main purpose "to serve as an advisory council on economic and social questions."[17] A similar arrangement characterized some other European parliamentary upper houses, particularly in the Mediterranean basin, since at least the mid-nineteenth century. The issue was put to the French people in a referendum and they rejected it. De Gaulle then resigned, as he said he would should the public not approve the changes sought. A weakening of France's democratic basis was averted by this vote with a ratio of 52 percent to 48 percent. This was not an overwhelming majority for the rejection of de Gaulle's proposal, suggesting that millions of French voters actually found his idea attractive and appropriate.

A student of modern French politics, William Safran, saw the essence of the new republic's significance tied to its effectiveness: "The streamlining of institutional relationships that in the installation of the Fifth Republic brought about helped to 'unblock' the decision-making process and, if judged in terms of policy outputs, transformed the French political system into a relatively efficacious and responsive one."[18]

Policies directed toward decolonization initiated by de Gaulle led to an independent Algeria. Other initiatives resulted in rapprochement with West Germany, and to the successful rebuilding of France's war-torn economy. One direct by-product of these three initiatives has been relative political stability during the past thirty years. Nevertheless, many cross-tensions remain in the French social and political structures. We have only to recall the May Days of 1968 and the social protests of 1993. For that reason, a great deal of attention will be paid to contemporary French realities in Chapter 5. However, suffice it to point out that whether, in times of acute crisis, the Fifth Republic and the Constitution of 1958 would survive intact with its safeguards for preservation of French democracy remains an unanswered question.

The picture just painted of French politics might appear to some readers as an exaggeration of instability; an overstatement of reality. The French case does raise the possibility that instability, or turnover of governments and constitutions, does not necessarily mean that democracy is at risk. After all, the French kept creating new republics. To American and English people, churn means risk, given the fact that Anglo-Saxon and American democracies turn over their leaders less frequently, keep their constitutions far longer, and place more emphasis on the rule of law rather than on the leadership skills of kings, presidents, or prime ministers. The French case remains problematic, however, precisely because churn creates inefficiencies in public administration, with unwanted economic and social consequences for a nation that cherishes order. Witness the pattern of voting in France in the mid-1990s, when the French voter did not hesitate to vote parties in and out of power. There is also the nagging question, what happens if a French prime minister or president chooses a course different from de Gaulle's? Would French democracy be at risk?

THE ITALIAN EXPERIENCE

Describing Italy's flirtation with democracy is a difficult task.[19] Even more difficult is any attempt to trace early roots of democratic behavior in Italy's extraordinarily long and complex history. No linkages appeared between the popular governments of city–states in the Italian Middle Ages—which were eventually engulfed in oligarchical or imperial rule—and the evolution toward democracy which has occurred over the past century. In fact, seeds of democracy earlier than the mid-nineteenth century are puzzling more than anything else. Even Denis Mack Smith, who has long studied modern Italy, struggled with the issue, finally concluding that, "Centuries of foreign rule had left Italy not only without a nucleus around which a national movement could gather, but also without experience of free government."[20] The fact remains that liberal democratic institutions are of very recent vintage in Italy. Political unification of the "boot" into a nation state only became a reality in 1861, when an Italian Parliament came into existence to create a new kingdom of some 22 million souls. Both landlords and peasants generally reacted to this development with apathy, neither in favor of unification nor strongly supportive of democratic principles of government.

One result of a lack of common ideals shared by most Italians was that senior government administration between 1861 and 1896 proved very unstable. During that period, there were thirty-three different cabinets. Furthermore, in those thirty-five years, the number of eligible voters remained but a fraction of the total population. In the main, these voters and their political leaders were guided by deals made between small groups, with the vast majority of the adult population eliminated from national political life.[21] In the South, illiteracy, brigandage, deplorable economic and social conditions, and extant feudal realities, combined with intense individualism (almost anarchistic in character), renders any attempt to uncover solid underpinnings for democracy in the early years of the unification almost impossible. Even in 1996, it was the Mafia which exerted true control in Sicily, despite strenuous efforts by the government in Rome to break its power.

Unification, and whatever evolution eventually took place toward democracy, occurred through a parliamentary system, mainly the work of a few capable leaders such as Camillo di Cavour and later Giovanni Giolitti, but with members rarely elected freely. The Monarchy had little sympathy with any movement which threatened its controlling role. Nor were the monarchs blessed with outstanding marks of enlightened leadership. They were not even paladins of education. To this gloomy picture must be added the constant opposition of the Vatican to both unification and democracy in a country which was almost entirely Roman Catholic.[22] It really was not until after World War II that the Catholic tradition could express itself politically through the medium of the Christian Democrats entering the political life of the nation. The Vatican, although very active in attempting to persuade voters on particular issues, was practically devoid of direct political influence. As we will demonstrate in detail in Chapter 5, since World War II the Christian Democrats have been the single most dominating political force in the country. In short, the behavior of this kind of party is barely one generation old in the traditions of Italian politics. Even so, in recent elections it was practically obliterated, as we will explain later.

One of the most distinguishing characteristics of Italian government in the modern period is its continued volatile leadership. The turnover in cabinets, for instance, far exceeds that of any other Western European nation in the same period. Between June 1860 and October 1922 (when Benito Mussolini came to power), thirty-eight prime ministers attempted to rule in Italy. Even in the two years between the end of Mussolini's dictatorship and the termination of World War II, two prime ministers governed Italy, each with his own cabinet. In the first thirty-eight years following the end of the war (between June 1945 and August 1983), forty-four cabinets attempted to rule—fifty-five as of April 1996. This rate of turnover in the twentieth century actually exceeded that which occurred in the period from 1860 to 1896. So the volatility in leadership actually produced less leadership.

But why was there so much turnover? The large number of turnovers in the period from 1860 to 1996 was the result of fragile coalitions, unable to work together in the compromising "give-and-take" characteristics of effective democratic governments. The same has held true during the continued churn in government leadership that has occurred in the mid-1990s and was again clearly reflected in the national elections of April 1996. One consequence has been to offer no case to the Italian people of the benefits of true democracy in offering effective, results-oriented leadership. The extraordinary fragmentation of political activity also suggests the inability of the Italian population to coalesce around two or three parties in sufficient numbers to provide relatively long-term governance.[23]

The key dilemma is whether such a complex of conflicting regional economic and social philosophies can permit Italy's brand of uneasy democracy to survive should acute economic and social turmoil again afflict Europe. The concern is made especially urgent today, given the quick return of ethnic and regional politics evident in many parts of Europe since the end of the Cold War. What happened in Yugoslavia, across a short body of water from Italy, is a clear indicator that the region is not immune from such a concern. In fact, regionalism was an important issue in Italian politics in 1995–1996. Italy is more than just a neighbor of what used to be Yugoslavia; we have a situation in Italy where various minorities live (so far) under one flag.

Because the precariousness of democratic institutions in Italy is a function of social, economic, and political conditions which currently are undergoing great change and stress, Chapter 5 will extend the discussion of the Italian situation. The heightened churn now evident in Italian society is largely because of the enormous prosperity and social changes which have taken place there since the 1950s, and which have now reached a point that they cannot be ignored in any assessment of the future of democracy in Europe.

THE SPANISH EXPERIENCE

The experiences of the Germans, English, Scandinavians, Dutch, Swiss, French, and Italians confirm the importance of predispositions toward certain types of political behavior. Thus, one of the problems which arises in connection with the development of a methodology for assessing Spain's democratic future relates to the matter of political dispositions. On the one hand, the peninsula endured intensive Romanization for a period of more than 600 years, with sections of Iberia as Roman as Rome itself. On the other hand, the invasion of the Arabs and their initial wide dispersion throughout most of Spain, combined with 800 years of struggle leading to their expulsion just 500 years ago, led to the development of political and social attitudes showing variation in the component parts of Iberia. Put another way, intense regionalism and difficult nation state building complicated the Iberian historical traditions affecting politics.[24]

The fight, over many centuries, that marked relations between Christians and Moslems in Spain, in which Castile emerged as the spearhead of the movement to take back lands from the Moslem invaders, gave rise within this region to a democratic order far in advance of its evolution elsewhere in Europe. The repopulation of the Duero Valley, initially sparked by the Asturian–Leonese dynasty and continued in the expanding territories of Castile after securing its independence from the latter, consisted of free-minded peoples, in general from the Pyrenees and the Cantabrian range. They were a mountain folk accustomed to an independent way of life, and came from areas which either escaped Hispano–Visigothic subjugation or were only lightly touched by the relationship. In fact, some pockets of remote Basque valleys were still pagan at the time of the Arab invasion and governed their interrelationships on the basis of custom.[25] Even those people who fled from the large landed estates in Galicia untouched by the events of 711, and whose status in society was of a servile nature, had to be of a courageous and adventurous temperament to run the risk involved in flight.

Movement into unoccupied lands offered squatters the opportunity (with royal assent) to acquire property and a better way of life, provided they had the stamina and courage to develop these areas and fight off Islamic harassments. Galicians, returning Goths, Basques, Cantabrians, Franks from the north side of the Pyrenees, and Asturians were the main ethnic stocks which moved into the expanding frontier sectors. In spirit and ideals they were a very different people from those who remained content, under Islam, to adopt the new faith, abandoning their age-long traditions and attitudes. These had constituted the majority of Hispania's inhabitants, but once they fervently entered the Islamic fold they also paid the eventual penalty of retreat and expulsion in 1492. Finally, in 1609, the last of the Moriscos (Islamic peoples) were eliminated from Spain. The Mozarabs (Arabized Christians), who were greatly in the minority, remained in the peninsula as major remnants of the old ethnic strain. Even in Catalonia, in northeastern Iberia, where Islamic intrusion lasted barely ninety years, the area was repopulated with an influx of Franks, returning Goths, and probably fused Hispano–Romans, all of whom changed in substance the physical inheritance and character of the pre-Islamic inhabitants. Although it can be assumed that many Hispano–Romans remained in urban areas, how many retained their Christian faith or reneged remains unknown.[26]

Occupation of the newly conquered or previously abandoned lands led to the issuance of charters for hundreds of communities by the Asturian–Leonese and later by Castilian monarchs. These guaranteed self-government and a wide range of civil rights. So widespread was this issuance of charters, with the resultant emergence of thousands of small proprietors, that a feudal order never sank roots in Castile as deeply as this institution did elsewhere in Europe and in Catalonia. There never rose within Castile a class of large landowners sufficiently numerous and financially powerful to impose serfdom on the Castilians during the centuries of the Reconquest.[27]

The masses of people were essential to the monarchs for the defense of their kingdoms, and they recognized this reality. This factor was the main difference between Spain and the situation in feudal Europe, where charters were granted to cities by both monarchs and independent nobles. In the latter cases, the rationale was purely economic. In Castile, it arose from military necessity. In the relatively early stages of the Reconquest, cavalry was an important element in the composition of military forces, as there were not enough knights to guard the frontiers or to fill out royal contingents. Villagers and other commoners who owned horses and were willing to serve as soldiers were granted the status of village cavaliers (*caballeros villanos*), with privileges equal to those of the lower nobility (*infanzones*).[28] In Catalonia, where cities were also the recipient of charters granting a considerable degree of self-government, the need for defense was satisfied with the creation of the *ciutadans honrats*, who eventually became a powerful urban oligarchy.

By the time of the Catholic Kings in the fifteenth century (Ferdinand and Isabel, the Monarchs who are so associated with Christopher Columbus and the discovery of the New World), the stage had been set for the probable emergence of some democratic-like structure in the peninsula with its implications for changes in attitude toward government and law, modifying the Roman inheritance passed on through Hispano–Visigothic traditions and institutions. But the entry of the Hapsburgs into Spanish history, with their concept of empire derived from the Germanic dream of revising Charlemagne's aspirations, and with a Monarch at the same time serving as King of Spain and Emperor of the Holy Roman Empire, the course of Spanish political affairs changed drastically. The road toward absolutism began, and with it the throttling of Castilian and Catalonian democratic inclinations. Through the Habsburgs and, later, the Bourbons (1500s–1700s), remote attitudes toward the concept of total power as attributes of a monarchy and nation state, which had survived in Romanized areas of Europe, profoundly affected Spanish political development and popular behavior.[29]

For one thing, autocratic, centralist Castilian rule, more frequently than not, became the norm in modern Spanish political affairs. Strong monarchical rule characterized Hapsburg authority all through the sixteenth and seventeenth centuries. Bourbon rule after 1700 also stressed centralized administration, even in the face of continued regionalist resistance—a pattern of behavior which continued down into the twentieth century. As parliamentary authority and that of a prime minister grew, even in the second half of the nineteenth century, Castilian focus remained on centralized administration.[30]

This interpretation of more recent events is not an attempt to trivialize actions of the Spanish nation state in the nineteenth century, when, like most Western European governments, a parliament (*Cortes*) evolved into an important institution and the function of a prime minister and cabinet followed the Bourbon model with institutional behavior similar to what existed in, for example, France, Prussia, and even in Italy. But the events of the nineteenth century were not conducive to serious evolution toward democratic behavior. For one thing, the invasion of Spain in the early 1800s by the armies of Napoleon Bonaparte devastated the economy of the country, which required decades to recover. There was a minor flirtation with liberal political institutions in the period after the fall of Napoleon, but it was quickly capped by the return of Fernando VII as an absolutist monarch in the 1820s. The middle decades of the century illustrated a pattern of parliamentary and ministerial churn not dissimilar to the Italian experience. The First Republic (1873–1874) was an unmitigated disaster.[31] One footnote on the Constitution of 1869: It has whole passages lifted from the text of the Constitution of the United States, proving once again that indigenous conditions are more important influences on political behavior than outside imports because this document was tossed out with the republic it represented.

The last third of the nineteenth century had a number of features that almost lent themselves to comparison to Italy's situation. Antonio Canovas del Castillo and Praxedes Sagasta, each the head of their own party, literally took turns being prime ministers and dominating the *Cortes*, a body that had a very limited electorate to vote it in. Conditions remained this way, even after the death of these two politicians, down to the time of General Primo de Rivera's establishment of a military dictatorship (1923–1930). The short-lived Second Republic, which soon followed the failure of the dictatorship was, in hindsight, an exception to a long-standing tendency toward authoritarian rule in an ethnically pluralistic society in which the element of compromise and coordination so essential to democratic forms of government failed to survive. For that matter, similar patterns were evident in Italian political affairs and, to only a slightly lesser degree, in French politics.

As we will explore in considerable detail in Chapters 6 and 7, the reemergence of the monarchy under King Juan Carlos and the creation of a democratic structure after General Franco's death, following over thirty years of dictatorship, is an extraordinary political phenomenon for Spain and has caught the attention of Europe and all of Latin America.

CONCLUSION

Given its previous experiences with representative government, one has to ask the question: Would the Spanish democratic structure survive acute economic duress or social turmoil? The answer, as with the Italian, French, and German cases, lies in a careful understanding of the handed-down values, traditions, and modern economic and social realities at work.

The essential common ingredient in Southern Europe is a body of experiences that includes highly unstable parliamentary rule, a penchant for the "quick fix" by using a dictator or highly authoritarian measures, and, often, a legal tradition that fostered centralized nation states in highly charged ethnic plutocratic nations (France excluded, because of having the most homogeneous ethnic social structures). Once again, however, we find that paying attention to what ethnic groups came and went over time is important, not because of who the individuals were, but out of a realization that different ethnic groups bring with them unique social, cultural, and legal attitudes which perdure for very long periods of time.

NOTES

1. Henry W. Ehrmann, *Politics in France* (Boston: Little, Brown, 1968), 68.

2. Particularly influential on us was Volume 1 of Fernand Braudel, *The Identity of France* (New York: Harper and Row, 1988).

3. Ernest John Knapton, *France* (New York: Charles Scribner's Sons, 1971), 330.

4. Ibid., 362.

5. Ibid., 371.

6. Ibid., 372.

7. H. A. C. Collingham, *The July Monarchy: A Political History of France, 1830–1848* (London: Longman, 1988).

8. Knapton, *France*, 391.

9. Ibid., 394.

10. Theodore Zeldin, *The Political System of Napoleon III* (London: Macmillan, 1958).

11. Henry Kissinger, *Diplomacy* (New York: Simon and Schuster, 1994), 136.

12. Ibid.

13. Many historians have studied the political Right in modern France. Most useful to us in exploring the delicate path of modern French democratic behavior were Robert D. Anderson, *France, 1870–1914: Politics and Society* (London: Routledge, 1977); Michael Burns, *Rural Society and French Politics: Boulangism and the Dreyfus Affair, 1886–1900* (Princeton, N.J.: Princeton University Press, 1984); William D. Irvine, *The Boulanger Affair Reconsidered: Royalism, Boulangism, and the Origins of the Radical Right in France* (New York: Oxford University Press, 1989); Peter M. Rutkoff, *Revanche and Revision: The Ligue des Patriotes and the Origins of the Radical Right in France, 1882–1900* (Athens: Ohio State University Press, 1981); David Thompson, *Democracy in France since 1870* (London: Oxford University Press, 1964); and Eugene J. Weber, *Action Francaise* (Stanford: Stanford University Press, 1962).

14. Knapton, *France*, 436.

15. Ibid.

16. Ian Lustick, *State-Building Failure in British Ireland and French Algeria* (Berkeley: Institute of International Studies, University of California, 1985); Jacques R. Goutor, *Algeria and France, 1830–1963* (Muncie, Ind.: Ball State University Press, 1965).

17. Knapton, *France*, 556.

18. William Safran, *The French Polity* (London: Longman, 1991), 246.

19. The literature on Italian politics is vast. Useful introductions to the problems relevant to our chapter are J. K. Hyde, *Society and Politics in Medieval Italy: The Evolution of Civil Life, 1000–1350* (New York: St. Martin's Press, 1973), and F. Spotts and T. Weiser, *Italy: A Difficult Democracy* (Cambridge: Cambridge University Press, 1968), 1–16.

20. Denis Mack Smith, *Italy* (Ann Arbor: University of Michigan Press, 1959), 11.

21. Armand Patrucco, *The Critics of the Italian Parliamentary System, 1860–1915* (New York: Garland, 1991). This is one of the few studies to look at the problem of late nineteenth-century Italian government practices.

22. Ornella Pellegrino Confessora, *Cattolici col papa, leberali con lo Statuto: richerche sci conservatori nazionali (1863–1915)* (Rome: ELIA, 1973).

23. This is a well-recognized, ongoing problem to all who study Italian politics.

For example, see Pietro Barcellona, *La Republica en transformazione: problemi istituzionali del caso italiano* (Bari: De Donato, 1978); Samuel H. Barnes, *Representative in Italy: Institutionalized Tradition and Electoral Choice* (Chicago: University of Chicago Press, 1977); Giuseppe De Palma, *Political Syncretism in Italy: History, Coalition Strategies and the Present Crisis* (Berkeley and Los Angeles: University of California Press, 1977).

24. James N. Cortada and James W. Cortada, *An Introduction to Early Spain, 218 B.C.–1037 A.D.* (forthcoming), looks at these issues in Central Pyrenaic Iberia in detail.

25. Joaquin Arbeloa, *Los Origenes del Reino de Navarra*, 2 vols. (San Sebastian: Editorial Aunamendi, 1969); Jose Maria Lacarra, *Historia del Reino de Navarra en la Edad Media* (Pamplona: Caja de Ahorros de Navarra, 1975).

26. Thomas F. Glick, *Islamic and Christian Spain in the Early Middle Ages* (Princeton, N.J.: Princeton University Press, 1975); Claudio Sanchez Albornoz, *La España cristiana de los siglos VIII á XI* (Madrid: Espasa-Calpe, 1980), especially 1–60; Pierre Bonnassie, *La Catalogne*, 2 vols. (Toulouse: Publications de l'Universite de Toulouse-Le Marail, 1975), especially Vol. 1; Francisco Javier Fernández Conde, *La Iglesia de Asturias en la alta edad media* (Oviedo: Duputación de Oviedo, Instituto de Estudios Asturianos, 1972).

27. This subject has recently received excellent treatment. On Visigothic Spain, for example, see P. D. King, *Law and Society in the Visigothic Kingdom* (Cambridge: Cambridge University Press, 1972), and on local rights (*fueros*), see James F. Powers, *A Society Organized for War: Iberian Municipal Militias in the Central Middle Ages, 1000–1284* (Berkeley and Los Angeles: University of California Press, 1988). For a broader study, see Luis G. de Valdeavellano, *Curso de historía de las instituciones españolas* (Madrid: Revista de Occidente, 1968).

28. For life on the Spanish frontier, see Powers, *A Society Organized for War*, but also Charles J. Bishko, *Spanish and Portuguese Monastic History: 600–1300* (London: Valorum, 1984).

29. José Luis Bermejo Cabrero, *Estudios sobre la administracíon central española (siglos XVI y XVII)* (Madrid: Centro de Estudios Constitucionales, 1982); R. A. Stradling, *Philip IV and the Government of Spain, 1621–1665* (Cambridge: Cambridge University Press, 1988); John H. Elliott, *Imperial Spain, 1469–1716* (London: Edward Arnold, 1963), and John H. Elliott, *The Revolt of the Catalans: A Study in the Decline of Spain, 1598–1640* (Cambridge: Cambridge University Press, 1963).

30. John Lynch, *Bourbon Spain: 1700–1808* (Oxford: Basil Blackwell, 1989), 67–115, 157–164, 247–328; Raymond Carr, *Spain: 1808–1975* (Oxford: Oxford University Press, 1982), 348–355, 366–379, 564–602, 673–709.

31. Carr, *Spain*, 327–346.

—4—

Democracy and Authoritarianism: Germany

We Germans fear God, but nothing else in the world.
                                        —Otto von Bismarck

This chapter discusses the concepts of democracy and authoritarianism and then how they are reflected in the German experience. In addition, we review the role of women and children, and what impact growing up in West and East Germany has on the nation.

In the previous two chapters, we pointed out the fact that democratic structures or, more precisely, parliamentary forms of government, did collapse in Western Continental Europe (in Italy, Germany, Spain, and France) during the 1920s, 1930s, and 1940s. Also a casualty of the time was democratic philosophy, when confronted with extraordinary social, economic, and political strains. Beginning with this chapter, and for the rest of this book, we will focus primarily on specific countries, looking at recent trends that assess how democracy is doing and suggest how its future may be calculated. While we have argued so far that one should look at democracy's performance and prospects against a longer time horizon than is normally done, we also believe that recent experiences and current realities can be added to the soup to make sense of the issue. Now, we will deal with democracy as it operates in the post–World War II period. In addition, since so much more information is available on what went on in Europe in the second half of the twentieth century, we now need to focus more precisely our perspective on the role of handed-down values and assessments of democratic behavior if we are to make sense of recent trends in European political behavior.

Our concern for the recent past is highlighted by the fact that, since the end of World War II, in different time periods, there has been a remarkable resurgence of democracy in the very countries where dictatorships had flowered. But to assume confidently that Germany, France, Italy, and Spain, not to mention smaller European countries, can weather future severe economic and political crises without the danger of collapsing flies in the face of past experience and is simply a dangerous tempting of fate. That is one of our key messages. Too many unappreciated variables come into play, such as the influence of national psyches and the kind and quality of leadership which would emerge or be in place at the time of an acute crisis. In the 1930s, Hitler came to power in a major nation while the collection of cabinet ministers in France are generally thought by historians to have been the most incompetent in modern times. On the other hand, great leadership can also emerge, as was the case with Winston Churchill in Great Britain and, to draw on a more contemporary example, perhaps King Juan Carlos in Spain during the late 1970s and the 1980s. The point is, many variables affect the quality and resilience of a nation's democracy. Just because a nation embraces democracy's government trappings does not mean that this form of government will remain in place, despite all the best intentions in the world, particularly in the halls of American and European governments. Our statement is even more so the case if a society does not have the necessary social and cultural predispositions (e.g., handed-down values) necessary to make democracy work, or at least work sufficiently well enough to keep.

ON ASSESSING THE HEALTH OF DEMOCRACY

A noted political scientist, Samuel P. Huntington, cataloged the variety of theories and variables that students of democracy and the process of democratization have most frequently used to understand this particular form of government.[1] In the process, he developed a list of the variables that are seen as essential to the promotion and welfare of democracy:

1. A high overall level of economic wealth.
2. Relatively equal distribution of income and wealth.
3. A market economy.
4. Economic development and social modernization.
5. A feudal aristocracy at some point in the history of society.
6. The absence of feudalism in the society.
7. A strong bourgeoisie ("no bourgeois, no democracy" in Barrington Moore's formulation).

8. A strong middle class.
9. High levels of literacy and education.
10. An instrumental rather than consummatory culture.
11. Protestantism.
12. Social pluralism and strong intermediate groups.
13. The development of political contestation before the expansion of political participation.
14. Democratic authority structures within social groups, particularly those closely connected to politics.
15. Low levels of civil violence.
16. Low levels of political polarization and extremism.
17. Political leaders committed to democracy.
18. Experience as a British colony.
19. Traditions of toleration and compromise.
20. Occupation by a pro-democratic power.
21. Influence by a pro-democratic power.
22. Elite desire to emulate democratic nations.
23. Traditions of respect for law and individual rights.
24. Communal (ethnic, racial, religious) homogeneity.
25. Communal (ethnic, racial, religious) heterogeneity.
26. Consensus on political and social values.
27. Absence of consensus on political and social values.[2]

This is a fascinating list of what political scientists believe are circumstances allowing for a democracy to thrive. Huntington's comment on the list is that "the multiplicity of theories and the diversity of experience suggest the probable validity" of a group of six propositions:[3]

1. No single factor is sufficient to explain the development of democracy in all countries or in a single country.
2. No single factor is necessary to the development of democracy in all countries.
3. Democratization in each country is the result of a combination of causes.
4. The combination of causes producing democracy varies from country to country.
5. The combination of causes generally responsible for one wave of democratization differs from that responsible for the other waves.
6. The causes responsible for the initial regime changes in a democratization wave are likely to differ from those responsible for later changes in that wave.[4]

Huntington's observations represent a useful theoretical backdrop for the assessment of any democracy that would be acceptable to many political scientists and government officials. It is, in short, a nice place to begin.

THE IMPORTANCE OF UNDERSTANDING
HANDED-DOWN VALUES

However, while Huntington is very much on target, what needs to be added to his list is a heavier emphasis on the role that handed-down values and attitudes within family traditions have on the predisposition of a society either to entertain the notion of democracy or to sustain that form of government. This idea of handed-down values is key to our thinking, and an added dimension we feel crucial to the discussion about the successful prospects of any democracy. Related to the role of handed-down values is the importance of intra-familial behavioral patterns, since these extend the practices of home-created beliefs and behavior to a larger group. It is in understanding the forces of change (economic, social, educational, and legal) on the family that one can begin to understand the prospects of democracy in Europe.

Pertinent to our belief in the importance of handed-down values are two points in Huntington's long list: Number 19, "traditions of toleration and compromise," and Number 23, "traditions of respect for law and individual rights." They are important because, in a society that is ripe for democratic institutions or wants to preserve that form of government, these two sets of traditions receive an early start in the home. Intra-familial relations anchored in such beliefs and practices inculcate attitudes in children which spill over into political philosophy and community participation in adulthood. In the United States and many other societies, there are various folk sayings that capture the essence of this concept; for example, when you hear someone say, "Your mother taught you everything you needed to know," or, more recently, captured in the title of a best-selling book, *All I Really Need to Know I Learned in Kindergarten*.[5] Whether children, in time, ape their parents' particular political coloration or not is beside the point if these two traditions are part of the offsprings' psyche. It can be reasonably assumed, for this hypothesis to prove valid, that the pattern of child upbringing in such an atmosphere is characteristic of the vast majority of a nation's populace.

If the experience at home is reinforced by parallel exposure at school, the basis for democracy as a way of eventual national political life would be strengthened. The seed of democracy is always planted in the home. For this reason, any desire to understand how to influence the national course of democracy in any country really requires the application of the skills of a social psychologist and political sociologist. In our research, we found a paucity of material that applies this approach to the study of democracy. Such studies of familial patterns of behavior as they relate to subsequent political attitudes and activities need to be conducted for Western Europe to better understand their nature.

The German experience is a case in point. Here we have two Germanies that, when put together into one nation by Bismarck in the nineteenth century, already had long-standing differences in their political, religious, and social traditions; and which spent the period from the 1940s to the late 1980s apart, with profoundly different types of governments, and are now attempting to make democracy work. One can immediately see the enormous risk for democracy, yet only by getting into the details of family life can anyone expect to understand specifically what young Germans, yet to be adults, can be expected to act out, let alone what German leaders need to do to reinforce democratic principles. Specifically, the next wave of studies on democracy must, from a practical point of view, focus on identifying father–mother, parent–child, and sibling behavioral patterns which could negatively or positively affect a child's eventual propensity for acceptance or rejection of democracy.

European sociologists have done considerable research into family patterns, particularly with regard to women's rapidly changing roles; indeed, we have relied extensively on this body of research in assessing democracy in Germany, Italy, France, and Spain. But rarely have these studies tied findings to democracy's prospects. Sensitivity to familial evolution since the end of World War II is especially notable in Germany, where extraordinary efforts have been made to assure survival of democracy. But German official and private measures have relied mainly on economic policy and legislation to safeguard the nation's democracy.

The idea of understanding and stressing the linkage between what happens in the family and school and a nation's political philosophy and goals is not a new one. German sociologist Ingeborg Weber-Kellermann has pointed out that "Nazi policymakers were not the only ones concerned with connections between family life and political agendas in the 1930s." He mentions that emigres Max Horkheimer, Erich Fromm, and Herbert Marcuse "published many of their studies on authority relations in the family after their emigration in the mid 1930s." Further, Weber-Kellermann points out the following:

These views argued that the political system of authoritarian rule had a basis in the early childhood experiences in the family, and particularly in the strict patriarchal family of German tradition. This group of social psychologists succeeded in illustrating the interdependence between authoritarian family socialization and Fascism and in discovering how smoothly the dictators of their time exploited psychological mechanisms.[6]

Similar concern for democracy, but on a much broader scale with regard to the five major continental democracies, would be of value to the governments concerned, as their publics would have a better understanding of themselves.

Contemporary anthropologists and sociologists frown on studies concerned with overall national character or traits. This view is understandable because of the great advances made in basing social studies on empirical data and refined methodologies. Most of the conclusions reached concerning national character of a half century or so ago were heavily dependant on subjective judgment. Yet, many of these had considerable validity because of close knowledge of cultures studied by specialists of the day. Certainly, no serious student of modern society could deny the splendid work of Ruth Benedict and her associates in helping to crack the Japanese values code. The drafting of resultant tracts led to the surrender of thousands of Japanese soldiers during World War II.[7]

While we do not propose a return to the approach followed by previous generations of anthropologists and sociologists, there is a need not to reject entirely their body of work. As any clear thinking foreign resident in a country knows, easily recognizable national traits are identifiable. In fact, whether a diplomat, student, or businessperson, knowledge of these traits are sought and essential in order to engage effectively in binational or multinational negotiations or conversations. We harp on this point because, in addition to hundreds of studies and doctoral dissertations by social science scholars, there are other important works by highly knowledgeable authors who are not sociologists or anthropologists. For example, British journalist John Ardagh's work on Germany, and Italian writer Luigi Barzini's work on Italy, help one to understand the evolution of democracy in these two countries.[8] Certain clearly discernible national traits affecting democracy's future become readily apparent (e.g., authoritarian behavior in Germany, rooted in the past in varying intensity, and marked individualism in Italy, with low regard for government). Nevertheless, the truly significant task must be carried out by sociologists, such as social psychologists and political psychologists. Ideally, comparative studies could be done to arrive at a fuller list of the preconditions for the success of democracy that, in effect, adds to Huntington's list of twenty-seven in a more comprehensive and basic manner.

THE IMPORTANCE OF CHILDREN IN DEMOCRACY'S FUTURE

A good place to begin applying notions of handed-down values and national traits is with children, because any discussion about the prospects of democracy must increasingly focus on the future citizens of a democratic society: today's children. Because children are society's messages, to be delivered at a time when we are no longer present, the source of their behavior obviously is the home and, to an important degree, the school. Both institutions have undergone profound changes in the second half of the twentieth century in Germany and across all of Western Europe. The absence of war affecting the major European states; the achievement of women's rights; extraordinary advances in technology, communications, computers, business practices, and medicine; and the impressive increase in the numbers of students at all levels of education have produced remarkable improvements in the quality of life in Europe. Also, two generations of Western Europeans have now been spared the horrors of war and have enjoyed an economic and social security never before experienced. Obviously, these circumstances have brought about important changes in social mores and political attitudes which have been thoroughly examined by both European and American political scientists, economists, and sociologists.

Nevertheless, we do not know a great deal about what effect these transformations have had on familial mores, child raising, and consequences relative to children's eventual attitudes toward democracy. We recently saw a dramatic example of this gap in knowledge in the form of behavior by German "skinheads," who have displayed a virulent and violent hatred for nonethnic residents in Germany (e.g., Turkish workers and Eastern Europeans), to the great surprise and horror of many around the world. Proper studies of families would offer a better understanding of why this is so, and even offer an early warning system for officials who want to either reinforce democracy or replace it with another form of government.

We imply no value judgment as to whether democracy is a "good" or "bad" form of government in defining the value of understanding how familial activities influence political attitudes. There are fundamental issues at stake. For example, if compromise has become a family trait instead of rigid authoritarianism, children will be better prepared in adulthood to favor democratic political and social values. On the contrary, if a "father knows best" and "don't speak until permitted" philosophy prevails, adult attitudes may be negative about the "give and take" essential to democracy.

The complexity of the type of information required from studying familial mores to enlighten people on political issues should not be underestimated. Social scientist Frank A. Pinner described the issues associated with this kind of analysis:

The long-term objective of any student of political socialization is to specify how experiences account for personality orientations, and in what way the latter explain specifically political dispositions and actions. We are still a long way from this goal. Many of the available studies describe either relationships between social orientations and specifically political attitudes. In the first case, the probable political effects of general social orientations can only be guessed; whereas in the second, the social experiences underlying general social orientations remain obscure.

Insofar as researchers do attempt to link political orientation to individual experience, their work often suffers from a methodological difficulty. In the tradition of anthropological case studies, the writers merely demonstrate the simultaneous presence, in some one culture, of a certain pattern of child-raising together with some particular set of political orientations. But they do not demonstrate empirically that within the culture they are considering there is a relationship between certain child-raising practices and the individual political orientations. Nor do they use the—however questionable—method of ecological correlations to show that cultures with different child-raising patterns also exhibit different political patterns.[9]

Although his comments were published in 1972, the situation remains relatively unchanged. In Western Europe, particularly in Germany, France, Italy, and Spain, cultural, linguistic, historical, economic, and political diversity renders the establishment of an empirical basis for the development of broadly applicable theoretical frameworks a daunting task. What would be required is an extension of comparative political sociology, both on a national scale and interrelated with Europe's key continental democracies. With the creation of the European Community, the need becomes even more urgent, and the results are probably a critical success factor for the survival of any serious efforts to propel the unification of Europe.

With children in particular, some work has begun which suggests that this line of research is, in fact, very revealing. Research on the issue of children and their possible eventual attitudes toward political participation has been done by R. W. Connell in Australia, in the United States by Fred I. Greenstein, Robert D. Hess, Judith V. Torney, and Anthony M. Orum, and by the eminent Swiss educational psychologist, the late Jean Piaget.[10]

Women are keys to our understanding of how children are being brought up and about their exposure to new social thinking and attitudes. What they teach children probably holds a direct link to the long-term survivability of democracy in Western Europe. Women's roles in Western Europe have undergone profound changes since World War II, and in particular since the late 1960s. Large numbers have gone on to universities, won great human-rights victories, and entered better-paid labor markets and professions, all representing sharp departures from the living patterns of their mothers and grandmothers. Their new way of life also affects husband–wife relations and the education of the children. Given the tradition of authoritarianism of *kinder, kirche, kuche,* which reached its extreme in Hitler's Germany but also existed to a lesser extent elsewhere in Western Europe, it is improbable that women would support antidemocratic politics. The remarkable development in the contemporary role of women in each of the countries we study is all the more reason for identifying handed-down values in the home and in school.

GERMAN EXPERIENCE

So what does this mix of ideas about national traits, children, women, and social experience say about Germany? Political scientist David P. Conradt, in a recently published essay concerning Germany, reminds us that, "In little more than a century Germany has had an empire (1871–1918), an unstable democratic republic (1919–1933), a totalitarian dictatorship (1933–1945), a military occupation (1945–1949), two separate states (1949–1990), a federal republic in the West and a one-party Communist state in the East and since 1990 a single federal state."[11] To this summary we should add that united Germany covers about 138,000 square miles, barely 4,300 square miles more than the 133,630 square miles of the combined areas of the adjoining states of Nebraska and Iowa in the United States, or, as Conradt mentions, approximately half the size of Texas.

By way of further comparison, in 1989 the population of West Germany was 62 million and that of East Germany 16.9 million, for a total of some 78.6 million after unification.[12] In contrast, the population of Nebraska and

Iowa combined totaled 4,355,140 in 1990. If we draw on Texas for further contrast, in 1990, half of its population would amount to 8,493,255.[13] Thus, only two generations after World War II, Germany has emerged once again as Western Europe's most populous nation (France had 56.2 million; Britain, 57.2 million; and Italy, 57.5 million in 1989).[14] Because of its remarkable recovery, Germany is also the strongest economic power in Europe. Militarily, it has the largest army in Western Europe, but within the framework of NATO and with the concurrence of the Allies.

What its strength means is that Germany is once again assuming its historic role of profoundly influencing the politics, economics, and culture of Central Europe. More than just the military and political roles of dominating the area or jostling between France to the west and Russia to the east, there is the pervasive influence of Germany on everything in the area, including the dispositions of many smaller nations toward one form of government or another.[15] In looking toward the late 1990s and into the twenty-first century, Henry Kissinger, himself raised a German, wrote in 1994,

Germany will insist on the political influence to which its military and economic power entitle it and will not be so emotionally dependent on American military and French political support.

The emerging generation [German] has no personal recollection of the war or of America's role in the rehabilitation of the devastated postwar Germany. It has no emotional reason to defer to supranational institutions or to subordinate its views either to America or to France.[16]

On a grand scale, Kissinger has pointed out that the German issue for all of Europe is one of integrating "a united Germany into the West and the relationship of the Atlantic Alliance to the new Russia," the two most important tasks facing contemporary European governments.[17]

With a third post–World War II generation now in childhood, the question of what is happening in German society and in the home which will help mold attitudes toward democracy when this generation reaches adulthood becomes paramount; it is indeed an issue of profound historical and international consequence. Answers to questions about these children can be hinted at by looking at the nation's educational system, the important role of women in German society, and the considerable diversity of traditional regional linguistic and cultural mores. Intra-familial relationships and discussions do touch upon each of these factors. There is no doubt in our minds that some aspects do seep into a child's subconscious and influence his or her behavior when entering the world as adults.

Because of the limited availability of information about what should be looked for in handed-down values in the German family and the linkage to thinking about democracy or its future, we will deal only with the authoritarian factor and the German penchant for adherence to the letter of the law. We do this, aware that we are skating on thin ice, in the hope of encouraging others to consider more broadly the issues such a debate raises. The good news is that a growing body of work in social studies has begun to appear, written by German social scientists in the post–World War II years, that enlightens the discussion and begins to suggest the issues involved.[18] With only a bit more expanded effort to link up with the issue of democracy, we can reach some conclusions of practical use to Germany's leaders and their voters. For the United States and the rest of Europe—keeping in mind Kissinger's statement that integrating a united Germany into the West is so important— one can arrive at better-informed policy decisions.

POLITICAL, ECONOMIC, AND SOCIAL REALITIES

One should remember that Germany's democracy was imposed through the efforts of French, British, and American military occupation on the western half of the nation, and the Communist system in East Germany by Soviet troops. While Germans cooperated in the process, since they had no option, the fact remains that political practices of the past half century essentially originated out of the impulse of occupation forces, not long-standing German political traditions.[19] Thus, in those portions of Germany where democracy was practiced, it was initially imposed. In addition to the factor of political diversity, there are intergenerational differences in social and political views which affect attitudes and value systems, particularly with respect to a family's father figure. A half century after World War II, Germans are still struggling with the issue of their identity within the framework of a new Europe (e.g., European Community). Generational diversities even engulf the Germans over the question of their nation's guilt and activities related to the establishment of a Nazi regime that caused World War II and the Holocaust. The showing of the movie *Schindler's List* in the 1990s once again illustrated the profound discomfort Germans still had with their political heritage. Further complications arise from the absorption of well over 16 million East Germans into a democratic and capitalist society; Germans who lived under a highly totalitarian regime between 1933 and 1989, and who, for at least two generations, were exposed to continuous antidemocracy propaganda.

Another consideration is that social welfare expenditures account for 48.2 percent of the Central government's expenditures. These are very high when compared to those of France (46.4%), Italy (38.6%), United Kingdom (34.8%), and the United States (28.2%). Even Sweden, with clearly the highest welfare costs, does not expend that much more than unified Germany (55.9%).[20] In Sweden, the load is already having political and economic repercussions.[21] And in the French press of 1993 to 1995, questions were being raised about their nation's bill for welfare. What happens in Germany if economic conditions should require a contraction in public welfare expenditures? The evidence of Swedish and French voters, who are beginning to resist these levels of expenditures, suggests what a European government can afford politically; Germany is almost there.

That is the West German issue. What about the East German problem? These people were promised help in integrating themselves individually into a democratic unified Germany. What happens if that promise cannot be kept? Already we see a hint of the answer—a traditional German response—which is to criticize the support given to non-German workers. Findings of the sort suggested in this book could help Germans develop internal attitudinal programs which would add depth to democracy's resilience in times of stress such as Germany is experiencing today and can be expected to suffer over the next few years at a minimum.

There is also the effect of regional differences that go beyond recent East–West political experiences. With regard to diversity and cultural anthropological differences, John Ardagh stresses the fact that "variations between dialects are great" and, after citing examples, states, "Small wonder that a German visiting another region may find it hard to follow a conversation in a pub or train . . . this helps to explain why some Germans still think of distant parts of their country alien."[22]

Discuss the issue with Germans familiar with most parts of their country, and they will quickly confirm Ardagh's observation. The problem exists elsewhere, to be sure: in Italy, between southern and northern citizens; in Spain, between Andalusian Spaniards and Basque-speaking northerners; even in the United Kingdom, where Welsh cannot be understood by an Englishman. Linguistic diversity, be it in Germany or in any other European country with significant ethnic diversity (and that includes almost all European countries), has far-reaching implications for the study of familial handed-down values and consequences for democracy.

Linguist George Trager and anthropologist Edward T. Hall highlighted this circumstance many years ago. They noted "that language and culture were part and parcel of the same process, yet paradoxically, under certain restricted conditions, like the photon in physics, each could be analyzed as separate and distinct from the other; that is, language and culture reflect each other but are also discrete [individually distinct]."[23] A farmer in Catholic, rural, conservative Bavaria may not only have difficulty in being understood (for example, by someone in Cologne, Hamburg, or Berlin), but contemporary intra-familial conceptions of the father-image (patriarchal family structure) may differ to a significant degree. A predictable reaction to an acute economic crisis with a political solution would contain authoritarian features.

National television and radio, while they may facilitate homogenization of the German language, can only do so to a limited degree. The cases of France, Italy, Spain, and the Netherlands, where intensive use of national television and radio has existed for decades, has done little to destroy local peculiarities of speech and familial values. So there is little to expect, in the short term, in the use of television and radio to have all the Germans act and speak as one.

Furthermore, there are other social factors at work of profound importance. The most important of these to affect attitudes toward familial and public authoritarianism relates to differences arising from religious diversity. One normally associates discussions about religion in political affairs with such places as Catholic Italy or Catholic Spain, or even Protestant Britain, but the issue remains an equally important one in Germany. The fact is that Southern and Western Germany are predominantly Roman Catholic, while the North and East are overwhelmingly Protestant.[24] How much familial give-and-take occurs in these two major sections which could, in time, spill over into politics affecting democracy's future is another aspect requiring study, particularly by those advising national political leaders in Germany.

For centuries, relations between Catholics and Lutherans have been marked by severe conflict; at times, crippling and particularly brutal wars. While these tensions had eased considerably during the present and last centuries, up to the end of World War II they nevertheless remained a divisive factor. As a German-born American scholar reminded the authors, in Hitler's early rise to power an appreciable number of residents in the Catholic South rendered him greater support than many living in the Protestant North.[25] While we should not read too much into that observation, there were some differences of opinion regarding Hitler from one region to another. Interestingly, and in direct contrast with the separation of church and state which exists in the United States, a surcharge on German income taxes is earmarked for churches. Hence, the two major confessions are financially well off.

After World War II, for the first time in German history, partly because of guilt over events of the Hitler era and partly, probably, from Allied nudging, the Catholic and Lutheran Churches developed harmonious relations. Tensions, however, developed within each of the two major hierarchies, stemming from views about social, political, and economic questions in the body polity. But, for researchers and government officials, the key question related to what the third post–World War II generation hears in the home is whether this harmony could survive acute periods of crisis. Would they crack under intense social pressures and return to ancient tensions, thus complicating further the future for democracy? A look at some realities begins to suggest the problems of late twentieth-century Germany.

ROLE OF AUTHORITARIANISM

Traditional patriarchal family patterns continued throughout World War II under the Nazis and in the 1950s and 1960s. As Ingeborg Weber-Kellermann explains,

With economic recovery, severe deprivation disappeared. Some formerly employed wives and mothers returned to their household duties. In many families the husband and father again assumed breadwinner roles. Prestige was attached to the claim that my wife doesn't need to work. Once again these new arrangements were enshrined as the traditional family form.[26]

Weber-Kellermann refers to West Germany. In the eastern Communist area, a different situation was developing. The significance of Weber-Kellermann's comments is that the first post–World War II generation grew to adulthood in a family atmosphere in which paternal authoritarianism prevailed.

In contrast to their parent's upbringing, German youth, in addition to a home patriarchal atmosphere, were exposed to rapidly changing Western European social currents, unprecedented affluence leading to consumer splurges, the pervasive influence of television, and the Cold War shadow with its doomsday aura. Contact with foreign NATO troops, student exchanges, masses of foreign visitors, and perhaps their sheer numbers led to serious university disturbances in the 1960s and early 1970s.[27] Although there were numerous causes behind the movement initiated by "the Berlin branch of Students for a Democratic Society,"[28] rebellion against university faculty authoritarianism was a key factor. Eventually, spirits simmered down, and by the mid-1970s matters had returned to a more normal campus atmosphere; but only after important changes in the "functionability" of the universities were adopted.[29] Did this mean that the second post–World War II generation would be reared in a break with German authoritarianism at home and at school? The answer to this question is of great importance, because authoritarianism excludes compromise and is incompatible with the politics of democracy. This aspect is another reason why contemporary handed-down values in the home, as related to democracy, should be better understood.

What is emerging then is the coexistence of three generations of living Germans, each with possibly quite different attitudes. The oldest generation— those who were adults or teenagers during the Nazi period—clearly grew up in a highly authoritarian world, made strict by social, familial, educational, political, and military disciplines. A second generation, the German "Yuppies," grew up in the world of affluence and Cold War tensions that has been described; raised by the older generation, who had been very strict, but in rebellion to such strictures, as evidenced by their role as university students in the 1960s and 1970s. This generation is also the one that today is most critical of Germany's Nazi past. Then there is the third generation, now working its way through elementary school, high school, and university, which is being raised under yet even more different circumstances than their second-generation parents. The picture is complicated, but it is this third generation that must be understood better because they are the future owners of German democracy.

In Germany, as in France and Great Britain, education for this generation is biased in favor of the middle and upper classes. Children wind up in a track system difficult to change. John Ardagh commented on the evolution of schools from the rigid discipline of pre–World War II days (first generation) to a considerably liberalized atmosphere (particularly after some reforms of 1968, which, of course, primarily affected third-generation children). Relations between teachers and pupils in elementary and secondary schools are today more relaxed, particularly as older, more autocratic teachers retire. Nevertheless, the very considerable range of nonacademic activity characteristic of British and American schools is mostly absent. He points out the "very little practical training in leadership or civics." Pupils "are taught about the Constitution and legal system and how the *Bund* and *Lander* operate, [but] are given little chance to rehearse democracy in practice." He stresses that "there is nothing to parallel the American system where a school becomes a parliament-in-embryo, nor the British one where senior pupils are in charge of discipline."[30]

Nevertheless, the assumption can be safely made that, both in the home and schools, the traditional German rigid, authoritarian behavioral pattern has eased a great deal, but probably not submerged, into a comfortable give-and-take framework. Given the penchant of Germans to observe the letter of the law, the combination of both traits raises the questions of what Germans would do if, in time of acute national distress, a strong father-figure emerges and pushes for antidemocratic actions and attitudes. Would they still comply in automatic reaction to laws which could undermine the present political structure? What happens in the home could very well point to the answer.

SOCIAL CHANGES

The aftermath of major wars, with their tremendous loss of life and disruption of normal family routine, inevitably brings about profound social changes for the vanquished as well as the victors. And ours has been a century of war on an unprecedented scale. Apart from the U.S. involvement in Vietnam and Korea, in which other allies participated, World Wars I and II wrought consequences which are still very evident. To these two conflicts must be added, on a titanic scale, the more than forty-five years of Cold War dueling between the West and the Soviet Union. While shooting was fortunately avoided, the enormous propaganda and economic dimensions acquired worldwide scope, with occasional regional proxy wars. The cost eventually brought down the Soviet Union and the eastern Communist states. It left the United States with a staggering national debt, the result of a "guns and butter" policy during the conflict. For Central and Eastern Europe, political chaos and economic havoc became the order of the day.

At the end of World War I, a defeated Germany had been spared devastation while family traditional patriarchal values remained relatively unchanged; during the Nazi years, they were actually reinforced. Germans had not lost their sense of identity; they merely blamed the politicians and the generals for surrendering to the Allies. World War II was another story. Not since the Thirty Years War (1618–1648), which ended only with the signing of the Treaty of Westphalia, involving the diplomatic interests of almost all of Western Europe, had there been such killings and vast destruction. In the 1600s, 35 percent of the population of the whole of Germany perished, leaving the surviving Germans bewildered, unsure of their destiny, and uncertain of their identity. The same could be said of the Germans who survived World War II. As of the early 1990s, almost a half century after World War II, Germans are still trying to understand what their place should be. At the moment, the consensus seems to be that being a part of the European Community is the solution. And, as Kissinger noted, this is the great task of Western Europe to facilitate, as important as determining how best to integrate Russia into a peaceful relationship with Europe as a whole.[31]

The fundamental conclusion to be drawn is that extensive and complex social changes accompanied the reconstruction of both Germanies. While an enormous corpus of scholarship has been devoted to practically all phases of these changes, briefly looking at the issue of authoritarianism and attitudes toward law (primarily within a familial environment) can yield some very practical insights.

Of the many social changes that followed World War II, none have been more important relative to the future of democracy than those affecting the role of women. The importance of women politically in Germany should not be underestimated. They obtained the vote in 1919, following the revolution which did away with the monarchy and brought in the Weimar Republic. It is worth noting what the distinguished historian of modern Germany, Gordon Craig, has to say about the early role of women and Hitler's ascendancy. He states that, after September 1930, the National Socialist Party (Nazis) "increased its popular vote from 809,000 to 6,400,000," and that "women voters constituted a large part of the total."[32] Craig further comments about this circumstance, which was very important in Hitler's rise to power based on winning a national election:

Despite the fact that the NSDAP [National Socialist German Workers Party] was consistently reactionary on all questions relating to women from employment to education, that it had no women in its executive organization or its Reichstag delegation, and that it made no bones about its blatant philosophy of male superiority, it attracted women voters because it promised to restore the position of the home and the family in a society whose growing economic troubles threatened them and to restore the dignity that was properly women's, as helpmate and supporter of her husband and as German mother, assuring the future of the German race.[33]

Although changes in the status of women in Germany during the last two generations have been considerable, the issue still remains about how these legal modifications affect current handed-down values in the home. Has the modern, educated German woman also absorbed into her personality the authoritarianism characteristic of her father's and grandfather's generations? Is she also committed to observe legal precepts literally, even when common sense points to alternative interpretations? With the somewhat greater balance in the home in sharing authority and responsibilities between husband and wife, is there evidence of compromise becoming an important factor? If there is, how would this relate to democracy in contemporary Germany, particularly in rearing the third post–World War II generation? Is it likely that an innate sense of conservation might lead German women to once again vote massively for ultra-conservative political parties in time of crisis, instead of Green parties in times of prosperity, as did their grandmothers and great grandmothers in Hitler's era?

Recent changes in German law have affected the status of women and therefore suggest additional pressures on them to change their attitudes toward a variety of subjects, much as their counterparts are doing in France, Italy, and Spain. To quote Professor Craig

When the rubble to which Germany had been reduced by Allied bombing had been cleared away, and the process of denazification completed to the satisfaction of the Occupying Powers, and political sovereignty granted to the West Germans, the Basic Law of their new Republic stated clearly in its third article: "Men and Women have equal rights." This was regarded in 1949 as being the completion and full realization of the process begun in 1919 with the granting of women's suffrage.[34]

The reality was that full implementation did not occur despite considerable progress later in educational facilities and employment, and profound changes in social mores.

In the section in Ardagh's book concerning women, sex, and children, written by his German wife, Katherine Ardagh, the slowness in the evolution of women's rights is noted. It was not until 1957 that women were given legal equality in marriage property rights in West Germany. They commented that, "Up until 1977 the Civil Code contained an astonishing clause that gave the wife sole responsibility for the household and permitted her to take a job only if her husband agreed and if it were compatible with her domestic duties! This was abolished by the 1977 Marriage Law which declared that such matters should be settled by joint agreement."[35]

Also, the guilt factor was removed in divorce cases, a burden which frequently fell on women and prejudiced alimony settlements. German women achieved, as the Ardaghs state, "virtual equality, in the private sphere." These legal changes provided important bridges for women to new roles and status in society and, therefore, are important early signals of changing familial values. What now needs to happen is for government officials and scholars to understand how this new equality will play out in familial interrelationships. Another issue is how much equality women actually get in the labor market, politics, and professions in a very much male-dominated society. While the Ardaghs documented progress, they also called out the fact that it was at a very slow pace.[36]

In East Germany, women's status in terms of equality with men was much more advanced than in the Federal Republic (West Germany). The Communist regime's commitment to the creation of a trained labor force to help rebuild their devastated country led to full participation of women in the labor force and to appropriate training and education.[37] In fact, the East Germans were so advanced in women's rights in comparison to West Germany that at the time of the unification, when details were being worked out, the social policies of the East Germans became a retardant in finalizing plans. The fact was that the West Germans were more backward than the East Germans when it came to women's rights. The irony of this circumstance is that democratic institutions are probably more facilitated in their development if women do have political, social, and economic parity with men.

The changes that occurred in West Germany were quite dramatic concerning attitudes toward marriage. This shift in cultural mores and how handed-down values affect the third post–World War II generation is another area that suggest a prognosis for democracy's future. At this writing, no hard data are available for numbers of men and women living together outside of formal marriage for any part of Germany. According to various experts on the country, there is probably a very large number of couples living this way.[38] More important, there is a high level of social and legal tolerance for cohabitation and no legal stigma attached to the progeny of such unions or those of single mothers. The implications for traditional familial values in Germany are enormous, to say the least.

Nevertheless, formal marriages in West Germany for the years 1987 through 1990 showed a small upward trend (see Table 4.1). Data for 1991 reflect a downward figure, but these could be adjusted when firmer facts are available. One source placed the peak in marriages as having occurred in 1962, with 530,000 such unions, which dropped to 328,000 in 1978. Allenbach Institute surveys reported that the number of people who thought marriage was "a

TABLE 4.1
Marriages in Germany, 1987–1991

Year	West Germany	East Germany
1987	382,564	141,283
1988	397,738	137,165
1989	398,608	130,989
1990	414,475	---------
1991*	400,253	---------

Source: United Nations, Demographic Yearbook (New York: United
   Nations, 1992), 492.
*Estimated.

necessary institution, not out-of-date" fell from 89 to 64 percent between 1949 and 1985. Data for East Germany revealed a year-to-year decline between 1987 and 1989.[39] More recent data for this part of Germany are not yet available, so conclusions about trends would be almost a guess at this time.

Women's notable increase in educational levels, and easier entrance into the labor market (thus lessening or even eliminating economic dependence on a husband), are all factors which account for the present levels of divorce (see Table 4.2). According to the Ardaghs, the rough divorce rate of one out of every three marriages is about the same as in the United Kingdom.

CONCLUSION

Germany is crucial to the survival of democratic values in Western Europe because of its size and economic power. Furthermore, its intellectual influence well beyond its borders is enormous. German thinking and patterns of behavior have affected events in Eastern Europe for centuries. There is no evidence to suggest that this influence will decrease in the decades to come. The German penchant for thoroughness and Germany's position as an advanced welfare state raises not only social questions, but also the issue of what happens if the cost exceeds Germany's financial capacity to foot the bill for these social programs. As of the mid-1990s, there is a heated debate underway in Germany precisely over the affordability of such programs. How would Germany face belt-tightening exigencies in light of the authoritarianism deep in the German social psyche? The third post–World War II generation

TABLE 4.2
Divorces in Germany, 1987–1990

Year	West Germany		East Germany	
	Number	Percentage	Number	Percentage
1987	129,850	34	50,640	35
1988	128,729	32	49,380	36
1989	126,628	31	50,063	38
1990	122,869	30	--------	----

Source: United Nations, *Demographic Yearbook* (New York: United Nations, 1992), 509.
Percentages were calculated to suggest relative number of German marriages ending in divorce.

will probably have to face this dilemma. What has permeated its subconscious through intra-familial behavior and conversation must be very much taken into account in any appreciation of the possible options.

Other issues that, in time, will manifest themselves as influences on the social fabric of this nation include the effect of using contraception and declining German birth rates. In societies where this has occurred, for example, the quality of the lives of children has been of greater concern because society as a whole can afford to invest more in these young people. What will happen in Germany, and what will be the result on fourth-generation children in their views and actions concerning democracy within the context of our concern regarding the role of authoritarianism?

In contrast to this concern about German authoritarianism, there is the individualism of the French and Italians, which are the main thematic elements of the next chapter. The theme of individualism is also present in Spain, the subject of Chapters 6 and 7. The French and Italian cases are particularly exciting to look at because, in both nations, revolutionary parties have had a greater influence than in the rest of Western and Northern Europe. For just as familial traditions and values affect the course of German authoritarianism, so too do the actions and beliefs of the family influence profoundly the direct connection between individualism and the violence so closely associated to it.

NOTES

1. Samuel P. Huntington, *The Third Wave* (Norman: University of Oklahoma Press, 1993), 37.

2. Ibid.

3. Ibid., 38.

4. Ibid.

5. Robert Fulghum, *All I Really Need to Know I Learned in Kindergarten: Uncommon Thoughts on Common Things* (New York: Ivy Books, 1986).

6. Ingeborg Weber-Kellermann, "The German Family between Private Life and Politics," vol. 5 in *A History of Private Life*, ed. Antoine Prost and Gerard Vincent (Cambridge, Mass.: Harvard University Press, 1991), 523–525.

7. The observation was made in one of the seminars on cultural anthropology attended by James N. Cortada in the late 1940s at the U.S. Department of State's Foreign Service Institute. At the time, lecturers were influenced by Ruth Benedict and her associates, leading authorities in studying Japanese cultural values leading to the widespread surrender of Japan. For comments on Benedict's research during World War II, see Edward T. Hall, *An Anthropology of Everyday Life* (New York: Doubleday, 1992), 201.

8. John Ardagh, *Germany and the Germans* (London: Penguin, 1991).

9. John C. Pierce and Richard A. Pride, eds., *Cross-National Micro-Analysis*, vol. 2 (Beverly Hills, Calif.: Sage, 1972); Frank A. Pinner, "Parental Overprotection and Political Distrust," Ibid., 77–109.

10. R. W. Connell, *The Child's Construction of Politics* (Melbourne: Melbourne University Press, 1971); Fred I. Greenstein, *Children and Politics*, rev. ed. (New Haven: Yale University Press, 1965); Anthony M. Orum, ed., *The Seeds of Politics: Youth and Politics in America* (Englewood Cliffs, N.J.: Prentice-Hall, 1972); Robert D. Hess

and Judith V. Torney, *The Development of Political Attitudes in Children* (Chicago: Aldine, 1967); Howard E. Gruber and J. Jacques Voneche, eds., *The Essential Piaget* (New York: Basic Books, 1977).

11. M. Donald Hancock et al., *Politics in Western Europe* (Chatham, N.J.: Chatham House, 1993).

12. United Nations, "World Statistics in Brief," in *United Nations Statistical Pocketbook* (New York: United Nations, 1992), 28–29.

13. U.S. census figures for 1990 are presented conveniently by states in *The World Almanac* (New York: Pharos Books, 1992), 74–75.

14. United Nations, "World Statistics," 27, 38, 80.

15. A little-publicized incident occurred at the time that the unification of Germany was being considered in 1990, which reflects how at least some Europeans take seriously handed-down values and national trends in behavior. The British Prime Minister at the time, Margaret Thatcher, needed to understand the implications of a united Germany and, after the usual round of consultations with British officials and cabinet ministers, called a quiet weekend meeting of distinguished historians of the Nazi period in German history to discuss their perceptions of what the unification would mean for European and British security.

16. Henry Kissinger, *Diplomacy* (New York: Simon and Schuster, 1994), 821.

17. Ibid., 823.

18. Weber-Kellermann, "The German Family," 524–525.

19. Gordon H. Craig, *The Germans* (New York: Meridian, 1991), 36–50.

20. See chart showing comparative percentage of central government for social welfare costs in France, Germany, Italy, Sweden, the United Kingdom, and the United States, in Zariski, "Who Has the Power and How Did They Get It?" in *Politics in Western Europe*, 345.

21. Ibid., 345, 395–396.

22. Ardagh, *Germany and the Germans*, 26–27.

23. Edward T. Hall, *An Anthropology of Everyday Life* (New York: Doubleday, 1993), 212.

24. David P. Conradt, "The Context of German Politics," in *Politics in Western Europe*, 203.

25. Karla Baer, conversation with author, Orange, Va., June 1994.

26. Weber-Kellermann, "The German Family," 525.

27. Craig, *The Germans*, 184–188.

28. Ibid., 184.

29. Ibid., 188–189.

30. Ardagh, *Germany and the Germans*, 236–245.

31. Kissinger, *Diplomacy*, 820–822.

32. Craig, *The Germans*, 164.

33. Ibid.

34. Ibid., 166.

35. Ardagh, *Germany and the Germans*, 191.

36. Ibid., 191–194.

37. Weber-Kellermann, "The German Family," 525–526.

38. Ibid., 528–530.

39. Ardagh, *Germany and the Germans*, 195–196.

—5—

Democracy and Individualism: France and Italy

Individualism Λ doctrine that the interests of the individual are or
ought to be ethically paramount.

—Webster's Dictionary

*This chapter defines the concept of individualism in a democracy
and demonstrates how this is played out in French and Italian
political structures. This chapter also discusses the role of education, children, women, and changes in demographics influencing
the fate of democracy in these two nations.*

France and Italy are two very large, very visible democracies. To the contemporary observer, they might appear on the surface to be long-standing members of democracy's inner circle, complete with core cultural values that
reinforce the attraction to democracy. While to the untrained eye such is the
case, there have been many profound changes in these countries in the twentieth century, and particularly in the past forty years, that influence the ebb
and flow of representative government. While many factors are at work to
define the nature of democracy in France and Italy, we believe that a central
characteristic that rises above the daily flow of events—in education, marriage, women in the workplace, internal immigration from countryside to urban centers, and so forth—is a fundamental national trait: political and personal
individualism. The role of individualism should not be lost in the crowd of
other political, economic, and social issues which crowd our agenda on the
prospects of democracy.

THE IDEA CALLED INDIVIDUALISM

Steven Lukes, at the very beginning of his well-known work on individualism, quotes the great German sociologist, Karl Mannheim: "We shall begin with the fact that the same word, or the same concept in most cases, means very different things when used by differently situated persons."[1] Lukes follows with an observation: "'Individualism,' like 'socialism' and 'communism,' is a nineteenth-century word. In seeking to identify its various distinct traditions of use I shall concentrate on its nineteenth-century meanings."[2] Lukes then argued that "the main purpose here is to indicate both the variety and the directions of the main paths traced during the term's rich semantic history. The interest of such an account is, however, neither merely semantic nor merely historical. The meanings of words generally encapsulate ideas, even theories."[3] Our examination of the major Western European societies reinforces the wisdom of his approach.

In his book, Lukes lists eleven "basic ideas of individualism":

- The Dignity of Man
- Autonomy
- Privacy
- Self-Development
- The Abstract Individual
- Political Individualism
- Economic Individualism
- Religious Individualism
- Ethical Individualism
- Epistemological Individualism
- Methodological Individualism.[4]

All of these modes can directly or indirectly relate to democracy, since political philosophy in its various shades of interpretation concerns primarily the individual. Nowhere are such considerations so obvious as in the cases of France and Italy. But we also cite Lukes's classification to suggest the wide range of thought that can and should exist in connection with individualism as a social, political, or economic theme.

To further the spectrum covered by individualism, think about the ideas in the opening paragraph in Pierre Birnbaum's and Jean Leca's book on the subject:

A specter is haunting the West's intellectuals—the specter of individualism. Individualism has indeed, many spectral qualities: indeterminate shape, avocative power, and a myriad of other qualities attributed to it and which allow it to take many forms on a scale which ranges from benevolence to terror according to perceptions of it.[5]

It is not surprising that every major writer in the past three centuries interested in political, social, and economic affairs has dealt with the issue of individualism in one form or another. And there is the additional complication that they have rarely agreed on the topic. The array of thoughts on the subject are almost bewildering.

As a social and political philosophy in its multiple facets, individualism has been very important in the evolution of political parties and actions in France, Italy, and Spain. For that reason, it is important to touch upon the notion of individualism as a commonly accepted trait in these three countries, even though it exists in different forms and in varying degrees. How the third post–World War II generation is being reared and what it hears at home as reflections of individualistic behavior will be a factor in their attitude toward democracy when they reach adulthood. Or, to state the case conversely, as a result of their upbringing, they could reject democracy and its principles. In Germany, voters elected Hitler to power, and both the institutions of government and the people were prepared to surrender the principles of democracy in exchange for his vision of the future. Attitudes can work both for and against democratic ideals.

Implicit in democratic social and political theory is concern with liberty and equality. To the extent that liberty is given priority over equality in political party programs and behavior, we see acceptance of liberal democratic thinking accompanied by clearly discernible facets of individualism. Where emphasis on equality is preeminent and consideration for individualism is on a low footing, the direction is collectivist thinking.[6] The result is fascism, communism, and various shades of socialism. Political parties and thinking in France, Italy, and Spain may fall at either extreme, or in-between. However, the obvious danger is that this kind of pluralism helps contribute to political instability.

In his discussion of individualism and collectivism, social scientist J. Roland Pennock observed a pattern that reinforces our emphasis on learning about intra-familial communications to which the young are exposed:

I know of no individualist who denies that men are influenced by ideas "imposed" from without as well as those not "imposed." No one who admits the most obvious facts of family life could take such a position. Our ideas of how we should behave are of course influenced, to say the least, by what we are taught in the home. Families may bear marked distinguishing characteristics for generations.[7]

Snobbishness, parental attitudes toward servants in the home and garden or lack of parental attitudes, degree of husband–wife tensions, and settlement of sibling disputes are but a few examples of what goes on in the home affecting a child's character and eventual attitudes toward life. In Western Europe, adult political behavior has ranged between extreme individualism (e.g., anarchism in Spain in the 1930s or what Ernest Hemingway used to call Spanish behavior, "Viva Yo") and extreme collectivism (e.g., fascism, communism), with contemporary leanings falling in-between, but tending to either left or right of center. Proponents of particular political philosophies in this continuum all claim that what they support are aspects of democracy. The future, however, will depend on how valid Pennock's comments apply to the generation now in kindergarten and primary school.[8]

Of overriding importance is the impact on today's children of electronic devices, such as television, video tapes, computers at home and in school, and other technological facilities. How are these devices and their attendant social messages dealt with in the family circle? We know from sales statistics of these technologies that they are entering the lives of children at a rate equal to what happened in the United States during the late 1970s and throughout the 1980s. To what extent are these devices dehumanizing influences or social facilitators? As we have learned in the United States, these are not causal concerns; they profoundly influence the debate on the nature of future children and adults. The role of something so specific as increased automation in the workplace (e.g., robotics on the factory floor and PCs in the office) will have an economic effect on tomorrow's adults. What the family's capabilities are to cope with such a future has a significant bearing on the individualism–collectivism continuum. In short, no discussion of future political circumstances in such countries as France, Italy, or Spain are possible without keeping in mind the role of individualism.[9]

THE FRENCH ESSENCE

With respect to France, the issue of handed-down values and their relationship to the third post–World War II generation now in childhood is of extreme importance, given the profound social and economic changes that have overtaken that nation over the past five decades. The problem is complicated by the diversity of traits characteristic of the French. Yet even talking about the French, or for that matter any group of people, as having "traits" is anathema to many thinkers in the Western world who are caught up in the neo–New Age religion of individualism. However, even the French speak of their "national" characteristics.

Intense French nationalism; affinity for the concept of French honor and glory (epitomized by General de Gaulle); the tendency to thriftiness and hoarding of gold; volatile political behavior, at times paradoxical; and distrust of government institutions, while at the same time regarding government employment highly desirable and respectable, are but a few traits involving degrees of individualism in a generic sense and individuality in a narrower meaning evident in French society.

French scholar Sanche de Gramont commented extensively on the issue under the rubric of "Common Attitudes":

Crossing dissimilar regions, one becomes aware that beyond regional customs there are common attitudes, an elusive but tangible Frenchness. Some of these attitudes are changing, and everywhere one feels the demands of the present scraping at the encrusted way of life. How do the French reconcile traditional values with belief in progress, that two-edged invention of the *Encyclopedistes*? After teaching at Nanterre in 1967, H. Stuart Hughes wrote about *triste Paris*, complaining that there were hardly any buses with platforms left. How to change and remain the same?[10]

Gramont also found a bond between the geographic and cultural analogy in his fellow countrymen:

The traveler finds signs and attitudes presenting themselves to his scrutiny like land-scapes: the demeaning national emblem, the noisy, self-satisfied barnyard strutter, peremptory and unproductive. The meaning of fraternity: it no more means that a Frenchman will love you like a brother than a crucifix over a bed means that the person who occupies it is a good Catholic. It is a decorative virtue. In its highest social form, fraternity is the Frenchman's inalienable right not to dislike you.[11]

In addition, Gramont captured a sense of Frenchness that is difficult to ignore:

Voltaire, the shopkeeper's philosopher: Don't ask for too much, mind your own busi-ness, find contentment in smallness, avoid quixotic pursuits. The rationale of the shop-keeper: I am my own boss, no one's beast of burden, and I see the money coming in. French distaste for the mediocrity of the shopkeeper mentality: Saint Exupery saying that we are living in a time when the Cathedrals have been taken over by the little old ladies who rent the chairs. The need to *rouspeter*, which Larousse defines as "cho-leric-resistance." Obstinacy in sterile discussion. The Frenchman is defined more in opposition to than in agreement with his society.[12]

Anyone who has lived in France would see the truth in another of Gramont's observations: "France is a nation which operates largely on multiple circuits of favoritism—the Resistance, political parties, professions, old school tie, social background, clubs, geographical origin, kinship, and many others. No night of August 4 can ever banish the era of privileges: whenever there is a queue, there is someone being let in the back way."[13]

Even Charles de Gaulle could not resist commenting on the essence of his countrymen: "Every Frenchman wants to enjoy one or more privileges; that's why he shows his passion for equality."[14]

We have taken you at some length through a sampling of comments con-cerning French traits because they all focus on some aspect of individualism. We also recognize that this is a term which, since the last century, has carried a pejorative stigma, in contrast to the notion of individuality, which has been subject of respect.[15] We do so to emphasize the importance of learning about changing values within a very complex frame, to which the young are ex-posed in the home and later in school. A generation of anthropologists, social psychologists, political sociologists, and political scientists would be required to fill in the details correlating French essence to political behavior—an exer-cise that would make sense if the French wanted to change existing patterns of political behavior.

France, about twice the size of Germany, is the third largest country in Europe after Russia and the Ukraine. About half the nation's territory consists of a wide fertile plain, a fact which has contributed to its self-sufficiency in food and the political importance of a large rural sector. In common with the other Western European nations, France has enjoyed two generations of unprecedented prosperity, a circumstance which has resulted in marked social changes, a sharp rise in living standards, and important demographic shifts from the countryside to the cities.

Dramatic changes in housing is a prime example of developments since World War II. French social scientist Antoine Prost studied data in the 1954 census which reflected the "striking image of the primitive state of French housing" in that year. He observed that, "Of 13.4 million homes, scarcely more than one-half (58.4%) had running water; only one-quarter (26.6%) boasted indoor toilets; and only one in ten (10.4%) were equipped with a bathtub or shower or central heating." In 1953, houses were built at the rate of 100,000 units per year; six years later, 300,000; and 400,000 in 1965. Between 1972 and 1975, 500,000 new homes were constructed annually. These units were mostly apartments on the outskirts of major cities. All were fully equipped with modern conveniences. As Prost remarks, "For millions of French families unable to afford a home of their own, the new apartment buildings represented a veritable look into modernity."[16]

With sufficient space being conducive to considerably greater familial privacy, and the second and third post–World War II generations benefiting from drastically improved living standards, new values must be and are emerging. Political leaders in France need to ask what these new values are. They must understand how the new conditions affect relations within the family units. We would add the following questions: How is dissent dealt with? How will the new environment affect the political and social attitudes of the third generation in adulthood, now that they enjoy bourgeois comforts? Since the French have a penchant for measuring many things, answers to these questions will probably be forthcoming. Most political scientists concur that, in the Western world, a stable middle class is a plus for the survival of democracy. Will these changes in living standards contribute to stability in French political life during the third generation's future? An issue that will have to be better understood in France, closely related to these changed circumstances, will be how they affect the French tendency toward liberty versus equality in public life. Already, a trend exists toward "attaching greater value to liberty than to equality."[17]

THE ROLE OF FRENCH EDUCATION

The French educational system since the last century has been entirely under the control of the Ministry of Education for primary and secondary schools (*lycees*), including intervention in the universities as a state monopoly. But, in the 1960s and 1970s, important liberalization and democratization took place. Curricula in some secondary schools were broadened to include technical fields geared to business and industrial needs. After the university students' outbreak in May 1968, Edgar Faure, Minister of Education, expanded autonomy within the universities to determine curricula, created new technical institutes, and formed what one observer called "American-style academic departments."[18] Nevertheless, the goals appear to have fallen short of expectancy because of chronic funding limitations, the baby-boom explosion leading to overcrowded facilities, and the lack of a sufficient number of jobs for the greatly increased number of university graduates.

An interesting aspect of a secular France, which maintains the separation of church and state in a nation where the majority is nominally Catholic (but with low church attendance), is the attitude of the national government toward parochial schools. Under laws passed in 1969, teachers in Catholic schools are paid from public funds when these institutions are under contract with the Ministry of Education. They cover from kindergarten through high school. About 15 to 20 percent of all school children attend these schools.

Access to careers which can lead to top positions in government, academe, and the great public and private business organizations is still mostly through one of the three elite universities. As Gramont observed, they "are run by the state for the state. The students in these schools are already salaried civil servants."[19] These are the Polytechnic, an outstanding engineering school under the authority of the Ministry of Defense, with a general as director; the Ecole Normale Superieure, which prepares future teachers for the *lycees* and universities; and the Ecole Nationale d'Administration, for the recruitment of high-ranking civil servants.[20] Entrance to these institutions, and academic survival, is through a process of rigorous competitive examinations.

However, one of the most far-reaching developments in French education concerns the expansion of nursery schools without any legal mandate or compulsory attendance. Prost considers this expansion to be of "great social significance."[21] Because he has correctly flagged an important issue in the evolution of modern French society, his argument is important to quote at length:

Previously the norm was precisely the opposite: to keep young children at home as long as possible and even to teach them to read at home. Nursery schools were for the children of the poor, whose mothers were obliged to work. A nursery school was nothing more than a baby-sitter. Now, however, it is widely believed that it is better for small children to be sent to nursery school than to remain at home with their mothers. Parents of the upper strata of society, especially the urban and the well-educated, have led the way, even in families where mother does not work. In 1982, 91 percent of all three-year-olds attended nursery schools, as did a third of two-year-olds. People have come to believe that the school is better than the family which is rapidly being supplanted.[22]

The process of placing greater responsibilities on school systems has continued unabated into the 1990s. Prost's observations accurately reflect what is happening. In the past, French children were kept away from other children and confined largely to the home. In fact, even play in the park was a restricted venture. How democratic interpersonal relationships, with so early a start, will affect the third post–World War II generation when it reaches adulthood is full of intriguing speculation. How will future handed-down values be affected?

THE MODERN FRENCH WOMAN

Another important change in French societal conditions has been the altered status of women. They first received the right to vote in 1945. Twenty years later, they received the right to open bank accounts without first obtaining permission from their husbands. In 1965, they also were allowed to dispose of property and to become legal heirs.[23] In addition to these changes came further significant participation of women in the economy.[24] William Safran, a political scientist, observed that in the ten years from the mid-1950s through the mid-1960s, participation by women in professional ranks grew by 70 percent. By 1980, 50 percent of the students in higher education were women and 20 percent of university and *lycee* faculty were women.[25]

Family planning and use of contraceptives by women is legal, as are abortions, which, incidentally, are covered by social security funding programs.[26] In his study of French society, Safran observed that "between 1970 and 1980, women achieved equality with men with respect to choice of domicile, authority over children, retention of surname, and initiative in divorce proceedings; in 1985 women were given equal rights in the administration of family property."[27]

Greater social tolerance for cohabitation, steadily improved education, and job participation increasing prospects for financial independence are trends which have weakened the institution of marriage. "In 1971, 416,500 marriages were celebrated," according to Prost.[28] From the data presented in Table 5.1, one can see that the decline is obvious, although numbers appear to have stabilized. As can be noted, the divorce rate is high. Not shown is how many divorcees who remarry are included in the marriage data. In comparing the figures in Table 5.1 with the peak marriage data for 1971, it would appear that the numbers of couples living together outside lawful wedlock must be considerable.[29]

Likewise, the data in Table 5.2 regarding births point to sizeable numbers probably being born to unmarried couples. According to Prost's analysis, the "percentage of children born out of wedlock doubled between 1970 and 1981, to one in eight."[30] In 1992, the national legislature passed a law granting the same legal status to children born in or out of wedlock, except with respect to inheritance.

The shift in societal values is bound to affect the attitudes of tomorrow's adults in a manner radically different from those characteristic of their traditionally minded grandparents. Hence, for political leaders and French citizens to understand their potential future political circumstances, they will

TABLE 5.1
French Marriages, 1987–1991, and Divorces, 1987–1990

Year	Marriages	Divorces
1987	265,177	106,527
1988	271,124	106,096
1989	279,900	106,295
1990	287,099	105,295
1991*	281,000	---------

Source: United Nations, Demographic Yearbook (New York:
United Nations, 1992), 492, 509.
*Estimated.

have to learn about the new familial relationships and how individualism and tolerance are affected. The question remains, how will this translate into future political life?

The statistics presented in Table 5.2 show the relative stability of population growth. Assuming no major change, such as a dramatic rise in foreign refugees or immigration, implications for the future include housing, schooling, and welfare demands. Presumably, budgetary pressures would lessen and weaken support for leftist political parties. On the other hand, unless French industry can steadily improve its productivity and competitiveness, a labor shortage in the next quarter century could hamper economic growth.

The profound changes in France in two generations raises many questions regarding the country's economic, social, and political future, particularly with regard to the new status and role of French women. The development of two wage earners in the middle class leading to sharing tasks is already affecting how children are reared and what they hear at home. How will this affect the future of democracy in France? Will the third post–World War II generation swing more toward the concept of liberty, or will it move in the direction of equality, with possible collectivist overtones? Given the evidence that French society is as inwardly concerned about its domestic affairs as at any time since the end of World War II, what role will this new generation want in some grand scheme of a unified, pan-European political construct?

FRENCH POLITICAL PATTERNS

No aspect of French life more dramatically reflects the many faceted shades of the country's "individualism and individuality" than the multiplicity of political parties and zigzags in voting patterns. More than a dozen parties are

TABLE 5.2
French Population, 1982–1991, and Births and Deaths, 1987–1991

Year	Total Population	Births	Deaths	Excess of Births over Deaths
1982	54,480,000	-------	-------	-------
1983	54,728,000	-------	-------	-------
1984	54,947,000	-------	-------	-------
1985	55,170,000	-------	-------	-------
1986	55,394,000	-------	-------	-------
1987	55,630,000	767,828	527,466	240,362
1988	55,884,000	771,268	524,600	246,668
1989	56,160,000	765,473	529,283	236,190
1990	56,440,000	762,407	526,201	236,206
1991*	57,049,000	759,000	526,000	233,000

Source: United Nations, Demographic Yearbook (New York: United Nations, 1992), 130, 275, 361.
*Estimated.

always likely to participate in any national election.[31] This pluralism contributes to the unpredictability of French politics and the future of democracy in times of acute stress, despite the current wide acceptance and support of and for the Fifth Republic. The financial burden of underwriting an extremely comprehensive social welfare program falls heavily on not only the tax revenues, but also private business. Without constant economic growth, it is difficult to see how this situation can survive without reaching a point of acute crisis in the not-so-distant future.

The possibility of the moment of truth arriving in the nearer rather than the distant future relates to the social welfare programs.[32] The extent of these benefits can be seen in a partial listing which appeared in a *Newsweek* article in 1993. The fact that this American news magazine focused on the topic only begins to hint at the extent of the debate underway in France:

Parent power: the government pays parents for having kids—$263 per month for three children, $418 for four. Children in school get their own perks, such as two weeks of Alpine skiing for $60 each.

The golden childhood: Public day care costs are as little as $2 a day. University tuition is $285 a year (scholarships are available).

Happy holidays: Five weeks of vacation is the minimum; many workers get six or seven. Many get a 13th month of pay for Christmas and a 14th for summer vacation.

So, fire me: Laid-off workers receive 60% of their pay for up to five years.

Death, where is your sting? A $6,250 stipend is provided for burial costs.[33]

How long can the French economy support these benefits? What will be the voter's reaction if subsequent governments try to bring them into closer balance with economic reality? And what will the children hear at home about such a prospect?

An example illustrating the swings in French voting behavior and growing concerns for the nation's economy is the result of the parliamentary elections of March 28, 1993. One should bear in mind that, in the complex French political system, there are small and large political parties, some durable and others ephemeral, which, while coming under overall tags of left, center, or right at voting time, nevertheless have varying or differing ideologies and intense leadership rivalries. This kind of situation makes for temporary alliances fraught with the danger of disruption in domestic and foreign government policies. This is particularly the case if charismatic or semi-charismatic political leaders jockey for positions favorable to ministerial or presidential aspirations. Tensions at the top of government leadership become acute when the president, with specific constitutional powers, philosophically differs from stances of a parliament controlled by the opposition. The situation becomes further complicated if the prime minister has presidential aspirations and is also in competition with others in his own party or coalition. This is not an unusual situation.[34]

In the French political system, there is the possibility of two election rounds, a week apart, unless a candidate from a single member district has received an absolute majority of votes in the first ballot. If not, then a runoff occurs, with a candidate needing only a plurality of votes to win. The same system applies to both parliamentary and presidential elections.

In line with the procedure described, two ballots were held in the spring of 1993. In the March 28 second ballot, twelve parties participated. The result was a landslide victory for a coalition of center and center-right parties and a stunning defeat for the Socialists and their allies after twelve years in power. In the April 23, 1995 elections, 38 percent of the electorate this time voted outside of the mainstream parties, yet another direction for the French. When polled on why, voters responded that unemployment was too high and that they were frustrated with the inability of the government they had voted in barely two years earlier to do anything about it.[35] A similar frustration affected Italian voters in the 1990s, including the April 1996 elections. Reflecting a broad European concern, the voters had demonstrated quite a significant impatience with their current politicians. These parliamentary elections illustrate French individualism translated into politics. The existence of multiple parties reflects not only a variety of interests, but also the underlying individualism in French society. A deeper analysis would show the ephemeral nature of some splinter parties and the volatile performance at the ballot box over the years.

M. Donald Hancock perceptively mentions that, "From the point of view of national politics, one may identify six major ideological families within which political parties have been arranged—at least from the post–World War II period until recently: Communists and Socialists; Radical-Socialists and Catholics; and Conservatives and Gaullists. For the sake of analytic convenience, these may be grouped into the left, the center and the right."[36] He cautions that "each of the 'families' has tried to represent different social classes and/or different views regarding economic policy, executive–legislative relations, and the place of religion in politics."[37] This pattern of behavior has led to frequent departures by elected officials from positions which they held earlier to obtain voter support.

Regarding the results of the very important second runoff in 1993—because it exposes much of the fabric of French democratic behavior—the Center–Right coalition won 484 out of 577 parliamentary seats in France's National Assembly elections. As the reporter for the Reuter Agency stated on March 29,

The humiliated Socialist government and its allies won only 70 seats. Interior Ministry data show that the Gaullist Rally for the Republic (RPR) won 247 seats in the National Assembly, 34 more than its center–right ally the Union for French Democracy (UDF). Other conservatives won 24 seats. The Communist Party took 23 seats, while France's other main political groups, the ecologists and the far-right National Front, failed to secure any seats at all.[38]

The official French Ministry of Interior reported the results for the second round, which are presented in Table 5.3. Leaving aside the issue of how many seats were won and lost by the various political groups or parties, we draw your attention to the final numbers of votes cast and the percentages of the total. The fact is that the Socialists and their allies obtained 31.57 percent, which, added to the Communists' 4.61 percent, means that 36.18 percent of the voters were or are out of sympathy with the winning conservative coalition. Within the latter's ranks, the Gaullist RPR is committed to individualism, nationalism, and the state. The UDF, a loose group of centrist parties, has, as a basic policy, support for a pro-European posture. Other small groups, such as the National Front (FRN), are further to the right.[39] The ideological splintering (without going into the detail of intraparty divergences) points to the individualistic tendencies of the voters and support for candidates based on perception of personalities rather than essential ideologies. This hypothesis is in line with the French penchant for the "man on horseback" in times of trouble.

In the 1995 presidential elections, Jacques Chirac, age sixty-two and conservative mayor of Paris for eighteen years, won with 52.7 percent of all votes cast in metropolitan France against 47.3 percent for his Socialist opponent, Lionel

TABLE 5.3
French National Assembly Elections: Final Results, Second Round,
March 28, 1993

Party	Votes	Percentage	Seats
Center-Right Coalition			
Rally for the Republic (RPR)	5,832,987	28.27	247
Union for French Democracy (UDF)	5,331,935	25.84	213
Other	736,372	3.56	24
Totals	11,901,294	57.67	484
Leftist Coalition			
Socialist (SOC)	5,829,496	28.25	54
Miscellaneous Left	685,809	3.22	16
Totals	6,515,305	31.57	70
Other			
Communists	951,213	4.61	0
National Front (FRN)	1,168,150	5.66	0
Other (includes ecologists)	96,971	0.44	0
Grand Totals	20,632,933	99.95	577

Source: French Ministry of Interior data provided by French Embassy, Washington, D.C., to authors, August 11, 1993.

Jospin. Total votes were 15.5 million for Chirac and nearly 14 million for Jospin, with a majority of voters under thirty-five years of age favoring Chirac. Recall that as many as 80 percent of all members of Parliament in the 1993 elections were members of conservative parties. Chirac was declared the winner by his opponent on May 7, and on May 20 officially succeeded François Mitterand, age seventy-eight and very ill with cancer, ending fourteen years of Socialist domination. Chirac began his term in office facing the difficult problems stemming from 12 percent unemployment and a $60-billion government deficit. How he decides to solve these twin issues with necessary parliamentary support remained an open issue as of mid-1996.

The question for the future is whether, in view of the many changes in France since the end of World War II, the third generation—now children—will in adulthood move in a less individualistic direction politically because of their different upbringing and what they hear at home.

THE ITALIAN WAY

Like the French, the Italians share a preoccupation with various forms of individualism which is reflected in national political behavior. Therefore, the Italian case represents yet another way of looking at the role of individualism and other cultural penchants within the context of democracy's possibilities. Individualism, particularly among peasants in the southern "boot" and in Sicily, and devotion to the family are fundamental Italian traits.[40]

Individualism, ranging from anarchistic personal social behavior to undisciplined collectivism, and family as an overriding individualistic social entity points to very difficult sociological and political analyses. As political scientist Paul Ginsborg has put it,

Attachment to the family has probably been a more constant and less evanescent element in Italian popular consciousness than any other. Yet the question of how this devotion to family has influenced Italian history, or been shaped by it, has rarely been posed. The few scholars who have ventured on to this terrain have been disparaging in the extreme about the role of the Italian family.[41]

These realities have been, and continue to be, crucial elements in negative attitudes toward government and political leaders. Consequently, there is always a heavy reliance on personal and extended family relationships in the conduct of personal, business, and public affairs. There is little question that this pattern of behavior is predominant. To the extent that authoritarianism exists, it lies mainly within the family or family groupings, or in manager–employee relations.

Throughout the centuries, Italy has experienced repeated devastations. German, French, Spanish, and, in Sicily, earlier Norman, Arab, and Catalan invasions; internecine wars; and complications related to papal political policies wreaked havoc on Italy and its people for over 1,000 years. Even as recently as World War II, American and British troops invaded from the south and Germans from the north. Nevertheless, ingenuity, imagination, and an extraordinary ability for survival has enabled Italians, whether as citizens of city–states or, more recently, of a united nation, to rebound from terrible adversities.

In the early post–World War II years, Italy experienced an economic "miracle" comparable in magnitude to that in France and Germany. Italy has emerged as an economically advanced nation with a Gross National Product about equal to that of Great Britain.[42] In contrast to the other continental powers, where government was a driving force behind recovery, the reverse oc-curred in Italy. Nevertheless, while the Italian state cannot be said, in any meaningful sense, to have planned the great boom, it certainly contributed to it in many ways. Infrastructural works, such as the construction of *autostrada*, served as vital support for the private sector. Monetary stability, the nontaxation of business interests, and the maintenance of favorable lending rates by the Bank of Italy all helped to create the correct conditions for the accumulation of capital and its subsequent investment in industry.[43]

It was mostly private enterprise which produced the "miracle," aided by massive migrations from the countryside in the north and center, but espe-cially from the south and Sicily. Between 1955 and 1971, some 9,140,000 Italians were involved in interregional migration.[44] These extraordinarily large migrations, although those from the south were mostly illiterate or semi-liter-ate, provided labor at low cost. Devoid of union protection, speaking a dialect unintelligible to the Northerners (where industry had developed), initially living four or five men to a shelter or attic without hygiene facilities, and working very long hours—these workers, together with equally resilient man-agement, were responsible for Italy's remarkable achievement against all odds.

Eventually, private and public efforts were undertaken to industrialize the *Mezzogiorno* (south of Rome). But these proved to be of only limited success. In Sicily, poverty-stricken conditions essentially remained in the rural areas, re-lieved only by the heavy migration of youth to northern Italy, Germany, and France. The result was one of the most massive transfers of population in modern times of a peasantry to an industrialized and commercial area. Move-ment to the cities north of Rome was bound to produce profound social and economic changes affecting education, standards of living in general, women's status, trade-union relations, and broadened social welfare programs.

It is important not to lose sight of the fact that the Italian population has changed drastically over the past thirty years. The internal migration alone reached 9.1 million just in the period of 1955 to 1971. In the boom years of 1958 to 1963 alone, some 900,000 moved out of Southern Italy.[45] Put another way, almost one in five Italians uprooted themselves from their homes to move out of rural com-munities into rapidly growing urban centers, causing disconnections with tra-ditional values, social customs, and patterns of behavior. To place the size of Italy in perspective, the country has a population of some 57 million (as of 1989), about the same as France (56.2 million in 1989) and the United King-dom (57.2 million in 1989). Italy spreads over 116,303 square miles, larger than the United Kingdom but considerably smaller than France. The northern area and that south of Rome are marked by dialects that are mutually unintel-ligible, different outlooks, and marked degrees of variations in the cultural behavior of the two economically and socially disparate halves. The reader can imagine the level of complexity that social configuration presents, both for Italians attempting to apply their existing handed-down values in what, for many, are rapidly changing lifestyles, and for the analysts scratching their heads in an attempt to understand the future course of Italian politics.

POLITICAL AND CULTURAL CONSEQUENCES

The transition from a basically agricultural economy and a traditional way of life characteristic of such societies to a powerful industrialized economy and the shift in population requires that we speculate about the future outlook for today's Italian children.

The most obvious reality is that the intensity of family has loosened somewhat because of the mobility and greater affluence of Italians today. However, as the experience of other regions of Europe has proven, it will certainly take several more generations before fundamental attitudes toward familial relationships and inherent obligations to the family are significantly altered. Likewise, individualism has been an Italian trait for centuries, which recent changes in Italian lifestyle have not affected, so this characteristic should not vanish. For those interested in the future of Italy, the task is to determine how increased educational standards and opportunities, as well as better economic prospects, will affect how the third post–World War II generation feels about democracy when they reach adulthood. For example, what is it that these children now hear at home that will eventually influence their political views and actions?

We must remember that southern rural Italians were not so long ago either lacking in sympathy for democracy or apathetic toward it. In Italy, individualism is not necessarily an impediment to the rise of some kind of authoritarianism if economic disaster should ever strike. The regime of Benito Mussolini proved that. The absence of a tradition of democracy, the low level of social trust, and distrust of government and politicians makes this an ever-present danger. In fact, when compared to circumstances in the other major democracies— Germany, France, Great Britain, and Spain—the risk is greatest in Italy.

In politics, Italian individualism contributes to the problem of uncertain political stability. As political scientist Raphael Zariski points out, "The most important feature of Italian political culture has been its heterogeneity and its fragmentation."[46] For the purpose of highlighting the volatility of Italian politics, Table 5.4 displays the composition of the Chamber of Deputies resulting from the 1992 elections. Note that the Christian Democrats still emerged in a leadership position, one held since the political restructuring of Italy after World War II. On the one hand, we have a party that served as an umbrella for many coalitional arrangements that came and went over the years (dozens since World War II) and, on the other, clearly not a monolithic or stable proposition. In the following section, we contrast the political configuration of 1992 to that caused by the elections of 1994 to suggest that instability remains a chronic condition in Italian political affairs. Data for the 1996 elections, shown in Table 5.5, provide additional evidence of the pattern at work.

Zariski's count of the important 1992 elections suggested the high degree of fractionality in the political makeup of that year's election campaign. Other

TABLE 5.4
Italian Chamber of Deputies: Seats by Party and Percentage of Votes, 1992

Party	Seats	Percentage of Votes
Greens	16	2.8
Communists (Various)	142	21.7
Socialists	92	13.6
Social Democrats	16	2.7
Republicans	27	4.4
Christian Democrats	206	29.7
Liberals	17	2.8
Neo-Fascists	34	5.4
Others	80	16.9

Source: Raphael Zariski, "Italy," in *Politics in Western Europe*, ed. M. Donald Hancock et al. (Chatham, N.J.: Chatham House, 1993), 336–338.

data drawn from footnotes to Table 18.1 in Zariski's analysis of the 1992 electoral percentage vote revealed the following additional information:[47]

Two Communist Parties on the ballot: Democratic party of the left (PDS) and Communist Refoundation (A party of Orthodox Communists) polled 16.1 percent and 5.6 percent respectively for a total of 21.7 percent. Northern League (Lombardy regional group) 8.7 percent, Network (La Rete), anti-Mafia party Sicily, 1.9 percent, Panella Lists (former Radicals and Party of Pensioners) 1.2 percent, South Tyrol People's Party (German ethnic group in Bolzano Province) and Liga Veneta, each less than 1 percent.[48]

TABLE 5.5
Italian Chamber of Deputies: Seats by Party, 1996

Party	Number of Seats
Olive Tree	289
Communists	35
Northern League	59
Freedom Alliance	246
Other Parties	1

Source: Washington Post, April 24, 1996, p. A23.

In the years since the elections of 1992 for the Chamber of Deputies seats and in the Senate, Italy experienced an extremely serious crisis, one that threatens the very underpinning of the Republic. Corruption at the highest levels of government and business elites, involving about 5,000 individuals and a quarter of the Chamber of Deputies, became the subject of intense investigations by the government and the press. As a result of domestic political pressures, President Oscar Luigi Scalfaro dissolved the twenty-one-month-old parliament on January 16, 1994 in anticipation of elections in March. The immediate consequence of the national conscience being upset at the corruption was how the voters responded in the elections, held March 27 and 28, 1994. They completely eliminated the Christian Democrats as a party. Whereas, in 1992, 206 of this party's members had been elected to the Chamber of Deputies, in the 1994 elections they vanished from the scene. A new party called the Centrist Alliance Pact for Italy had been created, led by former Christian Democrats Mario Segni and Mino Martinazzoli, presumably in an attempt to regroup erstwhile Christian Democrats in a renewed political effort. However, this new political configuration garnished only enough votes to elect forty-six deputies and thirty-one senators, not enough to play an important king-making role in determining who would be the new prime minister.

The Progressive Alliance, which included the dominant party of the grouping, the Democratic Party of the Left (made up of moderate Communists), and other allies, such as the refounded Communists (extreme left), the Network (anti-Mafia movement in Sicily), the Greens (environmentalists), the Italian Socialist Party (closer to left-of-center), and the small leftist Democratic Alliance, scored second place in the contest with 213 deputies and 122 senators.

However, the startling surprise was the strength of the newly formed Rightest Alliance, led by Forza Italia, which was associated with the regional Northern League (mainly in Lombardy) and the neo-Fascist National Alliance (with strength in Southern Italy but also in Rome and growing nationally). The granddaughter of Benito Mussolini, Alessandra Mussolini, was reelected on this ticket to the Chamber of Deputies. The leading spirit of the Forza Italia and the Rightist Alliance is a self-made billionaire, Silvio Berlusconi, owner of three television stations, mass-market magazines, AC Milan (a top Italian soccer team), and other vast holdings. Berlusconi emerged as a national political figure about two months before the elections. To a large extent, he was able to exploit the use of his communications media empire and the mass-marketing expertise of his holdings to present the Italian voting public a new political persona—himself. His exploitation of technology and mass communications accounts for why he was able to create a national identity so quickly and so effectively. Along with projecting himself to the Italian voters as a fresh alternative, he promised that the candidates for the Chamber on the Forza Italia slate would also be new faces in the political arena. The strategy worked: the Rightist Alliance obtained 366 seats in the Chamber and 155 in the Senate. Others in the national race scored only four seats in the Chamber and seven in the Senate.

It would appear, therefore, that, clearly and rapidly, a different political force had marched onto the stage of Italian politics. From the figures cited, it is obvious that it was Berlusconi's Alliance that carried the day. However, Forza Italia by itself did not score enough to obtain the prime minister's job for Berlusconi. Support from the other two members of the Alliance would be necessary to overcome the leftist opposition led by the former Communists. Herein lies the compromise, involving Forza Italia's right-wing posture and philosophy, the strong sentiment in favor of autonomy by the Northern League, and the contrary stance of the National Alliance arguing for strength in a central government. The compromise that was reached called for a re-writing of the Constitution, providing for a federal Italy and a strong presidency. Obviously, discussions about the terms of a new Constitution, which would have to be submitted to public referendum, could be expected to be lengthy and acrimonious. But the result could be a far-reaching restructuring of Italy's political life and framework. It would not surprise us if Italy examined with care the Spanish formula for insight on how to establish autonomous regions in a federal state. Already, most political scientists looking at European governments and many European national political leaders have become familiar with the Spanish experience.

Much was made over the spring national elections in 1996 because they resulted in Communists sharing political power in the new government—a first among the industrialized countries studied in this book. Italy's right wing experienced a narrow loss to a center–left bloc called the "Olive Tree" coalition, led by economics professor Romano Prodi. Many observers became highly concerned because of the significant victory of the left, particularly of Communist candidates who had reshaped themselves into a party that looked and talked much like other mainstream European Social Democratic parties. But as with most previous governments, the new coalition was fragile, and officials faced the same social and economic problems that existed before the election. The public was still concerned about high unemployment, bloated government, scandals, and an expensive welfare system. Regionalist differences between the north and the south again played out in the elections.

As evidenced by what happened in just three elections (1992, 1994, and 1996) and Italy's political history over the past century, it should be obvious that the Italian political scene and system is the most complex in Europe. Today's parties range in philosophy from orthodox Communists at one end of the spectrum to neo-Fascists at the other. Between 1946 and April 1994, the Christian Democrats, which was always positioned as a moderately conservative group, had been in power; at times alone, or in association with other groups of mildly left-of-center Socialists. But within the total political range there are splinter sectors and regional groupings, and within each party or sector a variety of views and positions. While dominant, the Christian Democrats only polled 29.7 percent of the votes in the 1992 campaign, followed by the Communists with 21.7 percent, of which the more moderate Communists accounted for 16.1 percent and the orthodox 5.6 percent. As can be expected in a nation as marked by individualism as Italy, within the major parties there is also a considerable variance of views and jockeying for position. Even political deals between moderate or conservative elements and Communists occasionally take place.[49] Interestingly, within the Chamber of Deputies party discipline is strict and rebellion is severely punished, including (as the case may be) expulsion from a party. Despite political distrust of politics and low opinion of politicians, voter participation is high, at times involving 90 percent of the electorate.[50]

The uneasy alliance of Forza Italia and the Northern League, led by the volatile Umberto Bossi, which contributed greatly to Berlusconi's victory in the 1994 elections, came apart in December, when Bossi failed to support the Prime Minister in a parliamentary nonconfidence vote. Realizing that he no longer enjoyed a parliamentary majority, Berlusconi resigned his office on December 22, 1994, some seven months after coming to power. About a month later, President Scalfaro, veteran politician and member of the defunct Christian Democrats party, appointed Lamberto Dini, former Treasury Minister in the Berlusconi government, to form a cabinet of "technocrats" to solve Italy's problems. The Chamber of Deputies confirmed the new cabinet on January 25, 1995. Once again, Italy was being governed by a weak and politically colorless group as would occur again after the April 1996 elections.

In the regional elections held in April 1995, Berlusconi's conservatives, supported by the Forza Italia movement, more or less split the votes with their Leftist opponents led by the erstwhile Communist Party, the Democratic Party of the Left, and the same coalition that would do so well in the 1996 elections.

The bottom line is that Italy is continuing down a well-worn Italian path of volatile and unpredictable political leadership. It is that kind of instability that suggests this country lacks the kind of national political stability that is so crucial to the effective and efficient functioning of a democracy. In short, Italy's political behavior would make any observer of its affairs frustrated at best. And, as if political swings in elections were not unnerving enough in themselves, other factors also toy with Italy's political realities.

The problem of the Mafia in Sicily is one of those other dimensions of complexity in the Italian political scene. Many would argue that the Mafia has been a de facto shadow government for centuries. Beginning in the early 1990s, the national government moved energetically against this crime mob. Important senior Mafia bosses have been jailed, but violence has continued. An important development in late summer 1993 was the assassination of a Mafia-fighting priest, the Reverand Giuseppe Puglisi, in Palermo. This episode brought to prominence a new aspect, one that concerns the future position of the Catholic Church in the anti-Mafia campaign. A press report on the incident commented that, "For decades, the Italian church was seen as generally passive in its relationship with the mob."[51] However, Pope John Paul II, in an earlier visit to Sicily "thundered against organized crime."[52] The church has increasingly turned its back on the Mafia during the 1990s.

The problem of the Sicilian Mafia continues to be directly linked to the future of democracy on that island. The issue is important because Sicily has a population of 5.1 million (1988) and is an area where, as in other parts of southern Italy, efforts at economic development have not borne much fruit.

THE ROLE OF ITALIAN WOMEN

Another sector of the Italian scene which has experienced important changes in the years following World War II is the status of women. Some of the more basic facts concerning their changed legal status are the following: In 1945, women gained suffrage; in 1970, they were allowed to divorce; and, in 1975, they received the right to half of the assets amassed during marriage.

The law of 1975 stated that "spouses have equal rights and responsibilities, and marriage requires mutual consent."[53] This same legislation also abolished the vast majority of legal discriminations that had existed against children who were born out of wedlock.[54] Then, on May 22, 1978, after an intense national debate, women obtained the right to legal abortions.[55] This law, however, did require that women interested in obtaining an abortion had to consult with a social worker and a doctor, and then allow a seven-day "meditation" period to pass before having the medical procedure performed. Girls under the age of eighteen were required to obtain parental permission before having an abortion.[56] It would be difficult to exaggerate how radical a change this law represented, given the long-standing hostility of the Catholic Church toward abortion anywhere in the world, let alone in its own backyard. More than any other legal measure of the post–World War II period, the right to abortion symbolized and advertised the new role of Italian women.

While the abortion issue was high-profile evidence of the changing status of Italian women, more important for day-to-day activities was what happened to their employment, involvement in education, marriages, and divorces. Their participation in university training has increased steadily over the years. The evidence presented in Table 5.6 suggests that they have taken advantage of laws permitting divorces, although obviously not fulfilling the fears of those opposing divorce, who forecasted mass breakups of families. To the contrary, the data suggest that Italian women have been quite restrained in exercising their right to initiate divorce proceedings. Divorce is still a stigma in a nominally Catholic Italy where familial relationships are all-important.

The number of separations, other than divorce, is not known, nor how many couples live together outside of marriage. Italian social scientist Chiara Saraceno mentions that, "From 1965—six years before the introduction of divorce in 1971—to 1985, legal separations increased six-fold, equal to 12 percent of the marriages celebrated each year. This increase, which still indicates a lower rate of dissolution than in other European countries, has only been partially translated into divorce since the law was passed."[57] Divorce became legal at the start of the 1970s, in the midst of what was a massive

TABLE 5.6
Italian Marriages and Divorces, 1987–1990

Year	Marriages	Divorces
1987	305,328	27,072
1988	318,296	25,092
1989	311,613	30,314
1990	311,739	27,836

Source: United Nations, Demographic Yearbook (New York:
United Nations, 1992), 492, 509.

internal migration of Italians from rural to urban centers. As can reasonably be assumed, divorce became more frequent in the heavily industrialized and urbanized north than in the more rural and traditional south.[58] One can also assume that improvements in education and professional training of women, and their entry into better-paying employment opportunities, lessened their dependence on husbands and lovers.

Nevertheless, the labor market is still overwhelmingly male dominated, although this near monopoly is gradually lessening in the middle and upper levels. In the urban setting of the city of Trento, the situation of women in the labor market and their home responsibilities has been thoroughly studied by Saraceno. What she was able to document were very disadvantageous circumstances for women relative to men. Nonetheless, she also demonstrated that the lifestyles of women were fundamentally changing because they had moved, they were working, and they exercised their new-found legal rights.[59]

THE EFFECTS OF EDUCATION

Another important change in the social transformation in Italy since the late 1950s concerns education. Before the 1960s, at least 90 percent of Italians could only boast of up to five years of formal education.[60] During the 1960s, the national government established compulsory education for all children until the age of fourteen. Prior to that, children were only required to attend secondary education until the age of eleven.[61] At the same time that the number of years of education went up, the government also implemented a single system of middle school.[62] The consequence of these actions was an increase in the number of students completing middle school; and, as one observer of the process noted, "large numbers of girls received some form of secondary education."[63]

The magnitude of the effort that would be required to educate such a large population as that of Italy was daunting. In the northern and central parts of Italy, where hundreds of thousands of southerners had entered the labor market, the task before educators was overwhelming. Southern immigrants spoke dialects which were not mutually intelligible with the Italian spoken in schools. The assimilation of children either born in the *Mezzogiorno* or brought early in life to the urbanized industrialized northern and central sectors posed enormous difficulties. However, the compulsory education requirement resulted, over time, in a labor force with considerably enhanced literacy, an important factor in the evolution of Italian commerce and industry as it adopted the use of modern equipment, facilities, and business practices.

Another by-product of the dramatic expansion of education at all levels affects the interrelationships of Italian children. Chiara Saraceno describes what she discovered:

The experience of an education extended beyond childhood, and begun well before the age of obligatory schooling with the growth of kindergartens (and in certain areas, though to a lesser extent, of nursery schools), allows children and adolescents an experience of identification among peers that to some extent influences the way they exist in the family and behave as children. In other words, if being children is only to a limited degree an experience shared with a group of brothers and sisters, it is increasingly becoming an experience partially developed outside the home.[64]

She further observed that the social dynamics within home life began to alter as a result of children living at home longer

in such a way that for long periods family life takes on the features of a community of adults, with rights and duties marked by differing generational positions. This requires constant adjustment of expectations as well as of everyday life. The inherited culture of proper generational and family relationships was unprepared for these negotiations on rights and duties, on solidarity and autonomy, about which is communal and what personal. The result is that the imagination and patience of families and their members are tested every day.[65]

It is readily apparent from Saraceno's research that the third generation is being reared under conditions—and one might add improved financial well-being, at least in the North—drastically different from the way their parents and grandparents were brought up. This situation reinforces our argument in favor of paying close attention to what handed-down values are now developing in the Italian family in all social classes as indications of how adults of the future will react toward political issues and democracy.

Education has its effects in other ways as well. One of the most important is the effect of university training on Italian adults of tomorrow. The university student upheaval which swept through Germany and France in 1968 also entered the Italian scene, at times with considerable violence. An important consequence was the opening up of access to universities for graduates of secondary schools without having to take the dreaded entrance examinations. Paul Hofmann, who has looked at this situation, mentions that, "Whereas there were 270,000 university students in Italy in 1960, their number a quarter of a century later had quadrupled."[66] Simply put, all universities were swamped and academic standards considerably relaxed. In the mid-1980s, standards were tightened and degrees regained their respectability. One result of the open-door university policy of the late 1960s and early 1970s has been a great excess of graduates relative to employment opportunities.

THE ROLE OF THE CATHOLIC CHURCH

The Church has always and continues to play a profoundly influencing role in Italian society. Yet, as is happening throughout Western Europe, there is growing secularization, with church attendance declining. The mass demographic movement from the rural areas, where traditional attitudes were well entrenched along with the moral influence of the Church at least publicly acknowledged, to the cities apparently weakened participation in religious activities.

Evidence of the Catholic Church's lessened influence is everywhere. For a dramatic example, in 1981, Italy conducted a referendum concerning the repeal of the liberal abortion law. The Church opposed abortion and did not hesitate to use its considerable influence to affect the outcome of the vote. However, 68 percent of the voters chose to keep the abortion law in direct contradiction to the pressures placed on them by the Church to vote otherwise.[67] The Church opposed passage of the divorce law, yet that too overrode the wishes of the Vatican and the Italian church leadership. Control of education increasingly slipped out of the hands of the Church as the schools and universities were expanded over the past thirty years. To the consternation of many Church officials, the liberalization of social mores as reflected, for example, in television programming, movies, and music directed toward youthful audiences continued unabated all through the 1970s, the 1980s, and into the 1990s.

Whether the trend toward secularization has run its course is an open question. But what is not is the profound effect that the trend has had on the third generation. The only immediate issue is for Italians to understand the specifics of the influence of secularization. For example, what are the discussions and values to which children listen in homes today? How influential can the Church be expected to be in the future of Italian politics, particularly when it comes to issues concerning democratic institutions? There is little question that it will continue to play some role. The real issue is one of degree.

THE ROLE OF ITALIAN FEDERALISM

A main objective of this book has been to raise the need to consider handed-down values relative to the future of the countries discussed, and not to analyze political structures. However, in the case of Italy, there is some reason to also call attention to the nation's semifederalist schema because of its ongoing influence on affairs. Some research on the subject has been performed by political scientists.

After World War II, limited government restructuring occurred, leading to the creation of five special regions. In 1970, this number was increased to fifteen, each with similar constitutional structures and mandates. In general, expectations have been met. Relations between Rome and the regions remain fuzzy and still have a long way to go before the system works smoothly throughout the nation. Nevertheless, there has been a weakening of the Central government's role in some key areas of responsibility (e.g., urban affairs, agriculture, housing, local public works, vocational education). With the concurrent and substantial transfer of funds to the regional governments, a new experience in Italy's political history began. In the twenty years since the regional strategy was initiated, the experiment reflects a checkered record with varying levels of success. However, a key factor is the fact that election experience broadened. These regional governments are becoming an important arena for the practical training of politicians aspiring to elective office on the national scene. This pattern has been replicated most recently in Spain where, after the creation of a democratic government, regional governments were also established with similar responsibilities as those given to their Italian counterparts.

It is still not clear what the long-term effects of the existence of these government bodies will be on Italian or, for that matter, European democracy. From our perspective, one can ask how the third generation will eventually react to democratic philosophy from what they now hear at home and in school. Will both successful and unsuccessful experiences with these regional governments profoundly affect the reliance of the Italian people on democratic principles by which to govern their political lives? The message is clear, however: The experiences with these powerful federations cannot be ignored when pondering the future of Italian political life. There is a tendency, particularly by observers outside of Italy, to overlook these expanding institutions.[68] That is why we call your attention to them.

PERSPECTIVES ON FRANCE AND ITALY

It is primarily the responsibility of social psychologists and political scientists in France and Italy to examine what is going on in homes and to identify what new handed-down values are emerging. Historical forces notwithstanding, so many new changes have occurred in the social behavior of the current generation of parents, most of which we have touched upon in this chapter, that for the casual observer to hazard guesses about adult political leanings of today's children would be foolhardy. Nevertheless, in the case of France, the free interplay of French children, closer relations with their parents, and higher standards of living would seem to augur little transformation in that country's political structure for the next quarter century. This assessment assumes no French involvement in a major war or economic catastrophe.[69]

Italy, however, is a very different case. The severe tensions between the areas north of Rome and to the south could destroy Italian unity. Remember, this is a country that has only attempted to have a national state for the past 130-plus years, while France, Spain, and Great Britain have had national states for centuries. The efforts stemming from the 1994 elections at revising the Constitution to provide for expanded federalism may well determine the nation's destiny. The 1994 elections, regardless of party labels, showed the country supporting center and right-of-center political attitudes, with Communist-dominated parties still in second place. Somewhat alarming is the growth of neo-Fascism. Italy is the only European nation where this is happening, and it is the result of disorder and the persistence of poverty in the south. Clearly, the southerners are more inclined toward authoritarianism than the northerners. Does this mean that, in the next generation, democracy will be the way of political life favored north of Rome, with some kind of authoritarianism to the south, assuming Italian unity holds?

What the two nations of France and Italy show in common, however, is that it is difficult to generalize about multiple European states when it comes to assessing their political futures. What is also common to both is the source of much of their diversification: individualism. In both instances, that trait affects familial life, handed-down values, and reaction to local and national political issues. It is an underlying social attribute that should not be discounted or ignored by anyone who attempts to understand events in these countries or aspires to play a leadership role in them.

NOTES

1. Steven Lukes, *Individualism* (Oxford: Basil Blackwell, 1973), 1.
2. Ibid.
3. Ibid.
4. Ibid., 45–110.
5. Pierre Birnbaum and Jean Leca, eds., *Individualism: Theories and Methods* (Oxford: Clarendon Press, 1990), 1.
6. J. Roland Pennock, *Democratic Political Theory* (Princeton, N.J.: Princeton University Press, 1979), 16–120.
7. Ibid., 73.
8. Ibid., 74.
9. Scholarly literature concerning individualism and democracy is so voluminous that it proved impractical in a brief work such as ours to acknowledge it all. However, our thinking has been influenced by the following studies: Pennock, *Democratic Political Theory*; Lukes, *Individualism*; Brian M. Downing, *The Military Revolution and Political Change* (Princeton, N.J.: Princeton University Press, 1992); Giovanni Sartori, *The Theory of Democracy Revised* (Chatham, N.J.: Chatham House, 1987); Birnbaum and Leca, *Individualism*; Arend Lijphart, *Democracies* (New Haven: Yale University Press, 1984); John H. Herz, ed., *From Dictatorship to Democracy* (Westport, Conn.:

Greenwood Press, 1982); Charles Hampden-Tanner, *Radical Man* (Cambridge, Mass.: Schenkman, 1970); Robert A. Dahl, *Dilemmas of Pluralistic Democracy* (New Haven: Yale University Press, 1982); Barrington Moore, Jr., *Social Origins of Dictatorship and Democracy* (Boston: Beacon Press, 1966); Robert A. Dahl, *Democracy and Its Critics* (New Haven: Yale University Press, 1989); Alan MacFarlane, *The Origins of English Individualism* (Cambridge: Cambridge University Press, 1978); Anthony M. Orum, *Introduction to Political Sociology* (Englewood Cliffs, N.J.: Prentice-Hall, 1989); Samuel P. Huntington, *The Third Wave* (Norman: University of Oklahoma Press, 1991); and Tom Bottomore, *Political Sociology* (Minneapolis: University of Minnesota Press, 1993).

10. Sanche de Gramont, *The French: Portrait of a People* (New York: G. P. Putnam's Sons, 1969), 37.

11. Ibid., 38.

12. Ibid.

13. Ibid., 44. We assume that the author's reference to August 4 concerns the proposal of Viscount Noille in 1789 that taxes should be paid by all proportionately to their incomes. For details, see John Knapton, *France* (New York: Charles Scribner's Sons, 1971), 276–277.

14. Knapton, *France*, 276–277.

15. Lukes, *Individualism*, 7.

16. Antoine Prost, "Public and Private Spheres in France," in *A History of Private Life*, vol. 5, ed. Antoine Prost and Gerard Vincent (Cambridge, Mass.: Harvard University Press, 1991), 56–57.

17. Donald Hancock et al., *Politics in Western Europe* (Chatham, N.J.: Chatham House, 1993).

18. William Safran, *The French Polity* (London: Longman, 1991), 36.

19. Gramont, *The French*, 197–198.

20. Ibid.

21. Prost, "Public and Private Spheres," 71.

22. Ibid., 73.

23. Safran, *French Polity*, 38.

24. Ibid.

25. Ibid.

26. Ibid., 39.

27. Ibid.

28. Prost, "Public and Private Spheres," 83.

29. Ibid., 84.

30. Ibid., 197.

31. William Safran, "Who Has the Power and How Did They Get It?" in *Politics in Western Europe*, 129.

32. Ibid.

33. Safran, *French Polity*, 246.

34. Safran, "Who Has the Power and How Did They Get It?," 129.

35. PBS interview with staff from *Le Monde*, National Public Radio, 24 April 1995.

36. Safran, "Who Has the Power and How Did They Get It?," 129.

37. Ibid.

38. Report from French Embassy, Washington, D.C., August 11, 1993.

39. Ibid.

40. Paul Ginsberg, *A History of Contemporary Italy, 1943–1988* (London: Penguin, 1990), 2–3.

41. Ibid., 2.

42. Ibid., 1.

43. Ibid., 214.

44. Ibid., 219.

45. Ibid., 220.

46. Raphael Zariski, "Italy," in *Politics in Western Europe*, 307.

47. Ibid., 336–337.

48. Ibid., 335–355.

49. Ibid.

50. Ibid., 334–335.

51. *The Washington Post*, 26 September 1993, pp. A-41, A-45.

52. Ibid.

53. Sally Shreir, ed., *Women's Movements of the World* (London: Longman, 1988), 147.

54. Ginsberg, *History of Contemporary Italy*, 370.

55. Ibid., 394.

56. Chiara Saraceno, "The Italian Family," in Prost and Vincent, eds., *A History of Private Life*, vol. 5, 471. See also Pierpaolo Donati, ed., *Secondo Rapporto Sulla Famiglia en Italia* (Milano: Ediziono Paoline, 1991), 136–149.

57. Quoted in Paul Hofmann, *That Fine Italian Hand* (New York: Henry Holt, 1990), 118.

58. Chiara Saraceno, *Il Lavero Mal Diviso* (Bari: De Donato Editore Spa, 1990).

59. Zariski, "Italy," 305.

60. Ginsberg, *History of Contemporary Italy*, 270.

61. Ibid.

62. Ibid.

63. Saraceno, "The Italian Family," 494–495.

64. Ibid., 495.

65. Quoted in Hofmann, *That Fine Italian Hand*, 55.

66. Zariski, "Italy," 305.

67. Frederic Spotts and Theodor Wieser, *Italy, A Difficult Democracy* (Cambridge: Cambridge University Press, 1988), 226–230.

68. Robert D. Putnam, *Making Democracy Work: Civic Tradition in Modern Italy* (Princeton, N.J.: Princeton University Press, 1994), 17–62.

69. Recent French interest in energizing European military peacekeeping intervention in the Bosnian crisis suggests that a limited European war is not ridiculously out of the question.

—6—

Spain: Political Transition to Democracy

... Which I have earned with the sweat of my brows.
—Miguel de Cervantes

In this chapter, we describe the political evolution of Spain from a pre–Civil War republic to a forty-year dictatorship, to a federated democracy. The key question addressed is how can a dictatorship evolve into a successful democracy?

The peaceful transition from Franco's dictatorship to a pluralistic constitutional democratic monarchy—within the three-year period from Franco's death on November 20, 1975 to the adoption of the new Constitution in December 1978—is unique in Western European history. For that reason, details of how this evolved have drawn wide attention from Spanish and foreign scholars.[1] The transition is made more remarkable, given the fact that the nation had a history of regionalist problems that prevented cooperation on the order evident in other democratic nations and at a time of difficult economic conditions. However, while many have described the individual events of the 1970s and 1980s, it is the basis of Francoism that is of greatest importance. In this chapter, we will briefly review many of the key events but focus on showing that the features of Francoist rule made it possible for the relatively smooth shift to Spain's current democratic political philosophy. Basic evolutions in the politics of the nation in the forty-odd-year rule of the Caudillo facilitated the implementation of democracy.

There is, however, a dimension which is impossible to cover. From Franco's takeover in 1936 to the Constitution of 1978 there are two generations, without counting the one which fought the Civil War (1936–1939), which included those born in the latter part of the last century. Also to be considered are the noncombatants on both sides, who were affected severely by the conflict in economic, social, and family terms. We do not know systematically what conversations took place in the homes of these generations or about what sank into the subconscious of the young growing up during those forty years. What did the children hear during those long years when Spaniards in general grew apathetic toward politics?[2] What happened in family circles that led Spaniards in their twenties and forties to reflect greatly mitigated extremes in political attitudes, to the point that violence-prone anarchists in the labor movements of the 1920s and 1930s melded into relatively mild Socialist camps in the 1970s after Franco? The same rationale would apply to the far right. While we would agree that the brutality of war was a factor in moving political leaders and army commanders toward *convivencía*, with its tacit demands for compromise, there must also have been conversations in the home which were a factor in mellowing the anticompromistic feature of traditional Spanish political behavior.

CIVIL WAR ORIGINS OF THE FRANCO REGIME

It is impossible to understand Spanish politics in the second half of the twentieth century without having some familiarity with the origins of the Spanish Civil War. No event affects a nation longer than a civil war, and Spain is no exception. In the Spanish case in particular, the fact that the winning side (the Nationalists) ruled for some forty years, and thus kept alive many of the symbols for which they fought, simply reinforced the influence of that war on key leaders for decades. The fact that many in the rest of Europe had been so interested in the Civil War at the time it was fought, and then spent decades convinced that the wrong side won, also insured a long-standing interest in the consequences of the war. For example, for more than a decade many governments in Western Europe refused to have full diplomatic relations with Franco because he was, in the eyes of many Europeans, the last of the fascist dictators—equated with Mussolini and Hitler.[3]

At the outbreak of the rebellion, the generals on the Nationalist side, including Franco, had no clear idea of what kind of state would come into being after the war was won.[4] Stanley Payne, American historian and expert on modern Spanish political history, observed, "The conspirators were determined to establish an all-military directorate that would force the Republic into a more conservative mold. They did not intend to destroy the republican form of government, nor even necessarily to establish a corporative chamber. Furthermore, they were determined to have nothing to do with politicians and took none of them into their confidence."[5]

This approach had many of the same characteristics evident in earlier military interventions into Spanish politics. Throughout the nineteenth century, Spanish generals periodically would intervene "to save the nation" from political unrest. In fact, the sense of the military's higher loyalty to the nation over any particular government was a clearly understood tradition in Franco's generation. Payne's observation about what the generals expected to accomplish was very consistent with the aspirations of the previous half-dozen generations of Spanish military officers. The fact that circumstances led to a much broader and extensive role for the military in the creation and operation of a post–republic government was not foreseen in the spring of 1936. Their *pronunciamento* was intended to be a quick, surgical, political operation, without any expectation of a long and arduous civil war. It was their failure to pull off this fast uprising that led to the extended Civil War.

Throughout his long reign, Franco very adroitly balanced, from the beginning, the diverse elements supporting the regime by appointing to major positions personalities known to be either associated with the various political groups supporting his government or sympathetic toward these factions. However, Franco also attempted to make sure of their loyalty to him, and they were so positioned that they could not prove an effective threat to his control. He showed uncanny skill in adapting his choice of cabinet officers and immediate advisors to changing internal and foreign conditions.[6] To a limited extent, King Juan Carlos acquired similar skills, applying this strategy. Without detracting from his innate abilities, the king had obviously learned a great deal from Franco about how to balance the key players on Spain's political checkerboard.

Franco was not the initiator of the military revolt against the Second Republic, although he was fully aware about preparations and party to the military conspiracy. But he was fearful, and, as it turned out, quite correctly, that a major split in the army would occur and civil war might result.[7] On July 24, under the nominal presidency of elderly General Miguel Cabanellas (the oldest officer of that rank on active service in the army, a Mason, and ardent republican in principle), a National Defense Junta (*Junta de Defensa Nacional*) was created.

The Junta was enlarged to include Franco, who became a member in August along with other military figures.[8] Obviously, the immediate concern of the Junta was conduct of the war which, by now, clearly required a prolonged effort. By the autumn, it was readily apparent to the Junta and other Nationalist generals that a unified command was essential to coordinate and direct all military activities. Franco was appointed Commander-in-Chief (*Generalissimo*) without dissent. Shortly afterward, he also was named Chief of the Nationalist State (*Jefe del Gobierno del Estado Español*).[9]

With this appointment, Franco not only had authority to direct the war effort, but received total powers to rule the embryonic Nationalist State without having to clear his decisions with any person or official structured body.

He never relinquished these powers until the day he died in 1975. On October 1, 1936, on the same day he received all his powers, the National Defense Junta was dissolved and a new group created, known as the Technical Junta of the State (*Junta Tecnica del Estado*). The purpose of the Technical Junta was to deal with issues and developments which went beyond military considerations.[10] As the areas falling to Nationalist forces expanded, the need for such a body became apparent. However, under Franco's expanded powers all appointments were subject to his direct or indirect approval. The composition and nature of the Technical Junta did not as yet reflect Franco's thinking with regard to the political direction of the new Nationalist State.

The Technical Junta was presided over by a president, and the group was required to submit decisions for approval to Franco as Chief of State unless he delegated authority within certain limits. Close military friends and advisors to the Caudillo dominated the membership on this Junta. On January 30, 1938, Franco formed his first government with the basic trappings of state.[11]

The Technical Junta consisted of "Commissions," each of which was headed by a president. Although the Junta was under a general, the Commissions were composed mainly of civilian specialists. For example, Andres Amado y Reygondaud, a respected financial expert, took charge of the Treasury. Culture and Education became the province of a well-known playwright, José Peman y Pemartin. Other Commissions were concerned with Communications and Public Works; Industry, Commerce, and Supply; Agriculture; Labor; Justice; and a Secretary for Foreign Affairs. Franco also created a General Secretariat attached to the Chief of State (Franco), comprised of experts in the various Commissions, to serve primarily in an advisory and liaison capacity. The post of Governor General was established to deal with civilian provincial matters and civil governors. Subsequently, a Secretary of War was designated.[12]

By the end of November 1936, the conflict had become internationalized, with Germans and Italians helping the Nationalists and the Soviets and international brigades of volunteers from many nations helping the republicans.[13]

In view of the military progress made in 1936 and 1937 and the complicated international aspects of the conflict, it became apparent that the Technical Junta had become inadequate for governing the now-expanded areas. Franco, therefore, promulgated a law on January 30, 1938 which immediately eliminated the Technical Junta and organized the government administratively.[14] Underlying part of Franco's rationale for this reorganization was his unwavering belief that the war would be won, despite the fact that the fighting was far from over. On the republican side, by contrast, dissension and lack of coordination in the Republic's war effort inspired growing pessimism in its sectors about the chances of victory. Although the January measure was essentially an administrative reorganization, in effect it was, provisionally, the first Franco government. Nevertheless, its primary function was still related to the Nationalist war effort.

It consisted of a presidency vested in the Chief of State (Franco), eleven ministers, and one cabinet-level position. The law also created a vice president.[15] Franco was moving toward development of a normal government, prepared to handle the broad range of issues that face any well-established regime. He also followed a practice evident throughout his tenure of staffing his cabinet with a mixture of personal advisors and colleagues, along with technical experts knowledgeable about the areas of their ministries.

A rose is a rose, regardless of what it may be called. Politicians continued to be politicians and vied with each other for dominant positions and blessings from Franco, the Caudillo of Spain. Based on pre–Civil War connections, a brief review of the political leanings of the first cabinet shows how Franco performed his political balancing act. But first, one short comment about the Monarchists is necessary because of their importance throughout Franco's life. Alphonsine Monarchists were those who favored restoration of the monarchy when the war was won, with Prince Juan de Borbon, Alfonso XIII's son, as king. Although Alfonso had departed Spain in a hurry, he never abdicated. The Carlists, who were much fewer in numbers and located mainly in Navarre, were ardent Catholics and regionalists. They supported the return of a monarch, but in the person of Carlos Hugo, a member of a collateral branch of the royal family. Supporters of Don Juan and Carlos Hugo were seriously at odds with each other. The Carlist militia (*Requetes*) were among Franco's finest forces, and it was very important for him to accommodate their presence, as well as that of the Alphonsine Monarchists, within the cabinet. And, of course, with a war going on the key positions had to be held by generals in whom Franco had implicit confidence as to their personal loyalty to him. The same was true with regard to the Falange leaders who were given important leadership roles, both within the organization and in government.

THE CHARACTERISTICS OF FRANCO CABINETS

Support for Franco generally came from diverse political constituencies. They included a broad military basis (the main prop of the uprising), Monarchists, Falange, the Catholic hierarchy, Carlists, and, as political scientist E. Ramón Arango adds, "the great landowners, the powerful business interests, certain members of the aristocracy, and later the Opus Dei, a sociopolitical religious group."[16] Franco's skill in reconciling men who held strong viewpoints and were not prone to compromise was extraordinary. In part, aside from any charisma he might have had, he did so by not allowing any one personality in the cabinet to pose a threat to his total authority. Nor did he permit any particular group to become strong enough to threaten his control of the regime. He did this by changing ministers who were becoming too powerful and reducing the power of groups that became too influential by elevating others. In dealing with international relations, he appointed ministers generally well suited for their responsibilities.

Franco used cabinet designations as a means of affording entry into the government of new political sectors when changing social, economic, and political circumstances so required. This was particularly the case when middle-income levels expanded in relation to the economic boom of the 1960s, impelled by economic technocrats. He also had the habit of sacking high-level cabinet or other government officials, for whatever reason, without any prior warning. In some instances, receivers of "pink slips" would be kicked upstairs, transferred to relatively unimportant positions, or simply dropped into obscurity. A case in point was his dismissal of his brother-in-law, Ramón Serrano Suñer, on September 2, 1942.[17]

During the Civil War, bickering remained relatively muted, mainly because supporters were fearful of losing the war through disunity and because Franco placed all in the Nationalist camp under a so-called, yet not fully defined, National Movement with the mystique of a crusade. To understand the political system which evolved, one may aptly quote historian Sir Raymond Carr with regard to competing support groups or families that warrant our attention: "The Army; the political groups representing the Church; the Falange Movement; the Francoist monarchists, the technocrats and the civil servants."[18] Although the first cabinet placed defense responsibilities in the hands of trusted career generals, the main props of the Nationalist government, other than the military, were also represented in the group.

Falangist militia represented a sizeable element and an essential part of the Nationalist forces, but they also wanted to create a state based on their political philosophy, headed by one of their own as Chief of State with Franco as Generalissimo of the armed forces. The Monarchists likewise had visions of a restored Alphonsine Monarchy with Don Juan de Borbon as king. The Traditionalists (Carlists), while limited to areas under their influence, also had their own agenda. It was in order to avoid a split at the top in the direction of the war, and not fall into the disruptive patterns which had so weakened the Republic's efforts, that Franco maintained the dual responsibilities of Chief of State (head of government) and supreme military commander. He ruthlessly aborted any attempt to sandbag this duality, during and after the war. Franco's decisive and rapid actions prevented serious Falange attempts at mutiny for example. They were reduced to just one more important factor in the regime, providing the outward political facade with limited political input over the next three decades.[19]

Thus, there developed a pattern of ideological inclinations on the part of the Spanish politicians and groups, but without strong party affiliations, since political parties as such were outlawed with all political groupings coming under the rubric of the National Movement. This pattern would last for the duration of Franco's regime.

It was a complicated balancing act. For example, during World War II, Count Francisco Jordana was known for his pro-British sentiments, while Serrano Suñer was known for his fervent pro-Axis sympathies. Jordana became foreign minister when international conditions changed, making it attractive for Franco to have someone running the Foreign Ministry who was perceived to be less alligned with the Axis than had been the case before. The Carlists, with their intense Catholicism, were also in the picture. The Falangists, with their thousands of armed militia serving at the front, had their paladins in Fernandez Cuesta and Serrano Suñer. Cabinet positions for needed technical skills were also in evidence. When the war ended and another government reorganization was decreed on August 8, 1939, the Ministry of Defense was divided into three portfolios: Army, Air Force, and Navy. From that point on, until changes after Franco's death, there were always three trusted senior military officers in all of the Caudillo's cabinets. Thus, regardless of the extent to which, over time, the regime eased its control over Spanish life, Franco's control of the army as protector of the regime never ceased.

For the rest of Franco's lifetime, the basic formula of balance in the cabinet reflecting the basic tendencies from the start of the regime's creation was preserved. The last cabinet—the seventeenth—was formed upon the death of Admiral Luis Carrero Blanco under the presidency of hard-line but colorless Carlos Arias Navarro. By then, the cabinet was close to twice the size of the original grouping, mainly because of expansion in the number of technocrats concerned with the growth of the economy. Because of failing health, Franco, who had held in his hands the triple functions of Chief of State, Head or President (prime minister) of the government, and Generalissimo of the Armed Forces, surrendered the Presidency on June 9, 1973 by appointing his long-time associate and alter ego, Admiral Carrero Blanco, to this position.

The Caudillo believed that, with Carrero Blanco, there would be no question about continuation of a future government after his demise which would preserve the kind of regime he had established. Arias Navarro's appointment as his replacement came as a surprise, not only in the upper echelons of government, but for the public in general. He was born in 1908 and trained as a lawyer. During the Civil War, he served in a judicial capacity with the armed forces, having been given the honorary rank of captain. After the Civil War, he served successively as Civil Governor of Leon, Santa Cruz de Tenerife, and Navarre; Director General of Security; Mayor of Madrid; and Minister of the Interior in Carrero Blanco's cabinet. King Juan Carlos initially retained him as President of the government (prime minister). But since Arias Navarro was unable to cope with the various political currents and violence that came subsequent to Franco's death, he was replaced by Adolfo Suarez Gonzalez, Minister of the Movement at the time of the appointment.

FRANCO: INADVERTENT GODFATHER
OF SPANISH DEMOCRACY

Much has been written about the Falange and fascism in Spain; nevertheless, their role in defining Spain's political future has been far exaggerated. Franco unwittingly set the basis for the eventual return of a constitutional monarchy based on liberal Western democratic principles. Whether Franco's rule lasted almost forty years or would have collapsed in the event of a much earlier death is essentially irrelevant to our hypothesis. Pilar, the Caudillo's sister, observed, "The fact is that the distaste of the Generalissimo towards the Republic was very great. Paco [Franco] in that era was totally a Monarchist. All his life. He had been a personal friend of His Majesty Don Alfonso XIII, who cared for him and expected much from him."[20]

As Pilar testified, Franco was a Monarchist, but the "*instauración*" which he envisaged as his succession had to be a monarchy based on the principles of "organic democracy" established by him. And, of course, a restored Republic was out of the question. He would not consider the return of a monarchy such as that which collapsed in 1931, that is to say, a liberal parliamentary institution based on political party participation. He repeatedly made this point clear in many statements over the years.[21] Yet, by the same token, he recognized the legitimacy of the Alfonsine line. Since he considered the pretender, Don Juan (Alfonso XIII's son), too partisan a supporter of liberal doctrines and the Western European type of party politics, which he considered would be disastrous for Spain, Franco ruled him out of the running. Franco proposed to Don Juan that he be allowed to prepare the pretender's son, Juan Carlos, for the responsibility. The crux of the matter rested in Juan Carlos's residency and education in Spain. When, in time, Don Juan reluctantly agreed to Franco's demand, this was the plan which eventually led to Juan Carlos's designation as successor and, after Franco's death, King of Spain. This is a dramatic example of a European leader understanding the importance of child rearing as a way to influence future political paradigms.

In the spring of 1937, in view of Franco's hidden agenda in favor of a restored monarchy, circumstances required that a legal structure be created under which all Nationalist groups would be covered as a single party, dependent on Franco as Caudillo of both it and the military effort. Dissension among his supporters, which could lead to disaster, had to be avoided. Faced with the dilemma of how to go about finding a solution which would not commit him to a definite political direction once the war was over, he turned to his brilliant brother-in-law, who had arrived in Salamanca in February 1937 after escaping imprisonment in Madrid.

Ramón Serrano Suñer had gone to the Spanish School in Bologna, Italy before studying law in Madrid. During his Italian stay, he came to greatly admire Mussolini and his fascist doctrine. When Franco turned to him for a resolution of his early political problem of finding a way to create an effective political structure, Serrano Suñer wrote Decree Number 255 of April 19, 1937.[22] Effective as of that date, all political parties, as such, were banned. The Decree unified the two most numerous groups with militia in the field. The Falange and Carlist Traditionalists were unified under the rubric of the Spanish Traditionalist Phalanx (*Falange Española Tradicionalists*, or FET) and National-Syndicalist Junta (*Juntas de Ofensiva Nacional-Sindicalista*, or JONS), with Franco as supreme leader. Through a subsequent communication by the Monarchists, that faction adhered to the unification move, placing its military units under the new organization.[23]

Since the officials of the FET and JONS were appointed at all levels either directly by Franco or with his consent, he controlled the political life in Nationalist Spain and later in the entire nation. Dionisio Ridruejo, prominent Falangist in the early days of the unification move who, many years later, became an advocate of democracy, stated in his memoirs that the Falangists hoped that, as a result of unification and establishment of a single party, they would be the predominate factor and convert the party into a totalitarian instrument for political action. Instead, according to Ridruejo, Franco seized control and renovated a Fascist party, but he was no fascist.[24]

While keeping in his hands total control of the only party permitted to function, Franco thwarted any prospect of Spain becoming a totalitarian state in the image of Italy or Germany and became essentially a military dictator until the end of his life. Had he permitted the Falange to take control of the political life of the nation, it would have been impossible for democracy to emerge after his death, or for that matter an *instauración* of the Alphonsine dynasty. We doubt that many students of Spanish affairs would agree with the view that without total military defeat the Nazi and fascist grips in Germany and Italy could have been terminated. It would have been likewise in Spain. That is why we conclude that Franco's decision regarding how he would grip power, using the strategy of the single party and long vacillating about his eventual successor after declaring Spain a kingdom in 1947, made the transition to democracy a distinct possibility. Obviously, Franco did not see the future in this fashion, but sought continuation (*continuismo*) of his regime on the principles of the Falange adopted at the time of the unification (Decree Number 255), with his version of organic democracy lasting indefinitely.

Another characteristic of his method of cabinet control (appointing individuals who, though having disparate opinions and linkages to rival groups with different political aspirations, contributed to subsequent political accommodations) was the practice of forcing their de facto cooperation. This was done by giving his ministers almost dictatorial powers in their respective portfolios. They knew that chances of getting their initiatives implemented rested on some measure of cooperation, or a veto by one minister could lead to a stand-off, with Franco throwing them both out. Over a period of nearly forty years, this reality forced a certain mellowing in the traditional Spanish politician's knack for no compromise. When the transition era began, many of the personalities involved were veterans of the Franco administration and had developed a degree of self-control in political duelling which they carried on in the new political environment of King Juan Carlos's reign.

To be sure, some did not survive the transition. Carlos Arias Navarro did not have the skill to deal with the widespread social and political unrest which followed Carrero Blanco's assassination by Basque terrorists in December 1973. Franco, debilitated by age and illness, could not firmly grasp anew the reins of day-to-day government. It was not until Adolfo Suarez came into the picture, with his wide experience gained through rising up the political ladder (although he was not a Falangist) and subsequent dealings with a broad coterie of politicians, that a relatively smooth transition began to take shape.

Franco was aware that, from time to time, adjustments in foreign and domestic policies were necessary, and in his long tenure in office he indeed made changes, mainly through composition of the cabinet. In his hope of perpetuating the organic nature of the political system that he had created, Franco acquiesced to passage of the Organic Law of the State, which, in turn, was submitted to a national referendum in 1966 and overwhelmingly approved. In the view of some of Franco's key advisors, the law battened down the legal hatches of his regime but also allowed for what they believed would be gradual changes. The key to the survival of Francoism, however, rested in the Head of State who, in effect, held veto power. When King Juan Carlos determined to move in the direction of Liberal Democracy, aided by the wily Adolfo Suarez and Torcuato Fernández-Miranda, they drew on the mechanisms provided in the Organic Law. The death of Francoism became fact and the legal bridge to a constitutional parliamentary democratic monarchy became a reality. In short, the transition to democracy was conducted within the framework of Franco's own legal handiwork.[25]

THE BIRTH OF SPANISH DEMOCRACY

The immediate task facing King Juan Carlos after Arias Navarro was pushed out of the government was to persuade the Cortes (Spanish legislature) to commit suicide by passing a law or laws providing for political party participation in a universal election process leading to a new freely elected Cortes. Such measures would have to be submitted to a national referendum. The task for the new Cortes would then include drafting a Constitution structuring the new state of affairs, a charter which also had to be subjected to a referendum. If these measures met with public approval, democracy would become a reality in Spain.

Following Franco's death, Juan Carlos was forced by circumstances, in an extremely complicated and risky situation, to continue with Arias Navarro as prime minister. By July 1, 1976, it was apparent that Arias Navarro was well over his head in dealing with the unstable situation and a restless and edgy military nervously observing the gradually unfolding public chaos. Under the King's pressure, Arias Navarro resigned as of that date. Juan Carlos, who obviously had developed his own agenda in favor of adopting a policy and philosophy leading to a democratic state, appointed Suarez as Arias Navarro's successor. Amidst wide popular acclaim, movement began immediately toward the objectives cited earlier. Journalist John Hooper described the challenge facing the government: "The problem for Suarez and the members of this Administration was that while they now enjoyed tremendous popularity they did not belong to any of the political parties that were shaping up to contest the election [for the Cortes]."[26]

In November 1976, a potpourri of parties, with little bases and, to some extent, reminiscent of semisocial clubs headed by both Francoist former supporters and opposition leaders of a mild sort, emerged initially as the Popular Party (*Partido Popular*) and later as a centrist group, the Union of Democratic Center (*Unión de Centro Democrático*, or UCD) headed by Adolfo Suarez. However, the party had no common ideological base, and by the time of the third round of general elections in 1982 more or less self-destructed, with victory going to the Spanish Socialist Worker's Party (*Partido Obrero Socialista*, or PSOE). The whipping of the UCD in those elections was so severe that it vanished from the political arena. Furthermore, the Falange, out of some 21 million votes cast, received only 0.01 percent of the total. So much for the future of Fascism in Spain. The Communist Party of Spain (PCE) scored a bit over 4.1 percent of all votes cast, while similar groups under other labels received negligible totals. The transition period ended with the results of the 1982 General Elections, in which the electorate indicated a preference for political moderation, whether to the left or the right.

RECENT TRENDS

Participation in Spain's national and regional elections has been marked by a multiplicity of parties and, in the general or national elections, by high turnouts. In the 1993 elections, slightly over 77 percent of eligible voters went to the polls. About eighty-six national and regional parties fielded candidates. In 1992, 80 percent of the electorate had voted, and in the 1986 and 1989 elections, 70 percent cast their votes. Despite the plurality of interests and preferences reflected in the many contenders in the four cited national elections, the main rivalry has been between the Spanish Socialist Worker's Party, the victor in four last elections with its more or less European Social Democratic philosophy, and conservative coalitions. In the 1989 and 1993 elections, the latter emerged as the Popular Party (PP).

In the 1989 elections, the PSOE gathered 39.6 percent of the vote, while the PP followed with 25.8 percent. In the 1993 battle, the PSOE obtained 38.68 percent, about the same ratio as in 1989, although it wound up with fewer deputies in the Cortes. The PP improved its position drastically, with 34.82 percent of the total and an increase in the Chamber of Deputies of the Cortes. In these two elections, the next nearest competitor was the United Left (IU), a coalition of Marxist-oriented parties overshadowed by the dominant Spanish Communist Party. In 1989, the IU accounted for only 9.05 percent of the vote, and 9.57 percent in 1993.

Tables 6.1 through 6.4 show, in greater detail, the results of the national elections from 1982 through 1993. The data illustrate the enormous turnout for these elections, proof positive of how seriously the Spanish electorate has

TABLE 6.1
Spanish National Elections: October 28, 1982

Parties	Votes	Percentage	Seats Deputies	Senate
Spanish Socialist Workers' Party (PSOE)	10,127,392	48.4	202	134
Democratic Coalition-Popular Alliance (CDAP)	5,478,543	26.1	106	54
Union of the Democratic Center (UCD)	1,494,667	7.1	12	4
Communist Party of Spain-Unified Socialist Party of Catalonia (PCE-PSUC)	865,267	4.1	4	0
Convergence and Union (CIU)	772,726	3.6	12	7
Democratic and Social Center (CDS)	604,309	2.8	2	0
Basque Nationalist Party (PNV)	395,656	1.8	8	7
Basque Homeland and Freedom Party (HB)	210,601	1.1	2	0
Republican Left of Catalonia (ERC)	138,116	0.6	1	0
Basque Left (EE)	100,326	0.5	1	0
Others (46 parties)	736,375	5.9	0	0
Totals	20,923,978	100	350	206

Source: Bernat Muniesa and Mercedes Cabo Rigol, "Historia," in *Enciclopedia Universal Ilustrada, Europeo Americana: Suplemento 1981–1982* (Madrid: Espasa-Calpe, 1985), 571–572.
Notes: PSOE = Partido Socialista Obrero Español; CDAP = Coalición Democratica-Alianza Popular; UCD = Unión de Centro Democrático; PCE-PSUC = Partido Comunista de España-Partit Socialista Unificat de Catalunya; CIU = Convergencia i Unio; CDS = Centro Democrático y Social; PNV = Partido Nacional Vasco; HB = Herri Batsuna; ERC = Esquerra Republicana de Catalunya; EE = Euskadiko Eskerra.

TABLE 6.2
Spanish National Elections: June 22, 1986

Parties	Votes	Percentage	Seats	
			Deputies	Senate
Spanish Socialist Workers' Party (PSOE)	8,901,718	44.35	184	124
Popular Coalition (CP)	5,247,677	26.15	105	63
Democratic and Social Center (CDS)	1,838,799	9.16	19	3
Convergence and Union (CIU)	1,014,258	5.05	18	8
Basque Nationalist Party (PNV)	309,610	1.54	6	7
Basque Homeland and Freedom Party (HB)	231,722	1.15	5	1
Basque Left (EE)	107,053	0.53	2	0
Galician Coalition (CG)	79,972	0.40	1	0
Regionalist Aragonese Party (PAR)	73,044	0.36	1	0
Canary Independence Association (AIC)	65,664	0.33	1	1
Valencian Union (UV)	64,403	0.32	1	0
Others	1,199,705	6.06	0	1*
Totals	20,069,129	100	350	208

Source: Bernat Muniesa and Isabel de Cabo, "Historia," in Enciclopedia Universal Ilustrada, Europeo Americana: Suplemento 1985–1986 (Madrid: Espasa-Calpe, 1989), 604.
Notes: *For a Mallorca group. The Spanish names of parties new to this election are CP = Coalición Popular; CG = Coalición Galega; PAR = Partido Aragones Regionalists; AIC = Independiente Canaria; UV = Unión Valenciana.

been recently about its duty to vote. Not included in these tables are some forty-six other senators, appointed by Spain's regional governments in accordance with Article 69 of the 1978 Constitution. Nonetheless, the will of the Spanish electorate, and its taste in parties, is evident.

Despite the considerable number of parties taking part in national elections, the actual numbers of deputies in the Cortes by party affiliation is lim-

TABLE 6.3
Spanish National Elections: October 29, 1989

Parties	Votes	Percentage	Seats Deputies	Senate
Spanish Socialist Workers' Party (PSOE)	8,088,072	39.56	176	108
Popular Party (PP)	5,282,877	25.84	106	77
United Left (IU)	1,851,080	9.05	17	1
Democratic and Social Center (CDS)	1,617,104	7.91	14	1
Convergence and Union (CIU)	1,030,476	5.04	18	10
Basque Nationalist Party (PNV)	253,769	1.24	5	4
Basque Homeland and Freedom Party (HB)	216,822	1.06	4	3
Andalusian Party (PA)	212,807	1.04	2	0
Basque Nationalist (EA)	135,595	0.67	2	0
Basque Left (EE)	105,217	0.51	2	0
Regionalist Aragonese Party (PAR)	71,628	0.35	1	0
Canaris Group of Independents (AIC)	64,989	0.32	1	0
Others	933,637	4.66	0	0
Totals	19,864,073	97.20*	348*	204

Source: Bernat Muniesa and Isabel de Cabo, "Historia," in *Enciclopedia Universal Ilustrada, Europeo Americana: Suplemento 1989–1990* (Madrid: Espasa-Calpe, 1992), 592.
Notes: *Does not include votes annulled or blank or other small parties with negligible impact. The Spanish names of parties new to this election are PP = Partido Popular; IU = Izquierda Unida; PA = Partido Andalusia; EA = Eusko Alkartasuna; AIC = Agrupación de Independientes de Canarias.

ited to leading groups in these four tables. Spain adopted the d'Hondt formula of proportional representation, which favors large parties against smaller ones. The method appears to function well, and avoids the confusion of political alliances which emerge from time to time only relative to particular

TABLE 6.4
Spanish National Elections: June 6, 1993

Parties	Votes	Percentage	Seats Deputies	Senate
Spanish Socialist Workers' Party (PSOE)	9,076,218	38.68	159	96
Popular Party (PP)	8,169,585	34.82	141	93
United Left (IU)	2,246,107	9.57	18	0
Convergence and Union (CIU)	1,162,534	4.95	17	10
Basque Nationalist Party (PNV)	290,386	1.24	5	3
Canary Coalition (CC)	206,953	0.88	4	5
Basque Homeland and Freedom Party (HB)	206,296	0.88	2	1
Others	1,939,614	9.98	4	0
Totals	23,297,693	101*	350	208

Source: "Elecciones Generales," ABC, 8 June 1993, pp. 33, 36.
Notes: *Total exceeds 100 percent because of rounding. The Spanish name of the party new to this election is CC = Coalición Canaria.

issues and then dissolves after a vote.[27] Thus, the emerging Spanish political pattern is different from what appears in Italy and perhaps can be characterized as more similar to that in France.

In general terms, both the PSOE and PP parties are relatively moderate in their respective positions, left of center in the case of the PSOE and right of center for the PP. The more radical IU, with only about 9 percent of the vote, does not appear to have any chance of acquiring substantial influence in the Cortes in the foreseeable future. Besides, smaller political groups, such as Convergence and Union (CIU) in Catalonia, are moderately conservative in outlook and add to stability in the Cortes.

The elections in March 1996, coming a month before the Italian national elections, reflected similar concerns on the part of the electorate for reforms in government and improvement in employment and a growing moderation in the views of the electorate. As Italians would in the next month, voters spread their support across many parties. José María Aznar's Popular Party narrowly defeated Felipe Gonzalez's Socialist Party, which was plagued by scandals. Yet, Aznar did not gain an absolute majority in the Cortes and thus had to form alliances with regional parties, just as was occurring in Italy. Aznar, leader of a coalition of conservative parties, won election within the Congress of Deputies as Prime Minister on May 4, the first conservative to fill that seat in thirteen years. He had to rule with a fragile coalition government and attack fundamental problems, like Spain's 22.7 percent unemployment rate—the highest in Western Europe. Since Aznar made concessions to win his prime ministership, he began his new role supporting positions that had existed during the Gonzalez period.

THE FUTURE OF SPANISH DEMOCRACY

With the pre–Civil War issue of anticlericalism out of serious consideration and the Catholic Church's support for plurality of worship, the large growth of the middle class, higher standards of education, the entry of Spain into European organizations, and the army a participant in NATO, the prospects for the long-term survival of democracy in Spain appear good. The only development which could shatter that upbeat outlook would be if one of the autonomous regions were granted full independence. In such an instance, the military would quickly intervene, since by the 1978 Constitution it is committed to the territorial integrity of Spain.

Spaniards are becoming accustomed to democracy and are increasingly sympathetic to it as a political system. A poll conducted in May 1993 revealed that 67 percent of Spaniards were "satisfied with democracy," compared with 43 percent in 1984.[28] Another survey, entitled *Report on Young People in Spain 1992*, covered the results of 5,000 interviews of males and females between the ages of fifteen and twenty-nine in Spain, and an additional 1,000 in the Canary Islands. Among the extensive attitudes examined was that toward politics. The researchers from Madrid's Cumplutense University found that, "With a level of interest in politics even lower than the population as a whole, Spanish young people are passive in their voting intentions and only show a certain interest for environmentalism. Membership of youth associations continues to be very low, more so than in the previous decade, and women show a greater tendency to join than men."[29]

During the Franco years, Spaniards became generally indifferent to politics. Is there a connection between the apolitical behavior of the children and grandchildren and that of the Franco-era generation? What did they hear, or not hear, at home that might have contributed, or contributes, to the intensified apathy toward politics in today's fifteen- to twenty-nine-year-old generation? Can one assume that this lack of interest is a contributing factor in the electorate's support for moderation in its voting patterns, as well as rejection of radicalism and other extremes? Or are they just teenagers, like we see in the United States—momentarily apolitical as they focus most of their attention on their social affairs? More to the point, as the fifteen- to twenty-nine-year-old group rear their children, will the latter be influenced by their parents' probable lack of warmth for political discussions? There is evidence of some interest borne out by the higher voter turnout, but the debates seem to lack the passion and the will evident in the 1920s and 1930s. If this benign approach to politics continues, the prospect for democracy in Spain can be considered positive. But, on the other hand, if apathy reaches too great an extreme, then unobserved corruption could seep into successive administrations, leading to dangerous instability and possibly to sympathy or yearning for an avenging dictator. The experience of the Italians from 1992 to 1994 in dealing with corruption in government is too obvious to ignore. It begs the question of whether the Spanish could also respond with a "throw the rascals out" reaction.

Another aspect of special interest in the *Report on Young People*, because of handed-down values relative to family relationships, is the following comment by the researchers:

Young people in Spain account for 24.75 percent of the total population. Ten years ago it was 23 percent and in the next decade the figure will drop to 19 percent. In 1992, 75 percent of young people lived in their family home, with their parents and brothers and sisters. The situation was highly valued by the vast majority, according to figures from the report. 92 percent state without reservation that their family and their health are the two most important things in their lives and what they are most satisfied with.[30]

This observation is as valid today as it would have been at the beginning of this century or in the previous several hundred years. However, in contemporary Spain, with its rather weak welfare programs, it is the family which continues to provide a cushion against economic and medical adversity. The role of the family goes far to explain why Spain's youth remain relatively apathetic with regard to politics, despite the highest unemployment among the countries of the European Community (22.1%). The young can still enjoy following their favorite soccer teams on television and radio; those in the middle class still have the wherewithal to support their social lives.

Another important factor which works for the survival of Spanish democracy concerns the likelihood of little population increase and its implied stabilization of the labor force. Demographic movements—whether up, down, or stable—have profound consequences for political trends, since they directly affect employment policies, welfare programs, and educational availabilities. One has only to look at what great population growth has done to the finances of California, the cities of New York and Washington, D.C., or nations like Brazil and Mexico. Table 6.5, concerning marriages, and Table 6.6, showing births and deaths, substantiate the hypothesis that Spanish population growth will be relatively stable for the foreseeable future. It is readily apparent that marriage levels show little movement in the three years for which data are available. Solsten and Meditz note that, "The marriage rate has de-

TABLE 6.5
Spanish Marriages, 1987–1990,
Select Years

1987	210,098
1988	214,898
1989	----------
1990*	214,805

Source: United Nations, *Demographic
  Yearbook* (New York: United Nations,
  1992), 492–510.
Note: *Estimated.

TABLE 6.6
Spanish Births and Deaths,
1988–1990

Year	Births	Deaths
1988	421,098	309,364
1989	----------	----------
1990	396,353	330,959

Source: United Nations, *Demographic
  Yearbook* (New York: United Nations,
  1992), 275, 361.
Note: See Tables 6.3 and 6.4 for
  comparison to total votes.

clined steadily since the mid-1970s. After holding steady at 7 per 1000 or
more for over 100 years, the marriage rate declined to about 5 per 1000 in
1982, a level observed in West Germany and Italy only a few years earlier."[31]
Why this leveling off has been happening is not absolutely known, but from
our observations while traveling in Spain from the 1960s onward, the number
of couples living together who are not married probably provides the majority of the explanation.

Spain's low birth rate (close to zero growth) is probably the result of use of
the pill and other birth-control methods by Spanish women. As early as 1984,
the World Bank estimated that more than half of Spanish women of child-
bearing age resorted to birth control, despite admonishments to the contrary
by the Catholic Church.[32]

In 1993, three highly regarded Spanish education specialists from the University of Valencia and the Complutense University (Madrid) published an important and thorough analysis of the values held by children ages eight to thirteen. The views of these children are important because they provide a window into the future of Spain covering at least the first half of the twenty-first century. This survey was conducted in major cities, based on very detailed questionnaires regarding the children's attitudes toward just about everything affecting their lives. The results were further tabulated in a broad range of percentages and by sex. While elderly scholars familiar with traditional mores will quickly recognize many handed-down values, they would be surprised at changes which have appeared since their own childhood. Obviously, Spain's profound changes in the past forty years or so have had deep impacts on the psyche of the children surveyed if compared with attitudes of grandfathers and great grandfathers at the same age. It appears that the important shift in Spanish culture away from rigid anticompromise toward *convivencía* has taken root.[33]

In general, from the detailed study one receives the impression of a generation being brought, by influences at home and in school, to greatly value warm family ties, regard for authority based on mutual respect, favorable behavior toward reading and studies, and a high degree of tolerance for the views of classmates, a posture which echoed in the home. In one interesting instance, when queried about talking things over before resorting to aggression in playground conflicts, the overwhelming number strongly favored discussion. The richness of data available shows, in our opinion, the kind of survey that should be done in any society attempting to implement democratic institutions. The information gained will help social psychologists in cooperation with political scientists in any attempt to fathom the impact of children's views relative to influences on eventual adult political behavior. In fact, it would be extremely important if a similar survey were made of the fourteen to eighteen age group, for the same reason. One can only wonder whether the political postures of their parents concerning backing away from uncompromising stances can be the result of a similar upbringing. In any event, the results of the study conducted in 1992 add strength to our optimistic view of Spain's permanent adherence to the values of democracy.

CONCLUSION

As this chapter was being written, the news was filled with stories of Bosnia and Herzegovenia. Periodically, additional stories were aired on television and discussed in the newspapers about the old Soviet Union and its many ethnic groups attempting to establish new, more open governments. Germany was struggling with its difficult effort to merge East and West Germanies. The common themes seem to be regionalist aspirations, individual desires for a better quality of economic and social life, and, in the areas rife with war, peace. Does Spain have a lesson to teach other European and American societies?

Constancy of purpose by Francisco Franco over nearly forty years made it possible for social and political changes to be implemented and, possibly, remain permanent features of Spanish society. That enormous number of years dedicated to one approach is, we would think, the least that would be required to alter fundamental societal and historical forces. The long arm of history continues to reach out and bring rapid social change, and so it is in Spain. If there is a Spanish lesson, it is that a concentrated multigenerational commitment to altered behavior appears to be a prerequisite for change. Otherwise, existing patterns of sociopolitical behavior will dominate, despite intentions to the contrary of any particular party or politician. Spain is proof that a multigenerational approach is possible.

Second, the Spanish case suggests that multiple ethnic groups can live together under the umbrella of a democratic and national government providing local aspirations (e.g., preservation of language and culture, control over education and taxes) can be accommodated while taking advantage of the critical mass made possible by a large national government operating on behalf of a nation (e.g., within the European Community). Yet, even with tolerance of diverse ethnic communities, the element of compromise—of give-and-take—must exist in how various ethnic and regional groups deal with each other. Without that, there is Bosnia. The Spanish case is simplified, to be sure, by the lack of major religious rifts—nominally, Spaniards are Catholics. The Yugoslavian formula suffered from the same problem all other Balkan strategies had for centuries: the existence of Christian and Moslem communities. Both the Spanish case and that of Europe as a whole clearly teach us that religious issues can bring a people to its knees. In the Spanish case, it appears that, in the second half of the twentieth century, the hierarchy of the Spanish Catholic Church had learned this lesson well and acted accordingly.

Third, economics is a factor not to be ignored; for the truth is, it is easier to live in a democracy if economic conditions are relatively good. Even in Spain, where unemployment has been high during the reign of King Juan Carlos, families provided an economic backstop that protected at least two generations from desperation. It was, for example, no accident that throughout the Franco years, cabinet after cabinet made sure there were jobs for veterans (who knew how to use weapons), a matrix of labor union-like institutions to insure a modicum of job security, and economic stimulus to further economic growth of designated industrial zones and security in large metropolitan areas such as Barcelona, Madrid, and the industrial sectors of the Basque Country. The lesson seems obvious: Democratic politics is easier for a people not desperate for physical or economic security.

Fourth, it is not axiomatic that dictatorships and democracies are antithetical. As demonstrated above, an authoritarian regime can either consciously or subconsciously (as in the Spanish case) create the conditions necessary for the flowering of democracy. What the Franco government always recognized was that a key element of success for itself and the society it governed was a relatively free economy in which self-initiative could lead to personal prosperity and, most important, ownership of property. With ownership of property and the inherent responsibility for its protection and growth, one can build a democratic platform—the strategy frequently proposed for such underdeveloped Hispanic areas as Central and Latin America.[34]

The Spanish case is dramatic evidence of what some political scientists have concluded; namely, that a transition to democracy works if you transform the state into a democratic institution and not attempt to transform the nation to democracy. The state is the manageable unit within a society that serves as the vehicle by which representative government becomes a reality. The Spanish case has an additional corollary in that its introduction of a federalist strategy for accommodating ethnic aspirations confirmed the suspicions of many political scientists and historians that the federalist approach should be applied *after* the central government has been democratized. That approach facilitates the implementation of a federated model with built-in give-and-take features so crucial to the effective operation of democratic institutions.

To reinforce the flow of events in Spain, because they warrant understanding by those who would bring stability to other parts of Europe, Figure 6.1 presents the flow of events. Read left to right, Spain had, in the form of the Francoist political arena, a contained circle of activities in which groups performed and sought influence, learning give-and-take. This was followed by the conversion of the national government into a more representative one that, in turn, created the regionalist federated structure Spain has today. Above all of the transition from the Francoist to the federated environment was the consistent leadership of the King and his allies, who were committed to democratic evolution. Below this flow of events were the regional and ethnic activities and aspirations which were kept subservient to the national transition.

To be sure, the Spanish case leaves many difficult questions unanswered. For example, will Spain's new government contribute to a decline in strong regional identifications? Professor Juan Linz, in his surveys of attitudes of

FIGURE 6.1
Spain's Evolution from Authoritarian to Democratic Government

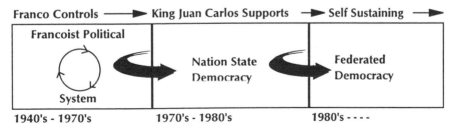

Franco Controls ⟶ King Juan Carlos Supports ⟶ Self Sustaining ⟶

Francoist Political System	Nation State Democracy	Federated Democracy

1940's - 1970's   1970's - 1980's   1980's - - - -

Regional Political Aspirations Increasingly Satisfied

Iberians in the early 1970s, noticed that large percentages of people living in northeastern Spain saw themselves as both Spaniards and Catalans. In recent years, they have seen themselves in much the same terms as during the years of the dictatorship. Will the Castilian-dominated national government tolerate restrictions on fellow Castilians as regionalist governments impose local mandates on their citizens? For example, in Barcelona, Catalan is the language in which all public education is conducted, meaning that any emigrant from southern Spain who puts a child into the local public schools will not have a choice in how that student is taught: They will receive their education in Catalan. Therefore, one could expect that child to grow up identifying with the local culture and not with their parents' Castilian heritage.

The Spanish experience with democracy is only just beginning, despite the fact that its transition from authoritarian to representative institutions has now been underway for nearly two decades.

NOTES

1. See, for example, Alejandro Muñoz Alonso, *Las Elecciones del cambio* (Barcelona: Editorial Argos Vergara, 1984); Victor M. Perez-Diaz, *The Return of Civil Society: The Emergence of Democratic Spain* (Cambridge, Mass.: Harvard University Press, 1993); Victor Alba, *Transition in Spain: From Franco to Democracy* (New Brunswick, N.J.: Transaction Books, 1978); Paul Preston, *The Triumph of Democracy in Spain* (London: Methuen, 1986); Raymond Carr and Juan Pablo Fusi, *Spain: Dictatorship to Democracy* (London: Allen Unwin, 1979); Eric Solsten and Sandra W. Meditz, eds., *Spain: A Country Study* (Washington, D.C.: U.S. Library of Congress, 1990); Geoffrey Pridham, ed., *Encouraging Democracy* (New York: St. Martin's Press, 1991), especially Chapter 7, "Spain's Transition: Domestic and External Linkages"; and Kenneth Maxwell and Steven Spiegel, *The New Spain* (New York: Council on Foreign Relations Press, 1994).

2. The only hint of the stories told are the few that have been collected in oral histories of the war. They suggest a public exhausted by war, threatened with loss of life or long prison terms in the 1940s if they questioned the status of politics and economic policies, and eager to get on with the task of rebuilding a badly damaged nation. James N. Cortada also spoke, between June and December 1949, with known republicans who had held official middle- and low-level positions in Barcelona during the Republic. See also Ronald Fraser, *Blood of Spain* (Harmondsworth, Middlesex: Penguin, 1981), and Ronald Fraser, *The Pueblo* (Newton Abbey, Devon: Readers Union, 1974).

3. On the background regarding the Civil War, see Hugh Thomas, *The Spanish Civil War* (New York: Harper and Row, 1977); Stanley G. Payne, *The Spanish Revolution* (New York: W. W. Norton, 1970); Manuel de Lara, ed., *Historia de España*, vol. 9 of *La Crisis del Estado: Dictadura, Republica, Guerra* (Barcelona: Editorial Labor, 1992), 243–545; Raymond Carr, *The Spanish Civil War* (New York: W. W. Norton, 1986); Gabriel Jackson, *The Spanish Republic and the Civil War* (Princeton, N.J.: Princeton University Press, 1965); James W. Cortada, ed., *Historical Dictionary of the Spanish Civil War, 1936–39* (Westport, Conn.: Greenwood Press, 1982); Stanley G. Payne, *Regimen de Franco, 1936–1975* (Madrid: Alianza, 1987); and Stanley G. Payne, *Spain's First Democracy: The Second Republic, 1931–1936* (Madison: University of Wisconsin Press, 1993).

4. J. P. Fusi, *Franco* (London: Unwin, Hyman, 1987), 17.

5. Stanley G. Payne, *Falange* (Stanford: Stanford University Press, 1962), 102.

6. Raimundo Fernández-Cuesta, *Testimonios, recuerdos y reflexiones* (Madrid: Ediciones Dyrsa, 1985), 155.

7. Fusi, *Franco*, 17–18.

8. Manuel Rubio Cabeza, *Diccionario de la Guerra Civil Española* (Barcelona: Planeta, 1987), vol. 2, 444–445.

9. Ibid., 445.

10. Ibid.

11. Ibid.

12. Ibid.; Joaquín Bardavio, *La Estructura de Poder en España: sociología política de un País* (Madrid: Iblico Europea de Ediciones, 1969), 9–10; Jose Tellado, ed., *Encyclopedia Universal Ilustrada Europeo Americana: Suplemento Anual, 1936–1939* (Madrid: Espasa-Calpe, 1944). Articles about the Civil War in this encyclopedia are detailed and scholarly.

13. Fusi, *Franco*, 27.

14. Rubio Cabeza, *Diccionario*, vol. 1, 381–382. See also Equipo Mundos, *Los 90 Ministros de Franco* (Barcelona: DOPESA, 1970), 19–67.

15. Equipo Mundos, *Los 90 Ministros de Franco*, 19–67.

16. E. Ramon Arango, *The Spanish Political System: Franco's Legacy* (Boulder, Colo.: Westwood, 1978), 122–123.

17. Pedro Sainz Rodriguez, *Testimonio y Recuerdos* (Barcelona: Planeta, 1978), 341; Ramon Serrano Suñer, *Memorias* (Barcelona: Planeta, 1977), 357–359; Fusi, *Franco*, 57.

18. Raymond Carr, *Spain: 1808–1975* (Oxford: Clarendon Press, 1982), 698.

19. Ibid., 675–676.

20. Pilar Franco, *Nosotros Los Franco* (Barcelona: Planeta, 1980), 90.

21. Ibid.; Francisco Franco, *Palabras del Caudillo: 19 abril 1937–31 diciembre 1938* (Barcelona: Edicions FE, 1939).

22. Fernado Diaz-Plaja, *La Guerra de España en sus Documentos* (Barcelona: Plaza y Janes, 1975), 285–296.

23. Serrano Suñer, *Memorias*, 181–185.

24. Dionisio Ridruejo, *Casi Unas Memorias* (Barcelona: Planeta, 1976), 114–116.

25. John Hooper, *The Spaniards* (London: Penguin, 1987), 35–46.

26. Ibid., 41.

27. Solsten and Meditz, *Spain*, 212; Arend Lijphart, *Democracies* (New Haven: Yale University Press, 1984), 153.

28. Spanish Embassy, *España 94, Information Bulletin of the Diplomatic Information Office*, 2nd series, 22, no. 239 (Washington, D.C.: Spanish Embassy, 1994), 8–9.

29. Ibid.

30. Ibid.

31. Solsten and Meditz, *Spain*, 110.

32. Ibid., 78.

33. Petra Maria Perez Alonso-Geta, Ricardo Marin Ibañez, and Gonzalo Vazquez Gomez, *Los Valores de los Niños Españoles 1992* (Madrid: CESMA, 1993).

34. James N. Cortada and James W. Cortada, *U.S. Foreign Policy in the Caribbean, Cuba, and Central America* (New York: Praeger, 1985).

—7—

Spain: Social Transition
to Democracy

My honor is dearer to me than my life.

—Miguel de Cervantes

This chapter discusses the economic and social underpinnings of Spain's democracy. It includes a review of changes to women, children, education, and the role of the Catholic Church.

The remarkable, not to say extraordinary, peaceful transformation of Spain from a centralist dictatorship to a federal, parliamentary monarchy and full-blown democracy, in less than a decade after General Francisco Franco's death in 1975, is one of the great surprises of post–World War II Europe. Much has been written about how this phenomenon came about.[1] And, given the absolute surprise this evolution to democracy created, the subject will no doubt continue to be the focus of study by Spanish and foreign scholars for years to come. They will also speculate as to its durability, particularly if grave economic crises should afflict the nation.

However, even more important than the interest of scholars and reporters should be that of European policy makers who have to struggle with nascent democratic aspirations in Eastern Europe, in what used to be the Soviet Union, across the Balkans in the old Yugoslavia, and even in places that have experienced significant change in the past half century (e.g., Italy and Portugal). The Spanish case is more than interesting, it is instructive. For that reason, it deserves more attention than we have devoted to such obvious areas as Great Britain, France, Germany, the Scandinavian countries, and Italy.

To understand what is happening in Spain, one must look at the situation from two interrelated perspectives: one political and one social. The two facets each influenced the other. In the case of social dynamics, five basic components made up the fundamental social transformations that made possible the cultural and behavioral move toward democracy: the role of individualism and pride, regionalism, the status of women, educational reforms, and the Church's role. Normally, in any discussion of Spain's evolution to democracy, one focuses on political actions, almost entirely ignoring these fundamental social considerations so essential to the process of change.[2] For that reason, this chapter considers primarily nonpolitical issues.

However, the political scientists and historians are correct in paying attention to the role of General Franco and his two generations of politicos, because they collectively facilitated creation of the conditions that made the flowering of democracy possible. In Chapter 6, we argue that it was the nature of Franco's government and how it operated that, over time, made it possible for democratic institutions to emerge out of the construct of Francoist administration. However, to emphasize the most important observation, it was the combination of sociocultural *and* political changes, one affecting the other, that not only made it possible for Spain to transform to a democratic government, but may sustain the effort, at least through the next generation. Our assumption is that no profound economic disruption will get in the way over the next generation; if one does, then the degree of change that is identified as having occurred will be severely threatened.

AN ECONOMIC RENAISSANCE

The changes which have taken place started in the Franco era against a backdrop of international influence on the course of Spanish affairs. Following the signing of a defense agreement with the United States in 1953, which ended Spain's political isolation in international, economic, and diplomatic affairs, the regime began developing liberal economic policies. These increasingly became similar in form and substance to those evident elsewhere in Europe. The first important wave of economic changes culminated in the Stabilization Plan of 1959, which removed a variety of restrictions imposed on economic activity, imposed wage freezes to shut off the possibility of inflation for a short period, introduced a devaluation of the Spanish peseta, fostered foreign investments in Spain, and moved Spanish financial and banking practices closer to those of mainstream Europe.[3] The result was nothing less than spectacular, helped along by a general economic boom in Europe during the 1960s. The Spanish economy grew faster than that of any other European nation during the early to mid-1960s.[4]

Millions of Europeans and Americans discovered Spain's sunbathed beaches, contributing greatly to the economic growth while exposing Spaniards to cultural mores and behavior drastically different from Spain's traditional handed-down values. The role of tourism could hardly be exaggerated, because each year, from the early 1960s to the 1990s, millions of tourists came to Spain. As the years passed, the parts of Spain these tourists visited extended beyond the beaches or Madrid to almost every province in the country, and even to remote villages.[5]

Further economic expansion in the 1980s brought Spain close to the levels in Italy and France. Beginning in the mid-1960s, hundreds of thousands of Spaniards found jobs in other parts of Western Europe, exposing them to the ways of life and value systems elsewhere on the continent. When they returned home, they brought new political, social, and economic ideas with them.[6]

Accompanying the economic miracle (as it has been called) were profound changes in practically all societal aspects. A few of the sectors affected included labor, education, the status of women, religious issues, political pluralism, a shift from intense central government control to diversification through the creation of autonomous regional structures, the downsizing and changing position of the armed forces, and the Europeanization of foreign policy.[7] In addition, massive population movements from the rural areas—as also happened in Italy—transformed Spain from a predominantly agricultural economy to an advanced industrial and commercial state. By 1986, from 23 percent of GDP in 1960, agriculture accounted for only 5 percent, and from 42 percent of workers employed in agriculture in 1960, only 13 percent were laboring in this sector in 1986.[8] Indeed, vast areas of rural Spain became as depopulated as in the Middle Ages.

Spain covers 196,700 square miles, including the Balearic and Canary Islands, as compared to Germany's 137,838 square miles, France's 211,208 square miles (including Corsica), and Italy's 116,314 square miles.[9] Spain's population had climbed to 39,025,000 in 1991, up from 30,558,896 in 1961, yet was less than that of Germany, France, or Italy. More important, the population growth had been most dramatic in the period since the early 1960s, providing Spain with two large generations of citizens whose experiences were the by-product of life in the second half of the twentieth century.[10] Using 1989 data for Spaniards born during the period of the democracy (up to ages fourteen), we see that 20 percent of the population has grown up in the post-Franco period. The numbers are actually larger if we use 1985 data, in which 24.3 percent of the population is under the age of fifteen.[11] This is the generation (those born in the 1980s) whose attitudes one should be most concerned with in forecasting political behavior patterns in the early decades of the twenty-first century, and is the subject of our examination of handed-down values and education.

INDIVIDUALISM

The issue of Spanish individualism is of great importance relative to Spain's political future and survival of its democracy. In this century, this characteristic ranged from the extremes of violence-prone anarchism to corporatism of a fascist stamp under Franco's government.[12]

Regardless of the reluctance of social scientists to accept identification of national traits unsupported by empirical studies, honor and pride can be considered quintessential Spanish traits. More important than proving the point through sociological studies (although that has started to be done in at least the case of Spain), is the fact that Spaniards believe they have national traits, among which is a great concern for personal pride and honor.[13] Honor and pride are, in combination, a form of egocentrism without a national counterpart elsewhere in Western Europe. It leads to heightened personal sensitivity, to an extent that makes compromise in political affairs difficult and complex. Although honor, pride, and shame are recognized Mediterranean characteristics, they acquired deepened significance.[14] This came about largely because of the 800 years of conflict with Islam, which ended only with the collapse of the Kingdom of Granada in 1492; this left behind social and cultural patterns of behavior still evident half a millennium later, a period of time shorter than that of the Reconquest. These traits were equally important among the Islamic hosts and probably crept into the Spanish Christian culture of the Middle Ages from that source. Whether they were an Islamic legacy or *sui generis* Spanish linked to chivalry derived from centuries of warfare, they are characteristics identifiable in Spanish culture down to the present.

Underlying Miguel de Cervantes's classic, *Don Quixote de la Mancha*, highlighting the issues of idealism and materialism, one can see that even in tilting at windmills the elderly mad knight acted from a profound sense of honor. Admiral Pascual Cervera's coming out of the harbor at Santiago de Cuba, with outmoded and undergunned warships, to face the ultramodern American fleet in the Spanish–American War (1898), was typical Spanish *Quixotismo*. Spanish history is replete with such instances.[15] In another dimension, the anarcho-syndicalist movement in the pre–Civil War period (1930s) was also a form of extreme individualism and *Quixotismo*. This movement was a type of Libertarian Communism which called for the abolition of government and counted between 700,000 and possibly 1 million followers, mostly from rural Andalusia and industrial Catalonia. This kind of individualism, leaving aside the political aspect, is mentioned by the great Spanish social commentator of the dawn of the twentieth century, Angel Ganivet, in his *Idearium Español*.[16] Ganivet, together with other brilliant Spanish intellectuals known as the "Generation of 98," critically examined Spain's dilemmas following their nation's defeat in the Spanish–American War and the loss of Cuba, Puerto Rico, and the Philippines. An important part of their debate concerned the identification of Spanish behavioral traits.

Yet, they were continuing a discussion that had been going on for centuries. The theme of honor and pride runs through Spanish literature from the Middle Ages to the present, and now, increasingly, in contemporary studies of social scientists. Recently, Fernando Diaz-Plaja, one of Spain's most distinguished writers, in his *The Spaniard and the Seven Deadly Sins*, whether by design or accident, discusses pride in the first chapter, treating it extensively.[17] In the Golden Ages (sixteenth and seventeenth centuries) of Spanish literature, writers such as Felix Lope de Vega, Spain's greatest playwright and a contemporary of William Shakespeare, wove the theme into his work,[18] as did Francisco de Quevedo, the latter in a pejorative manner.[19]

In the twentieth century, Spaniards continued to recognize honor and individualism as a critical, defining characteristic of Spaniards, as evident in Salvador de Madariaga's work contrasting Englishmen, Frenchmen, and Spaniards.[20] Madariaga also focused on "the tendency toward social, political, and moral disorder which has often been observed in societies of the Spanish race."[21] Spanish philospher José Ortega y Gasset, in his *Invertebrate Spain*, includes an entire chapter on "Spanish Pride."[22] He wrote that "pride is our national passion, our greatest sin."[23]

Foreign social scientists who, in recent times, have investigated life in specific Spanish communities in detail are beginning to document the existence and nature of these issues of honor and pride. Julian Pitts-Rivers, Stanley Brandes, and Ronald Fraser have produced interesting and well-documented studies which touch on pride or honor. All three investigations concerned areas in Andalusia, but much of what they observed can apply to other small rural communities.[24] Honor in Spanish society is so discernible a trait that even travel guides have carried relevant comments on the topic for several hundred years. Using one small example—a tour guide published in 1974—we see a lengthy discussion of Spanish manners, with considerable attention to how one should behave in front of different classes of people in order to preserve their sense of position. The point is made that despite the tourist boom, Spanish character has not changed much.[25] Our observations in Spain lead us to concur with this conclusion, even if attitudes and habits have been affected by changes such as those brought on by tourism. Another example, *Bazak's Guide to Spain*, addressed the issue this way: "And then there are those trite but true Spanish characteristics from which Hemingway derived his literary philosophy, such as cult of manliness, the tradition of honor, the disdain for fear, [and] the passion for independence."[26]

We have stressed the factors of honor and pride in Spanish society because they, and attitudes toward regionalism, are fundamental elements in considering the future of democracy in Spain. The twin issues of honor and pride are crucial because of their relationship to the traditional Spanish tendency of resisting compromise. In fact, a key cause of the Spanish Civil War was the rock-firm position of the principal politicians and societal leaders that made accommodation of various positions impossible.[27]

Historically, in times of debate, sensitivity about one's honor has led politicians and intellectuals to avoid personally offending proponents of opposite views. To resort to personal invective, as often occurs in the American political scene or academic circles, is to torpedo permanently any prospect of compromise or *convivencia*, a term which has crept into Spanish political lore since the 1970s; it implies, "living together or getting along together." Perez-Diaz mentions the terms *reforma pactada* and *ruptura pactada*, and states that, "It seems that the Spanish transition should indeed be understood as the result of bargaining among political elites."[28] His comment refers to debates concerning the new Constitution of 1978 and the Statutes for Regional Autonomies.

The drastic shift to bargaining from political, social, and economic polarization and intractability in the post-Franco years, and the sharply reduced penchant for refusing to compromise, stems largely from memories of the Civil War (1936–1939), when the loss of life exceeded 300,000 Spaniards. Scarcely any family escaped being touched by that horror. In addition, many citizens were concerned about the attitude of the armed forces. This worry intensified because of an attempt early in 1981 by Lieutenant Colonel Antonio Tejero Molina of the Civil Guards, who held representatives of the Cortes hostage in an attempted coup.[29] Tejero and a few other military officers, reflecting an aspect of honor and *Quixotismo*, sought to establish an authoritarian monarchy and destroy the nascent democracy. Only the rapid and courageous intervention of King Juan Carlos, who approached the key military commanders throughout Spain, foiled the attempt. It was the defining moment of the early years of the reign of King Juan Carlos because, through his actions, he clearly had taken the side of those who proposed a future characterized by democratic government. The scare prodded politicians, labor leaders, and businessmen to continue along the path of *convivencía*.

If one may wax philosophical, there seems to be, in the history of all nations, moments when circumstances and certain personalities in positions of leadership come together for better or worse. In Spain's case, the extraordinary juncture of King Juan Carlos and Adolfo Suarez as Prime Minister during the most crucial period of the transition to democracy led the nation in the direction of a firmly-based parliamentary monarchy and an apparently successful federal formula as a solution to the chronic problem of regionalism. The monarch had been reared under General Franco's guidance, who looked upon the young prince as the successor who would keep his regime and philosophies intact. Instead, the young King supported democracy along lines diametrically opposed to Franco's ideas.

THE ROLE OF REGIONALISM

Regionalism is a far more serious problem for the Spanish state than in France or Italy. The main reason lies in the remote past, when the remaining unconquered Iberian Christians sought refuge in the Cantabrian range from Islamic forces, which invaded the peninsula in 711 and swept rapidly throughout the country. Geographical realities then influenced the Reconquest. Spain is a very mountainous country with a central plateau, the *Meseta*, which is ringed by high mountains except for part of its western rim. Separating the *Meseta* from the lowlands along the Bay of Biscay is the Cantabrian range, which connects with the Pyrenees. With thinned-out forces, the invaders were not able to track down and destroy the Christian remnants which sought refuge in the Cantabrian mountains. It was from this range in the modern-day province of Santander (see Chapter 3) that the Reconquest began under the legendary Pelagius (Pelayo) as first King of Asturias. His forces included Cantabrians, Asturians, Galician mountaineers, and Mozarabs (Christians), as well as Visigoths also fleeing from the Arab-occupied *Meseta*. According to old but not necessarily accurate chronicles, Pelagius, founder of the eventual Asturian–Leonese Kingdom, reigned from 718 to 737.[30] From this most modest beginning, the mountaineer Christians, Basques, and, later, Frankish forces initiated a saga extending over nearly 800 years to the expulsion of Islam from Iberia.

During this epic struggle, as elsewhere in Europe, dynastic intermarriages led to the merging of diverse territories into kingdoms. But, in contrast with similar developments in France and Italy, the Iberian kings were in constant warfare with foreign foes—Arabs and Moors. In addition, the conflict of Christianity and Islam gradually led to a crusader's consciousness and intense Roman Catholicism. Regionalism, born from Catholicism and strife and repopulation of territories either abandoned by Islamic peoples or seized from Islam, has remained an important element affecting contemporary Spanish politics and structures.[31]

The vast majority of people living in Islamic Spain converted, in time, to the Muslim faith. With the ebbing of Islamic fortunes, these converted masses retreated also. When the expulsions finally came, they too left the peninsula. After the fall of the Nasrid Kingdom of Granada in 1492, some converted back to Christianity, leaving handed-down values and genetic inheritance to the Castilian conquerors who occupied Andalusia. An important fact to note is that the gradual repopulation of Spain was mostly the work of Europeans descending from the Cantabrian and Pyrenaic mountains. In the eastern wing of the Pyrenees, there were the Hispano-Romans, a people ethnically different from Basques and other Cantabrians, as well as Visigoths, who had sought refuge in Septimania (the Narbonne region in southern France), supported by Frankish military might.

Throughout the centuries of conflict between Christians and Muslims, the nascent Christian kingdoms and earldoms (*condados*) expanded into larger political units at the expense of Islam. Early in the first expansions, Leon absorbed Galicia, which nevertheless preserved its own personality; Castile developed into an earldom and later into a kingdom; and Aragon, a miniscule earldom in the Pyrenees, evolved into an important realm. Navarre, for centuries constituting a kingdom, failed to expand, partly because of inheritance subdivisions, partly because of inadequate surplus manpower, and partly owing to linguistic difficulties with the surrounding powers where variations of Latin derivatives were spoken. The Catalan Pyrenaic earldoms gradually came under the suzerainty of the Counts of Barcelona, equal in status with the other powers. Portugal developed from an earldom into a kingdom.

In all these centuries of absorption, individual traits and aspirations, language, customs, and laws were preserved. When, as a result of the marriage of Ferdinand of Aragon and Isabel of Castile, the various crowns were united, there was no attempt to develop a truly unified nation. It was not until the French Bourbons came to power, with Philip V in 1705, a grandson of Louis XIV of France, that the different regions were subjected to centralizing policies. Obviously, Philip had in mind the highly centralized French system. As recently as Franco's forty years of heavy-handed government, the Bourbon doctrine was intensively pursued. Ironically, with a Bourbon king now on the throne, reversal to a federation of semiautonomous regions has come into being. The message is clear: Handed-down values die hard.

The major regions which have been able to preserve their basic characteristics and languages include Galicia, in the northwestern corner of Spain; the Basque provinces, on the border with France; Catalonia, occupying the northeast corner; Castile, in central Spain; Valencia to the east; the Balearic islands, in the Mediterranean; and, to a lesser extent, Aragon, next to Catalonia. After considerable debate and unusual give-and-take, the Cortes approved a new Constitution which included articles dealing with the autonomous communities. A Basque Statute was passed in late 1979, and a Catalan Statute. A consensus was reached on "an extremely broad declaration of exclusive powers for the autonomous governments, with the sole cautionary introduction of an ambiguous clause. Without prejudice to the powers, which with similar exclusiveness, the Constitution grants to the central states for the same matters."[32]

Reorganization of Spain into regional autonomous communities was completed in 1983. It consists of seventeen groupings in addition to the traditional fifty provinces, but boundaries do not necessarily coincide. To quote from one study of how this arrangement works,

Each regional entity is governed by its own statute of autonomy. It has its own capital and a political structure based on a unicameral Legislative Assembly, elected by universal suffrage. This assembly chooses from among its members a president who is the highest representative of the community. Executive and administrative powers are exercised by the Council of Government, headed by the president and responsible to the assembly. There are also regional supreme courts. The regional supreme courts are subject to the Supreme Court in Madrid.[33]

These communities obtain funds from the central government, but also have the authority to levy taxes. While there are still many aspects to be worked out, results thus far have been positive. The approach is a bold effort to reconcile the interests of so diverse a nation, a country which really is a grouping of Spains. The system as designed, while not a copy of the federal structure of the United States, does have many features in common. Questions remain, however, that will be answered in the next few years: How will the next generation of Spaniards feel about what has been created? What new handed-down values are now being developed in Spanish homes? Will today's children, growing up in the shadow of *convivencía*, reflect, in adulthood, a more generous bend toward compromise than their forebears did? What role will honor and pride play as part of the compromise complex?

THE STATUS OF WOMEN

Another area of considerable change in Spain concerns the status of women. An old Spanish saying goes like this: *"El hombre gobierna y la mujer reina."* Translated it reads, "The man governs but the woman rules." The saying stems from the historical fact that despite the inferior legal position of women in Spanish society, women generally not only had actual control of the household and most of the say in rearing the children, but also exercised considerable influence over their husbands. In situations where extended family relationships were important, life could be made very miserable by the woman in the family if a husband's behavior proved too outrageous. Nevertheless, husbands had very great legal authority over their wives and their assets. The latter could not be sold without his consent, nor could she travel abroad unless her husband gave permission. Divorce was not possible, and legal separations too costly and time consuming to achieve. Contraception and abortion were prohibited and a sexual social double standard prevailed. Considerable leeway was usual for men, and stringent codes of behavior prevailed for women; yet prostitution was tolerated.

In the 1970s, the legal position of women changed drastically with the advent of democracy. Permission from the husband to work and leave the country was abolished in 1975. "Laws against adultery were revoked in 1978 and those articles of the civil code which put women at such a disadvantage with regard to their children and the family finances were replaced in 1981."[34] The Cortes legalized divorce in July 1981 and, in 1985, abortion under prescribed limits. In 1978, the sale of contraceptives became legal.

The increased entry of women into the workforce and universities emerged as another important development, particularly among the middle class, where mores had long called for women to remain at home. By 1984, 33 percent of adult women were in the workplace.[35] The statistics presented in Table 7.1 show the effects of the ratios of men to women in the labor market, changes which affect the role of women in Spanish society.

The data presented in Table 7.2 illustrate that, in 1991, the percentage of women in the total labor market was about 35 percent. In the following discussion on education in Spain, the increase of working women will be related to a steady growth in the numbers of women as students at all levels of education. The data in Table 7.2 demonstrate that the growth rate of women in the workforce between 1979 and the end of 1992 exceeds that of men for the same period. Also noteworthy are the total numbers of unemployed men and women in the years 1973 to 1992, reflected in Table 7.3. However, even though women comprise only slightly over one-third of the total labor available, when

TABLE 7.1
Labor Profile for Spain, 1991

	Millions of Workers	Percentage
Total Work Force	15,382	-----
Men	9,974	64.9
Women	5,408	35.1

Source: Organization for Economic Cooperation and Development
(OECD), *Employment Outlook* (Paris: OECD, 1993), 190–191.

Spain entered a slowdown phase in its economy, which intensified in 1990, 1991, and 1992, the rise in female unemployment in total numbers exceeded male unemployment quite markedly. Since the European economy was still in a recessionary stage in 1995, the trend probably will continue until a recovery gets well underway. Then, one should expect the proportion of women in the workforce to continue growing.

Tables 7.4 and 7.5 address what has been happening with marriages, divorces, births, and deaths. It is readily apparent that marriage levels show little movement in the last three years for which U.N. data are available. After holding steady at 7 per 1,000 or more for over 100 years, the marriage rate

TABLE 7.2
Workforce Growth Rates in Spain, 1973–1992 (percentages)

Years	Total	Men	Women
1973-75	0.4	0.8	-0.6
1975-79	-0.1	-0.1	0.0
1979-83	0.7	0.3	1.5
1983-90	1.5	0.3	1.5
1991	0.3	-0.2	3.9
1992	0.3	-0.9	2.6

Source: Organization for Economic Cooperation and
Development, *Employment Outlook* (Paris: OECD,
1993), 190–191, 193–194.
Note: 1992 figures estimated by OECD.

TABLE 7.3
Unemployment in Spain, 1973–1992 (in thousands)

Year	Total	Men	Women
1973	363	267	96
1975	625	471	154
1979	1,129	759	370
1983	2,351	1,521	830
1990	2,443	1,167	1,276
1991	2,466	1,193	1,273
1992	2,791	1,385	1,405

Source: Organization for Economic
Cooperation and Development,
Employment Outlook (Paris: OECD, 1993),
190–191, 193–194.
Note: 1992 figures estimated by OECD.

declined to about 5 per 1,000 in 1982, a level observed in West Germany and Italy only a few years earlier.[36] Why this leveling off has been happening is not really known, but from our observations in Spain, the number of couples living together outside of legal marriage may be the answer (as in the Italian

TABLE 7.4
Spanish Marriages, 1987–1991, and Divorces, 1991 (in thousands)

Year	Marriages	Divorces
1987	210,098	-------
1988	214,898	-------
1989	---------	-------
1990*	214,805	-------
1991*	---------	23,063

Source: United Nations, *Demographic
Yearbook* (New York: United Nations,
1992), 492–510.
Note: *Provisional.

TABLE 7.5
Spanish Population, 1982–1991, and Births and Deaths, 1987–1991

Year	Population (in millions)	Births (in thousands)	Deaths (in thousands)	Excess of Births over Deaths
1982	37,970	--------	--------	
1983	38,162	--------	--------	
1984	38,328	--------	--------	
1985	38,474	--------	--------	
1986	38,604	--------	--------	
1987	38,716	421,098	309,364	111,734
1988	38,809	415,844	318,848	96,996
1989	38,888	--------	--------	
1990	38,959	396,353	330,959	65,394
1991	39,025	--------	--------	

Source: United Nations, Demographic Yearbook (New York: United Nations, 1992), 131, 275, 361.

and French cases). Spain's low birth rate (close to zero growth at the moment) is largely because of the use of the pill by Spanish women. In 1984, the World Bank estimated that more than half of Spanish women of child-bearing age resorted to birth control.[37]

EDUCATIONAL CHANGES

Part of the reason women could participate in the economy, and particularly in those professions that require high school or university training, is because of substantial changes that occurred in the Spanish education system over the past two decades. As surprising as the smoothness of Spain's transition to democracy was, so too was the evolution of the nation's educational system and philosophy.

The transformation actually started in the Franco era, as did the initial efforts to broaden the rights of women. During the boom in the 1960s, technocrats in the government were sensitive to Spain's need for a labor force capable of participating with the necessary skills required by the expanding economy. The problem they faced was how to deal with the issue without being torpedoed by the extreme right and the hierarchy of the Catholic Church, which was fearful of losing its grip on the educational sector. Memories remained of the Second Republic's anticlericalism in the 1930s as it affected Catholic schools, a situation which contributed to the 1936 to 1939 Civil War. A detailed look at recent Spanish educational reforms focuses profoundly on how attitudes can and are being changed in the youth of Spain.

José Luis Villar Palasi, a university professor, was appointed Minister of Education and Science in 1968, following repeated and severely repressed university student unrest in the 1960s, a situation which led to his predecessor's resignation. Initially, Villar Palasi focused on the need for university reform, but it was readily apparent that a major overhaul of Spain's educational system was essential. Such an approach would permit the preparation of Spain's masses for incorporation into the country's short- and long-term economic requirements. No such comprehensive legislation for Spain's educational system had been undertaken since passage of the Moyano Law in 1857.

In 1969, a survey prepared by R. Diez Hochleitner resulted in enactment of the General Education Act (*Ley General De Educación*, or EGB). The reservations of the Church were assuaged by language that recognized the "special position of the Roman Catholic Church."[38] It could have its own schools and provide "religious education in State schools in accordance with the Concordat of 1953."[39]

After Franco's death in 1975 and adoption of the Constitution in 1978, subsequent modifications were developed within the broad framework of the 1970 reform. However, there were important changes in curriculum requirements and administrative structures to reflect the shift to democracy guaranteed by the Constitution and the creation of autonomous regions. The net effect was to bring Spain's current educational system in line with that of the other Western European democracies. One significant change was that the study of religion in state schools became optional. Catholic schools which agreed to follow requirements applicable to all state institutions, including free education, now enjoy official subsidies for payment of teachers. The arrangement appears to be similar in principle to that in France.[40]

Three laws were passed by the Cortes to implement the constitutional mandates: the 1983 Organic Act on University Reform (LRU), the 1985 Organic Act on the Right to Education (LODE), and the 1990 General Arrangement of the Educational Organic Act (LOGSE). The 1990 law repealed the 1970 General Act and was put into effect for the 1991–1992 academic year.

The 1990 law refined the existing system for nonuniversity levels in accordance with the following principles:

1. Personalized instruction, encouraging comprehensive education, encompassing knowledge, skills, and moral values in all walks of private, family, social, and working life.

2. Participation and collaboration of parents or guardians to contribute to better achieving educational objectives.

3. Effective equality of rights between the sexes, rejection of any kind of discrimination, and respect for all cultures.

4. Development of creative abilities and a critical mind.

5. Encouragement of habits of democratic behavior.

6. School self-government in teaching matter within the limits laid down by law, as well as teachers' research activities on the basis of their teaching experience.
7. Psychological and pedagogical care and educational and vocational guidance.
8. Active methodology ensuring the participation of pupils in teaching and learning processes.
9. Evaluation of teaching and learning processes, teaching institutions, and the different elements which make up the system.
10. Links with the social, economic, and cultural environment.
11. Education in respecting and protecting the environment.[41]

The Spanish government is extremely sensitive of the need to stress democracy in the nation's educational system and to throw in high relief the importance of elections and parent participation in the educational process. It holds that, "An education in the democratic values of freedom and participation, tolerance and solidarity, which are today universal values, is a primary objective, as these are what enable a full preparation for coexistence within society."[42] Clearly, the government understands the necessity of training its youth in the essentiality of injecting into the value system of Spanish cultural mores the spirit of compromise implicit in *convivencía*. Furthermore, in the public schools there are elected school boards (councils) composed of parents and others concerned with education, including teachers, students, and other staffs. Boards usually meet once a month, chaired by the school's principal or director. The principal is elected from among faculty members who volunteer for the job and serves a three-year term, after which he or she can either be reelected or return to teaching.

The structure of the system closely resembles what exists in the United States, but under different labels and divisions. Primary schools consist of eight grades divided into two stages (1 to 5 and 6 to 8). Religion classes are optional and, in the bilingual Autonomous Communities, the native language is included in the curriculum (e.g., Catalan, Basque, Galician). Starting in third grade, a foreign language is also required.

Following graduation from the eighth grade, students enter secondary school, which consists of two alternatives. One more or less parallels grades 9 to 11 of an American high school and leads to a baccalaureate diploma (BUP). For students going on to university, a University Orientation Course (*Curso de Orientación Universitaria*, or COU) is required, with an examination at the end of that year. Actually, the combination of grades 9 to 11 and the additional year is roughly equivalent to an American high school diploma. Graduates must then take a university entrance examination.

The alternative track involves vocational training at the secondary school level and is designed for students not preparing for university studies, or, as we would say in the United States, not college bound. These institutions are referred to as vocational schools or institutes and are centers for what is called Professional Formation (*Formación Professional*, or FP). Programs consist of two stages. The first is for students fifteen and sixteen who still must remain in school; they must take a labor baccalaureate examination (*Labor Bachillerato*) at the end of this stage. The second is optional for students over sixteen years of age and consists of more specialized training. The combination of both stages is roughly comparable to an American four-year vocational training curriculum. As in the primary school plan, classes in religion are optional.

An important aspect to note is that the Spanish educational system is consistent with objectives established by Europe's Council for Cultural Cooperation.[43] These concern language learning; teacher training; the promotion of Europeanization programs at secondary school levels, leading broadly to the study of geography, history, literature, natural and social sciences; and so forth.[44]

The higher education system consists mainly of thirty-six state University Schools (*Escuelas Universitarias*), in every province, and four private universities linked to organizations within the Catholic Church. As of now, there is a two-track approach in place. One is five- or six-year programs leading to liberal arts and professional degrees offered in the conventional departments (*facultades*), such as medicine, law, engineering, and philosophy. The other offering is generally available in branches connected with universities and covers three-year programs related mainly to the preparation of elementary school teachers, nursing, and a wide range of vocational fields.

The 1983 Organic Act on University Reform weakened control by the central government over universities, since by Spanish law all higher education, as well as primary and secondary, is under the Ministry of Education and Science. As one report of the situation put it, universities became

relatively free to offer new programs and to restructure themselves internally so long as they met the qualifications imposed on all state universities. The law also weakened (at least on paper) the control of the universities that had been exercised by the *catedraticos*, the senior professors who held the highly prestigious chairs in each department. The new law provided that control of the universities would shift to the *claustro constituyente* or university council made up of professors of all ranks, as well as administrators, staff, and occasionally, for certain purposes, students.[45]

Subsequently, five Royal Decrees were promulgated (one in 1990, four in 1991) calling for an expansion in the number and range of courses in Spanish universities. The purpose of these measures was to integrate Spanish higher education within the framework of the European Commission and to facilitate greater mobility between Spanish and other foreign graduates.[46] Actually, the legal basis which started the changes required by the 1990 and 1991 decrees was Royal Decree 1497 of November 27, 1987, which dealt with broadened programs, particularly of a vocational character.

The data in Table 7.6 reveal the dramatic changes in the numbers of Spanish youth benefiting from the transformed and broadened educational system. However, in 1984, women accounted for 48 percent of the student university population, a figure comparable to most other European countries, only four to six percentage points behind Italy, France, and Belgium.[47] A brief statistical report prepared by the United Nations shows that, in Spain, third-level (university) students per 10,000 population totalled 485 in 1985 and 533 in 1989, of which 48 percent were women for both years.[48] Given the higher numbers of women than men in the secondary school system for the academic year 1989–1990, this percentage would appear to be reasonably accurate. The assumption can be made that women permanently constitute at least half, if not a bit more by now, of the universities' student body.

The significance of the student population figures, particularly those shown in Table 7.6, is that they represent and augur a profound change in Spanish society and values, by virtue of the large numbers of people being channeled through the educational system. With a leap and a bound, the Spain of massive illiteracy is a thing of the past. Practically all of Spain's youth through the age of sixteen (both sexes) are in school under the nation's compulsory and free education laws, reflecting Spanish society's ardent embrace for what journalist John Hooper refers to as "A Thirst for Learning."[49] This means that, coupled with the broad availabilities in secondary education and offerings in the university system, Spain is developing a labor force technically prepared to enable the nation to continue its march as an industrially advanced nation. At the highest and middle government levels, it is on the road to having competent cadres of bureaucracy for both domestic service and to meet technical

TABLE 7.6
Spanish Student Population, 1979–1991

Academic Year	Preschool	Elementary	High School	Vocational	Higher Education	Total
1979-80	1,159,854	5,606,850	1,037,788	515,119	639,288	8,958,899
1980-81	1,182,425	5,606,452	1,091,197	558,271	649,098	9,087,443
1981-82	1,197,987	5,652,874	1,119,095	628,368	669,848	9,245,082
1982-83	1,187,617	5,633,518	1,117,600	650,770	692,152	9,281,657
1983-84	1,171,062	5,633,009	1,142,308	695,480	744,115	9,385,974
1984-85	1,145,968	5,640,938	1,182,154	726,000	785,880	9,480,840
1985-86	1,127,348	5,594,285	1,238,874	738,340	854,189	9,553,036
1986-87	1,084,752	5,575,719	1,278,269	751,995	902,380	9,593,115
1987-88	1,054,241	5,398,095	1,355,278	759,796	969,508	9,536,918
1988-89	1,010,765	5,263,518	1,476,491	781,748	1,027,018	9,559,540
1989-90	1,000,301	5,080,953	1,539,169	817,099	1,093,086	9,530,608
1990-91	986,964	4,881,699	1,589,921	850,456	1,137,228	9,446,268

Source: Ministerio de Educación y Ciencia, *Informe Nacional de Educación* (Madrid: Ministerio de Educación y Ciencia, 1992), 24.

commitments in the European community. Indeed, Spaniards have already served in important posts in the various European organizations.

One can also see from Table 7.7 that there are greater numbers of women in the secondary level of schooling than men, except in the vocational track, where the latter are more numerous. But the FP approach means terminal education, whereas the academic route keeps open the possibility of university careers. The sharply upgraded education of women in almost one generation is bound to affect, in some fashion, the traditional value systems of their mothers and grandmothers, particularly for those families who left miserable lives in rural Spain and moved to industrialized commercial centers. This expectation is made more real by what is happening in other Hispanic societies, where women did react differently than earlier generations to issues and values (e.g., in Puerto Rico, Costa Rica, and Mexico). Additional corollary evidence comes from birth statistics, which suggest a leveling off of Spanish population evident after women could practice birth control (thanks to the legal availability of contraceptive pills and devices).

What access to education means in terms of husband–wife, parent–child, and extended family relationships is difficult to know. What do children hear at home regarding settlement of family disputes, about the government, and about politicians? These are episodes that, by osmosis, reach their psyches and will affect their adult behavior in some ways. Will the home experience of the children of today, combined with greater education, produce a people sympathetic to democracy, *convivencía*, and tolerance? Or will they emerge with greater impatience and uncompromising attitudes at failing to achieve idealist goals, which would make them susceptible to charismatic extremists in times of trouble? While polls are useful in spotting momentary reactions, they have not yet been able to measure what goes on in the home which affects a child's behavior and thinking in adulthood.

THE CHANGING ROLE OF THE CATHOLIC CHURCH

In a 1982 interview with Monsignor Delicado Baeza, Archbishop of Valladolid, by Spanish journalist María Merida, the prelate commented

According to a historian's curious statistic, during the century from 1833 to 1936, we Spaniards have had over one hundred and thirty governments, nine constitutions, three dethronements, five civil wars, dozens of provisional regimes, and an almost incalculable number of revolutions which we can tentatively number as two thousand, or what amounts to the same thing, an attempt to remove the established authority every seventeen days as an average.[50]

The Archbishop's remarks were included in a response to María Merida's query about his view relative to Lt. Colonel Tejero's failed coup of February 23, 1981, when the latter held the Cortes hostage.

Regardless of whether the data cited by Baeza are accurate or only approximate, or even grossly exaggerated, the fact is that in those hundred years

TABLE 7.7
Spanish Student Population, by Age, Sex, and Grade Level, 1989–1990

Age	Total	Male	Female
	Preschool		
2	20,115	10,454	9,661
3	93,235	47,031	46,204
4	415,424	211,772	203,652
5	471,527	240,428	231,099
	Elementary		
6	505,998	260,076	245,922
7	536,192	275,915	260,277
8	562,875	289,323	273,552
9	590,763	303,573	287,190
10	617,270	317,095	300,175
11	650,672	334,099	316,270
12	661,877	340,293	321,584
13	670,179	343,094	327,085
14	220,644	125,679	94,965
15	64,485	37,972	26,511
	Secondary		
14	310,410	140,869	169,541
15	333,667	152,136	181,531
16	307,145	138,985	168,160
17	278,463	123,516	154,947
18	112,410	52,958	60,452
19	52,908	24,168	28,740
20 & over	75,872	36,151	39,721
	Vocational		
14	96,853	57,732	39,121
15	147,360	89,143	58,217
16	141,665	83,143	57,730
17	118,307	67,867	50,440
18	98,942	53,876	45,066
19	67,124	33,074	34,050
20 & over	146,848	68,477	78,371
	Secondary and Vocational		
14	407,263	198,601	208,662
15	481,027	241,279	239,748

Source: Ministerio de Educación y Ciencia, *Informe Nacional de Educación* (Madrid: Ministerio de Educación y Ciencia, 1992), 26–27.
Note: As of 1989–1990, there were 1,093,086 students in Spain's thirty-six state universities and affiliated institutions of higher learning, including four private universities connected with the Catholic Church.

a high level of political instability reigned in Spain. While social, political, and economic factors contributed to this reality, a crucial element in the unhappy picture was the anticlericalism which seeped into Spain during the Englightment era, particularly from France. As Spanish political scientist Victor M. Perez-Diaz observed, "The anticlericalism of the 1930s was heir to a tradition of popular anticlericalism with a bloody history dating from 1834–35 and from the *semana trágica*, the 'tragic week' of 1909."[51] This anticlerical crescendo reached its explosive point during the years of the Second Republic, provoking a situation which led to the Civil War of 1936 to 1939. However, it should be stressed that being anticlerical did not imply that one was automatically also anticatholic. The criticisms leveled were usually against the Catholic hierarchy and less against the theology of the Church.

With the advent of the Second Republic in 1931, the leaders of the new state launched an intensive charge against the Church, leaving the hierarchy and Catholic following disconcerted, as "they had adopted a wait-and-see" posture toward the Socialist-led new regime.[52] Fueled by anticlerical Socialist doctrine and masses of Anarchists from Andalusia and Anarcho-Sindicalists from Barcelona who called for the total destruction of the Church, the latter and its believers mobilized the rural peasantry elsewhere in Spain, the middle classes and professionals, as well as the aristocracy for defense of its institutions and faith. Perez-Diaz notes, "The burning of churches and convents almost within a month of the Republic being declared was an indication of the intention of some not merely to limit the Church but to destroy it, relying on the deliberate passivity of the government (as was demonstrated by the negative attitude of Azana and the Socialist ministers to the demands of Miguel Maura to use the forces of law and order)."[53]

For any democracy to survive, there must exist a mechanism which permits the resolution of deeply dividing issues, or civil war becomes inevitable. In the case of the Second Spanish Republic, the rapidly passed Constitution of 1931 provided a formula for the resolution of the other burning question, that of regionalism. But with regard to religion it aimed at the separation of church and state with provisions designed to cripple the position of Catholicism in Spain. Subsequently, laws were enacted calling for the abolition of church-run schools, a development that caused deep resentment in the middle classes and helped bring matters to a boiling point politically. Actually, the measures affecting Catholic schools were never implemented, if only for the reason that not enough schools existed to replace the institutions destined to be shut down, despite energetic measures to build state-owned schools. Also, there were not sufficient numbers of teachers to run them. The religious issue thus highly polarized the nation. Had the Constitution of 1931 dealt with the religious problem more gently and not threatened the existence of the Church as an institution deeply woven into the Spanish social pattern, quite possibly the Civil War would not have happened.

The mistake in 1931 was not repeated in the post-Franco Constitution of 1978.[54] The formula for dealing with the religious issue was carefully honed and accepted by the Spanish Church. Independence from the inherited "throne and altar" concept had shifted drastically in the decade or so before Franco's death, especially after Vatican Council II (1962–1965), which liberalized the Church on a universal basis. Already in the 1950s, young Spanish priests sent to study or visit Catholic centers in France, Germany, and Italy were startled to learn how archaic the Spanish Church had remained.[55] Before the Civil War, the mass of Spanish faithful viewed the hierarchy as equivalent to the Church, and the middle and upper classes as its constituency, a view held by lower-income laborers (mostly in Andalusia and in Barcelona) and, to some extent, by prominent intellectuals.[56]

In the early months of the Civil War, some 7,000 clergymen were killed, an event which led to the emergence of a crusade psychosis in the Church, in thousands of its followers in the middle and upper classes, and among masses in major rural areas. The revolt of the military under Franco took on almost medieval proportions, with the Catholic hierarchy aspiring for a "national church," a position which resulted in a tight merger between the Church and the Franco regime. For the latter, the attitude of the Church provided a much-needed basis for legitimacy. Franco responded by turning over to the Church enormous support in financing education, and giving it censorship authority to force media activities, films, and book publishing to conform to rigid Catholic values. This situation persisted through the early 1950s.[57]

With the return of many of the younger priests to Spain after their visits to other European countries, the questioning of the almost medieval stance of the hierarchy began to take root. In addition to the activities of these priests, there emerged a small number of bishops, such as Vicente Enrique Tarancon, with a similar feeling that the nation needed reconciliation of the two sides in the Civil War. The thinking of both groups, bolstered in time by the liberal philosophy sparked by Vatican II, eventually led to the gradual alienation of the Church from the regime, much to the latter's dismay. Franco personally had difficulty understanding this movement in the direction of Church independence from his regime. The situation reached a crucial turning point when, in 1971, now Cardinal Tarancon, a moderate, was elected president of the *Conferencía Episopal* (Episcopal Conference), which embraced all bishops.

From then on, a Church policy of independence from the regime developed to the point that, with Vatican support, the hierarchy moved in two directions. One was support for the liberal democracy created after Franco's death and the other was an active policy directed at the evolution of the Church in Spain, which included the episcopate, clergy, and laity as participants in churches and other related Catholic organizations and activities.

Under Tarancon's inspiration, the laity was discouraged from forming a political party with the designation of "Christian" in its name.[58] This permitted Catholics to participate in the socialist political parties, particularly since the latter's main group, *Partido Socialista Obrero Español* (POSE), had earlier dropped the reference to Marxism in defining itself. In acceptance of competition with other religions for the salvation of souls, the Church's political participation remained limited to that of any other pressure group: concern for specific legislation, such as that dealing with abortion, divorce, use of contraceptives, and other possible moral issues.[59] Cardinal Tarancon believed that the new situation revitalized the body of the Church through the participation of the laity in its functions, the dialogue between bishops and clergy, and the competitiveness of an open society even in the field of religion.[60]

From our interest in handed-down values, the fact of *convivencía* as an accepted behavioral pattern to be encouraged in the general Spanish political arena means that the bitterness which formerly led to conflict between Socialists and Catholics removes religion as a cause for social explosion. How do Spanish families discuss the new situation at home, and how do these interchanges affect the children's future thinking and behavior? Does the altered state of tradition with regard to religion lay the foundation for a child's reinforced attitude toward democracy? Or does he or she hear constant complaints at home about the efficiency of government and contrasts the latter to how the Church now functions? At present, according to an undated Spanish Embassy (Washington, D.C.) summary paper about education, "Approximately one third of the schools are private and more than half of these are religious. Most private schools (95%) are sponsored through public funds."[61] The influence of the Church on the young is still very considerable. Is anticlericalism still a topic at home? What models does the child see in husband–wife relationships, as well as that of siblings? Is there give and take? These are important questions, answers to which will contribute to an understanding of Spain's prospects for long-term democratic institutions.

The efficacy of the Constitution of 1978 as a means of removing religious conflict as a powder keg is evident from the comfortable working relations between the Church hierarchy and the Socialist government, an almost unthinkable prospect prior to the 1936 to 1939 Civil War. In fact, Cardinal L. Lias Yanes, president of the *Conferencía Episcopal* in the early to mid-1990s, stated that dialogue between the government and the Church was more candid than ever, particularly with the Minister of Justice, although no communication difficulties were encountered with other agencies.[62]

CONCLUSION

The Spanish case demonstrates that profound social changes of historic proportion occurred; changes that were bound to reflect new attitudes, different roles, and a political system more in tune with the fundamental nonpolitical changes underway. The most dramatic of these new changes was the alignment of the Church with the forces that were coming to power in the post-Franco era while playing down its traditional political role. But of almost equal importance were the extraordinary changes that resulted from mass migrations of workers from rural to urban communities and the broadened role of women in Spanish society. While the changes affected in education are nothing less than profound, by Spanish standards, their consequences are yet to be felt with the same impact as the changing role of women and the Church. Children educated in the new system have not yet grown up and had time to develop patterns of adult behavior.

Social changes evident in Spain had similar consequences to those found in Italy and, to a lesser extent, in Germany and France. If one concentrates on education and the role of women, the changes begin to form a common pattern across Western Europe, which ultimately reinforced the move to more democratic institutions (at least in Italy and Spain). But Spain, just as every country, has its own peculiar circumstances. Its intense regionalism, profoundly influenced by historic forces dating back centuries, and the role of the Church distinguish the Spanish situation from that of France, Great Britain, Germany, and even Italy, despite the fact that, at least in Italy and Great Britain, the roles of their local churches are not trivial.

As demonstrated by comments of Church leaders and actions of politicians, it becomes very obvious that what Spain teaches us is that with social upheavals come political consequences. Liberalization of previous social traditions does create an environment conducive to democracy's development. However, as we will argue in the rest of this book, actual implementation of democracy does not come from the masses. It originates from the state which, in response to changes in society, looks for more effective forms of government administration. That is why it is so important to understand the sociocultural aspects of a country's activities if one is to appreciate what is possible with democracy or even to attempt a forecast of its future.

NOTES

1. Year-to-year reviews, in considerable detail, regarding economic, legal, social, and political developments after Franco's death can be found in the *Enciclopedia Universal Ilustratada Europeo Americana*, 9 vols. for the years 1975–1992 (Madrid: Espasa-Calpe, 1981–1995). On the transition, see Richard Gillespie, *The Spanish Socialist Party* (Oxford: Clarendon Press, 1989); Paul Preston, *The Triumph of Democracy in Spain* (London: Methuen, 1986); Victor M. Perez-Diaz, *The Return of Civil Society: The Emergence of Democratic Spain* (Cambridge, Mass.: Harvard University Press, 1993); Adrian Shubert, *A Social History of Modern Spain* (London: Unwin Hyman, 1990); Kenneth Maxwell and Steven Spiegel, *The New Spain* (New York: Council on Foreign Relations Press, 1994); Howard R. Penniman and Eusebio M. Mujal-Leon, eds., *Spain at the Polls: 1977, 1979, and 1982* (Washington, D.C.: American Enterprise Institute for Public Policy Research, Duke University Press, 1985); John Hooper, *The Spaniards* (London: Penguin, 1987); Raymond Carr and Juan Pablo Fusi, *Spain: Dictatorship to Democracy* (London: Allen and Unwin, 1979); Sima Lieberman, *The Contemporary Spanish Economy* (London: Allen and Unwin, 1982); Stanley G. Payne, *Spanish Catholicism: A Historical Overview* (Madison: University

of Wisconsin Press, 1984); Eric Solsten and Sandra W. Meditz, eds., *Spain: A Country Study* (Washington, D.C.: Federal Research Division, Library of Congress, 1990). With the exception of Hooper's book, all include extensive bibliographies.

2. Even sociologists looking at contemporary political issues tend to overlook the sociocultural aspects. See, for example, James Petras, "Spanish Socialism: The Politics of Neoliberalism," in *Mediterranean Paradoxes: Politics and Social Structure in Southern Europe*, ed. James Kurth and James Petras (Oxford: Berg, 1993), 95–127.

3. Lieberman, *Contemporary Spanish Economy*, 199–264; Solsten and Meditz, *Spain*, 169–195.

4. Solsten and Meditz, *Spain*, 169–195.

5. Ibid., 192–195. A personal case illustrates this point: In 1968, one of the authors, James W. Cortada, visited a village deep in the Pyrenees near Andorra, and found that the villagers only spoke Catalan, except for one old Civil War veteran who had a working knowledge of Spanish. The other author, James N. Cortada, visited Andorra—just a few miles away from this village—in 1985, and found the ancient principality's main thoroughfare converted into one large shopping center with multiple languages spoken and local residents vastly outnumbered by visitors from all over the world.

6. Solsten and Meditz, *Spain*, 142.

7. Perez-Diaz, *Return of Civil Society*, 1–26.

8. Solsten and Meditz, *Spain*, 159.

9. Flora Lewis, *Europe: Road to Unity* (New York: Simon and Schuster, 1992), 546–549, 554.

10. Ibid.

11. United Nations, *World Statistics in Brief* (New York: United Nations, 1992), 70.

12. Manuel Tuñon de Lara, ed., *História de España*, vol. 9 of *La Crisis del Estado: Dictadura, República, Guerra* (Barcelona: Editorial Labor, 1982). For an account in English, see Hugh Thomas, *The Spanish Civil War* (New York: Harper and Row, 1977).

13. J. G. Peristany, ed., *Honour and Shame: The Values of Mediterranean Society* (Chicago: University of Chicago Press, 1974). Actually, there have been a number of empirical studies that have identified these as very important traits of those Spaniards studied. For example, see Stanley Brandes, *Metaphors of Masculinity: Sex and Status in Andalusian Folklore* (Philadelphia: University of Pennsylvania Press, 1990), which also includes a useful study of the critical studies.

14. For example, in the defense of the Alcazar in Toledo by Colonel José Moscardó, his son was captured by the forces loyal to the Republic in the 1936–1939 Civil War. When told by the opposing commander that the young man would be shot if the Alcazar was not surrendered, both father and son replied stoically in the negative. The Alcazar was a military academy with a total complement of 1,205 persons, including 555 adult noncombatants and 211 children. Subjected, over ten weeks, to a total of 10,000 shells and 500 bombs, and armed with only rifles and machine guns, the 261 cadets and 106 militarized civilians in the complement of the Alcazar held out until relieved by General Franco's forces. For details, see Cecil D. Eby, *The Siege of the Alcazar* (New York: Random House, 1965), 50–64.

15. Examples might include Phillip II's religious wars of the sixteenth century, Spain's desire to bring Catholicism to the Indians of the New World, and even the direct efforts of anarchists during the Spanish Civil War to link their ideals directly with Don Quixote.

16. Angel Ganivet, *Idearium Español* (Madrid, 1896).

17. Fernando Diaz-Plaja, *The Spaniard and the Seven Deadly Sins* (New York: Scribner's Sons, 1967), 11–88.

18. Vega, Lope Felix de, "La Llave de la Honra," vol. 34, tome 2 of *Comedias Escogidas de Fray Lope Felix de Vega* (Madrid: Biblioteca de Autores Españoles, 1950), 117–133; Angel Del Rio, *Literatura Española, Lope de Vega* (Madrid: C.S.I.C., 1962), 467–515, 515–526.

19. Del Rio, *Literatura Española*, 654–655; Guillermo Diaz-Plaja, *A History of Spanish Literature* (New York: New York University Press, 1971), 183.

20. Salvador de Madariaga, *Englishmen, Frenchmen, Spaniards* (London: Oxford University Press, 1949), 3–8, 46, 51, 82, 136.

21. Ibid., 50.

22. José Ortega y Gasset, *Invertebrate Spain* (New York: W. W. Norton, 1937), 143–157.

23. Ibid., 146.

24. Julian Pitts-Rivers, *The People of the Sierra* (Chicago: University of Chicago Press, 1971), 65–97; Stanley Brandes, *Metaphors of Masculinity*; Ronald Fraser, *The Pueblo* (Devon, England: Readers Union, 1974); and Ronald Fraser, *Blood of Spain* (New York: Pantheon, 1979).

25. Herbert W. Serra Williamson, *The Tourist Guide-Book of Spain* (Madrid: The Times of Spain, 1951), 45–51.

26. Robert E. Liss, *Bazak's Guide to Spain* (Tel Aviv: Bazak Israel Guidebook Publishers, 1974), 36.

27. Tuñon de Lara, Historia de España, 107–227.

28. Perez-Diaz, *Return of Civil Society*, 32.

29. Ibid., 203.

30. Stanley G. Payne, *Historia de España: La España Medieval* (Madrid: Editorial Playor, 1985), 52; Joseph F. O'Callaghan, *A History of Medieval Spain* (Ithaca, N.Y.: Cornell University Press, 1975), 98–99; Roger Collins, *Early Medieval Spain* (London: Macmillan Press, 1983), 225–231.

31. Luis G. de Valdeavellano, *Historia de España*, 2 vols. (Madrid: Alianza Editorial, 1980).

32. Perez-Diaz, *Return of Civil Society*, 200.

33. Solsten and Meritz, *Spain*, 224–225.

34. Hooper, *The Spaniards*, 197.

35. Solsten and Meditz, *Spain*, 108.

36. Ibid., 78, 110.

37. Ibid., 78.

38. John M. McNair, *Education for a Changing Spain* (Manchester, England: Manchester University Press, 1984), 33, 36.

39. Ibid., 36.

40. Ministerio de Educación y Ciencia, *The White Paper for the Reform of Educational System* (Madrid: Ministerio de Educación y Ciencia, 1990).

41. Ministerio de Educación y Ciencia, *Education National Report* (Geneva: International Conference on Education, 1992), 16.

42. Ibid., 86.

43. Ibid., 99.

44. Ibid., 99–100.

45. Solsten and Meditz, *Spain*, 122.

46. Ministerio de Educación y Ciencia, *Education National Report*, 99–103.

47. Solsten and Meditz, *Spain*, 118.

48. United Nations, *World Statistics*, 70.

49. Hooper, *The Spaniards*, 96–103.

50. María Merida, *Entrevista con La Iglesia* (Barcelona: Planeta, 1982), 167.

51. Perez-Diaz, *Return of Civil Society*, 128.

52. Ibid.

53. Ibid.

54. Peter J. Donaghy and Michael T. Newton, *Spain: A Guide to Political and Economic Institutions* (Cambridge: Cambridge University Press, 1989): Spanish Constitution of 1978, Basic Principles and Provisions, 2.3, p. 11 and The Church, p. 12.

55. Perez-Diaz, *Return of Civil Society*, 161.

56. J. L. Martin Descalzo, *Tarancon: El Cardinal Del Cambio* (Barcelona: Planeta, 1982), 66.

57. For a fascinating explanation of this topic, see ibid., 61–69, and, on the Church's role in the transition to democracy, 79–272. See also Merida, *Entrevista con La Iglesia*; and Perez-Diaz, *Return of Civil Society*, 109–183. For background on the religious aspects of the transition phase, see Stanley G. Payne, *El Catolicismo Español* (Barcelona: Planeta, 1984), 191–274.

58. Descalzo, *Tarancon*, 252–257.

59. Ibid., 247–257, 264–266.

60. Ibid., 139–142; Payne, *Catolicismo Español*, 268–273.

61. "Education," undated memorandum, Spanish Embassy, Washington, D.C. Reference is made to reforms scheduled to take place in 1992 and 1993. One can assume that the paper was prepared in 1990 or 1991, since some statistics presented in the document are similar to data from other sources published by the Ministerio de Educación y Ciencia in Madrid.

62. *ABC*, 12 October 1993, p. 76.

—8—

The Future of
European Democracy:
A Strategic Perspective

Politics is not an exact science.

—Otto von Bismarck

This chapter describes lessons about democracy's health, suggests what Europeans can do, along with the United States, as an extension of its historic foreign policy, and concludes with observations on the challenges faced. The perspective is of grand strategy, the agenda of nations.

Looking at the experiences with democracy of several European nations—France, Britain, Germany, Italy, and Spain—provides a baseline against which to reach conclusions about the future of democracy both in Western Europe and on the periphery, such as in the ex-Soviet Union, Eastern Europe, the Eastern Mediterranean, and Southeastern Europe (e.g., the old Yugoslavia). These nations are a baseline because their experience with democracies profoundly influence the thinking in other European and non-European nations wrestling with the issue of whether to implement democratic institutions and how. The influence is sufficient that if democratic institutions should retreat to any extent in these five Western European nations, one could confidently expect a more rapid rejection elsewhere of representative governments as a model by which to govern. The two notable exceptions, of course, would be the United States and Great Britain, which have proven over two centuries that Europe's ebb and flow relationship with democracy has not had a similar effect on them. So, the first consideration for those interested in the health and expanded use of democracy is understanding its condition in the five Western European countries.

The second reason for looking at these nations is that there is the opportunity to address the problem of how to reinforce democratic behavior outside of Europe. In the late twentieth century, democracy had become fashionable as the most widely discussed approach to governing people. The values and practices associated with democracy are discussed, implemented, and experimented with all over the world. Twenty million South Africans voted into power their first biracial government—in the land that for hundreds of years was the home of apartheid. The Japanese, who cherish social order above personal freedoms, stick to their post–World War II democratic institutions and force out of political office leaders found to be corrupt—a smaller version of the corruption problem existing in Italy, and with the same results. In Mexico, national presidential elections were held despite the assassination of the candidate the polls indicated was most likely to become the next president. And then there is Haiti, with its pseudo-democratic institutions, touted by the U.S. Government as a major area requiring the care and focus of the Clinton administration. In short, the world has an interest in democracy greater than it has ever exhibited before, and the examples that it either constantly looks at or aspires to mimic are the ones in the five European nations that we have studied and the United States. Therefore, any discussion about the future of democracy's evolution in Western Europe reaches into the center of a very important debate about the political structures of national governments over at least the next generation.

In Europe today, there is the problem of how to transform from autocratic to democratic institutions, especially in Central Europe. It is such a major problem for the late-twentieth-century world that academicians, journalists, and politicians are dealing with the topic. Each brings to the discussion their own discipline's perspective. Political scientists seem to view the world through events of the past half century and want to identify models of political formulations. Historians want to describe specific cases and leave it to the reader to draw analogous insights on contemporary and future events. Sociologists and cultural anthropologists have not linked handed-down values and other social phenomena to the question of effects on political behavior and have yet to wade in with any discussion about democracy in Europe. The political leader is the ultimate pragmatist, in that he or she is concerned about solving immediate short-term problems or they lose the next elections.

Yet, as we have attempted to demonstrate in this book, it takes a holistic approach, crossing many disciplines, to arrive at a better understanding of the prospects of democracy in Europe. Such an approach makes it possible to determine what actions a people, government, or leader must take, either to foster further development of democratic institutions or to retard or kill them.

WHAT STUDENTS OF DEMOCRACY HAVE TAUGHT US

The most obvious lesson is that democracy is a major political issue facing governments and nations globally, from Haiti to Singapore, from the ex-Soviet Union to China, from various Latin American countries to the heart of Africa. The disaster in Rwanda, where a reported 100,000 people were killed in the first month after the collapse of a reportedly "democratic" national government in 1994, reminds us of how high the stakes can be in the game of democracy. Democracy as a topic has engaged discussion for some 200 years; it has been framed differently in each age, but nonetheless grew in importance over time.

Where European democracies exist today, they emerged out of preexisting nation states. Democracies did not emerge out of "the people," but from evolutions of national governments, usually over a long period of time (e.g., as in the case of the British). The lesson of both historians and political scientists on this point is clear: Only states have created democratic institutions, not nations. Put in the form of a rule of thumb, nations, peoples, or ethnic groups do not build democratic institutions; it is the governments of nations, not people and ethnic groups, that create democratic institutions. Cavour, frequently French speaking and clearly not a revolutionary, while at the pinnacle of Italian political leadership made possible Italy's adoption of parliamentary governing practices in the 1860s, not the people. Franco, as head of the Spanish government, and later King Juan Carlos and his ministers, provided the leadership that led to the creation of Spain's democratic form of government. Bismarck, intending first to ensure Prussia's political influence in the Germanies and later Germany's growth as a political power, created the German State in the 1870s, not the people. Republics in France were not the result of revolutions or mass human activity, but the work of politicians writing constitutions and creating laws and regulations that took on the form of representative governments.

In fact, one could argue that "the people" get in the way of building democracies. People approach politics by either associating with a particular ethnic group aspiring to protect their cultural and economic advantages and identity (leading to regionalist politics), or with some nationalist ideology which deals less with the mechanics of democracy and more with sentiments. Thus, regionalism and nationalism, while both have received an extraordinary amount of attention, and no more so than now, have at best been a deterrent to the development of democracies and, more frequently, the most important impediment. One has only to look at the current troubles facing those in Russia and in what used to be Yugoslavia to see how regionalism and nationalism retard development of democratic institutions.

In each case where these were developed successfully, regionalism and nationalism played a secondary role. The Spanish case is very instructive when one looks at the order of events. Here was a country with a virulent

Basque nationalist movement, replete with bomb throwers and political parties, and the Catalans who aspired to enhance their economic advantages while preserving a culture nearly a thousand years old. But what happened follows.

Franco created institutions for various groups to work together at different levels (cultural, political, and economic) during the period from the 1940s to the 1960s. Then, King Juan Carlos and his cabinets orchestrated creation of a democratic constitution governing political activities of the nation in the late 1970s. Finally, the government created regional governments for seventeen parts of the nation, including local representative institutions for the Basques and the Catalans. In the case of Spain, nationalism and the federated option were sublimated to the greater requirement that a national state be transformed first.

In short, the political scientists have taught us that without a state you cannot organize a democracy. That explains, for example, why Hong Kong represents a difficult problem, with British institutions soon to reside next to those of China in an area that is a city, not a national government. The number of potential nations is far greater than the number of potential states. In Spain, one could argue that there are a minimum of three to seventeen potential states, if you look at various ethnic (that is to say, nationalistic) groups. In Great Britain, the count is at least three, in the old Yugoslavia at least four (possibly as many as six), while in the ex-Soviet Union the number runs to over two hundred.

The fact is the world is made up of states; and it is through states that forms of government, such as democracies, are developed and changed. Indeed, state building and nation building in Europe occurred almost side-by-side, yet independently of each other. We believe that the concurrent development of various cultures and national identities side-by-side with state building has caused most people to mix and match the two; in short, to confuse them as one process. History has taught us that Cavour, Bismarck, Franco, Gorbachev, and others did not confuse the two sets of activities.

Even great moments of trauma in Europe did not alter the centrality of the state. At the end of World War I, many new states were created, typically through treaties and the acceptance of Wilsonian concepts of self-determination. Few were nations, hence a major source of political problems in Europe throughout the twentieth century, particularly along the periphery of Western Europe. Put another way, thanks to the League of Nations and Woodrow Wilson, many states, not nations, gained independence. That experience also taught us that the disintegration of a state makes the creation or reinforcement of democracy impossible. The German and Italian experiences between the two world wars is a case in point. The disintegration of Yugoslavia and the Soviet Union are others. Can anyone doubt that the destruction of these two central states has retarded the introduction of democratic forms of government? Even Gorbachev failed to realize the importance of the state as a democratic facilitator. In fact, despite his image in the West, he used the rhetoric of democracy to fulfill his agenda and to preserve control. For example, elections were very undemocratic, often with no competition for elected seats.

The expansion of nationalism in late-twentieth-century Europe, like earlier bouts of this form of political behavior, actually got in the way. Poland's nineteenth-century struggle against Russian colonialism rallied around the phrase "Our and Your Freedom," a slogan used again in the 1970s and 1980s as a signal of the rise of a threat against the one institution that experience has shown could transform into democratic form. In hindsight, therefore, had the Soviet Union created democratic institutions first at the Soviet level, and then later, like Spain, local federated political structures, then the nation might have done better. The same holds true for Yugoslavia. Without national leadership, one sees the breakup of peoples into nationalist groups, as we have seen in Yugoslavia, the Soviet Union, and Czechoslovakia (into two parts) in recent times, and as we saw with the destruction of both the Turkish Empire and the Austro–Hungarian Empire at the end of World War I.

WHAT IT ALL MEANS

Our findings concerning the dynamics and future of democracy in the five countries we studied can be boiled down to six observations. We framed our six ideas with the intent that they would encourage students of democracy to study the subject with a far greater sociological and cultural–anthropological spin than they have before, while serving up observations to political leaders who have to worry about managing and influencing the evolution of this form of government.

First, social scientists are more or less in agreement that handed-down values are important in shaping adult beliefs and behavior, including views on political tendencies. The obvious point is that how we are raised at home and in school directly influences our attitudes toward the "public" side of our lives. In societies where family life is profoundly important, traditions and attitudes exist toward political, social, racial, and economic issues that frequently transcend generations. Thus, for example, if a family operates within some authoritarian structure at home, can we not expect at least some sympathy for a similar style of leadership in public affairs? In the United States, just as many families practice semidemocratic behavior (e.g., family discussions about where to take vacations or what next major purchase to make), creating an empathy for the give-and-take quality so essential to the successful application of democracy in North America, so too familial attitudes are important barometers of future political behavior. Our concern is that the link between home and public life today is not sufficiently understood.

Second, superimposed democratic systems in Germany and Italy appear to have taken root. As suggested in the discussion of the two countries, democratic institutions have been in place long enough and with sufficient positive results for the people of these nations to warrant the conclusion that democratic forms of government have proved attractive. Of particular importance is the fact that, in both cases, democracy has contributed to the emergence of a prosperous and substantial middle class—a factor essential to the survival of democracy. In a ground-breaking study by economic historian Nathan Rosenberg, in which he set out to answer the question of how the West got rich, he concluded that whenever a society shrank the role of government and church in dictating the nature of economic behavior, it was likely that prosperity would come. In case after case covering many centuries, he demonstrated that freedom to exercise economic initiative was essential to the creation of wealth and, more pertinent to our discussion, a stable middle class.[1] No form of government has provided a greater freedom of economic movement than democracy. The Italian and German cases are proof of Rosenberg's observation.

Third, notwithstanding democracy's success in Germany and Italy, it is too early to predict that this form of government will survive permanently in these countries. There is insufficient evidence to know with certainty to what extent authoritarianism has retreated in Germany. We do not know, for example, if it has retreated to the point where it would not threaten democratic institutions during periods of acute crisis. What is troublesome is the fact that East Germans, who have historically been less tolerant and more pessimistic than their fellow Germans in West Germany, have not experienced democracy since the days of the Weimer Republic, over two generations ago. Blend East Germans with West Germans and you have the makings of politically and socially turbulent conditions for the foreseeable future. Events of the past half decade in Germany cannot be ignored. The country is having difficulty melding together two economies and two political traditions. With the uncertainty of how things will turn out in front of us, one cannot assume that democracy is a given in Germany, Europe's largest democracy.

The Italian case also suffers from regionalist tensions. Can Italian unity and democracy survive the tensions between the areas north and south of Rome? The question is even more urgent if one just looks at southern Italy, where there is historically even less tolerance for the patterns of political behaviors required of a successful national government or a democracy. Thus, like the German experience, one could argue that one cannot assume with confidence that democracy is in Italy to stay. This is not to confuse, however, our earlier observation that democracy has been very successful so far.

Fourth, the weather-beaten phrase, "Plus ça change, plus c'est la meme chose," still applies to France. Bureaucracy, in general, is still a profound and stabilizing force in the political administration of the nation, regardless of which party is in power. Yet, children today are being raised quite differently from their grandparents and parents. Will this mean that eventually the *plus ça change* perspective no longer will apply? And if so, what does that mean for democracy? While democracy appears more rooted in France than in Germany or Italy, it too has a dark side. The variety of regions, the resort to concentrated personal leadership during moments of crisis, and a society whose social institutions are evolving rapidly suggest that the twists and turns of French democracy will have moments of enormous stress. The challenge for the nation will continue to be to preserve political stability within a democratic context. Yet, as with the German and Italian cases, there are no guarantees, just optimism that democracy will continue to thrive.

Fifth, Spain's surprisingly positive evolution and embrace of democracy might prove a beacon of democracy for other European governments, as it is for Latin America. While there is currently a euphoria evident whenever anybody talks about Spanish democracy, the cold sober facts confirm that democracy has done quite well in Spain. Many of the historically major political sources of power in the nation—the king, army, and Church—have thrown their considerable influence behind democracy and have supported it well. If Eastern European governments are looking for a model to study, the Spanish case is more attractive than those of the other Western European countries we have looked at. This is because Spain shares with Eastern and Southern Europe many of the same problems: regionalism, recent experience with civil war and heightened political activism, authoritarian government, and dramatic economic and social changes. The success with which Spain has approached the problem of regionalism through its creation of federated government structures is particularly attractive for Italians to consider as they deal with their own regionalist issues.

The Spanish experience with changing values is of particular importance for any nation on any continent working through the issue of how to implement democratic institutions. The reason for this is that in Spain new value systems are evolving which bring Spaniards closer to their Western European associates. This new closeness includes more commonly shared attitudes about the form of national government to have, how such administrations should operate, and all with a heavy dose of closer economic relations (e.g., through the EEC, United Europe). Spain's emergence from isolation is complete. More than just a part of NATO, Spain is a part of the European scene and, in some areas of activity, a leader in trends (e.g., music, architecture, women's clothing). With each succeeding set of elections in Spain during the 1990s, we observe voting patterns mimicking those of the rest of Western Europe. For example, in the municipal elections held in May 1995, like their counterparts all over Western Europe, the electorate voted more conservatively. The center-right party (*Partido Popular*) won 44.6 percent of the vote versus roughly 35 percent in 1991, while the Socialists went from 38 percent of the vote in 1991 to 31.5 percent in 1995. It was the same kind of pattern evident a few months earlier in France. In 1996, we saw similar vote conclusions and responses across a variety of local and national elections. But the key point is that because values that are conducive to patterns of democratic behavior have been changing over the past generation, the prospects for democracy's continued strengthening in Spain appear quite good.

Sixth, handed-down values may ultimately be the most important factor in determining the success or failure of democracy in Western Europe. People's personal opinions concerning their relationships with each other is of profound importance; yet, surprisingly, this notion is not well understood. Historians have hinted at the issue by looking at what dozens of generations of Europeans have done; political scientists have flirted with the topic by looking at patterns of behavior (usually over a short period of time, e.g., one generation); while sociologists have only recently started to study methodically how people interact in political contexts. A central theme of this book has been that handed-down values profoundly influence political attitudes, particularly as concerns democracy. To be more specific, conversations, ethics, morals, and other attitudes children are exposed to in the home or at school have the potential of profoundly affecting the course of democracy. These either bolster traditional handed-down values or give rise to new ones; both are possible and indeed are evident. The critical question is how these values will affect political outlook in adulthood. It is a question that has yet to be answered with the precision needed to make it possible for national leaders to guide their citizens either toward or away from democratic institutions.

Related to this observation about the role of handed-down values is the length of time it takes to make democracy a permanent feature. Democracy comes and stays when the mass of population in a nation is historically ready for it. Where people are not, prospects are weak. While governments can introduce democratic practices, the people must be ready. They either have a built-in propensity, as was recently demonstrated in what used to be Czechoslovakia, or the value of democracy has to be cultivated over several generations, as it appears is happening in Spain. The issue is thus a multigenerational one. The quick fix so desired by politicians will not do it. That is why we have to conclude, for example, that the jury is out on Russia's prospects of implementing democracy; and why the reader would probably agree with us that Iran, to pick a state run as closely to a medieval oligarchy as is possible to find at the end of the twentieth century, may be generations away from even seriously considering a democratic option.

EUROPEAN PARTICIPATION

Western European nations appear to be committed to democracy as a basic political dogma, implicitly accepting free elections as a means of choosing their ruling parties. But, based on their experiences just in this century, national leaders are also fully aware of the fragility of democratic systems. Uncontrolled disorders, acute economic downturns (with a consequent rise in unemployment), serious weakening of the middle classes, and disastrous military conflicts are situations which all have experienced in this century.

Leaders of the main political parties in Germany are particularly sensitive to stirrings among small numbers of neo-Nazi youths capable of extreme xenophobia resulting in violent anti-Turkish and anti-Semitic activities. Germans recall that Adolph Hitler rose to power through free elections.

For forty years, the Italians have held the Communist parties at bay, not only because of concern about their antiprivate, anticapitalist dogmas, but because of the danger of a Communist dictatorship. Even as recently as the 1994 elections, the revamped Communist parties failed to garnish significant numbers of votes, despite the collapse of the Christian Democrats. Nevertheless, the Communists remain the second strongest bloc in Italy and able to exercise their strength by entering the government after their success in the April 1996 elections.

Spain's experience with forty years of authoritarian government is still very recent in the memories of Spanish voters. They have reacted to proposed extreme political options of the right and the left with negligible support. In fact, their behavior at the polls is becoming increasingly predictable and moderate.

In France, with the collapse of the Soviet Union, the substantial bloc of Communist voters seems to be gradually dissolving into the predominant mainstream of democratically inclined Socialists. Still, disastrous situations could lead to growing support for a leader "on horseback," as has happened in both this and the past century.

While we have focused on the five principal Western European democracies, a shadow over their future looms because of Russia's uncertain prospects. They are all aware that free elections could bring to power a revised form of Communist dictatorship reeking of intense nationalist and imperialistic sentiments, a government that could also restrict the role of the Orthodox Church, despite the outcome of the July 1996 elections. Europeans are very much aware that Hitler solved Germany's acute unemployment problem by drawing on the nation's industrial–military complex for vast armament. The same could happen in Russia. Indeed, as Henry Kissinger recently pointed out, the old fears about Russia's role in Europe are back again.[2]

HOW TO SUPPORT THE GROWTH OF DEMOCRACY

How are democratic institutions to be encouraged, whether in Europe or elsewhere? Who decides? Should it be, "let the people determine?" Should it be all the people, some of the people, or a particular ethnic group? Which majority decides? Historical experience and theories of democratic behavior are not terribly useful in providing answers to these questions. Robert Dahl made that perfectly clear in his studies of democratic institutions.[3] There are many problems. For one thing, historical experience would indicate that even the people do not have clearly defined political identities. A Catalan is also a Spaniard, a Welshman also English, a Sicilian also an Italian. If anything, therefore, dual or multiple identities would have to be modified in order to create effective democratic institutions, if you accept the notion that the people should create democracy.

Another impediment is the problem of regionalism or localism, because these too militate against the creation of a national identity. The problem is that, often, different ethnic and cultural groups live in a territory. In Bosnia, you have Christians and Muslims living in the same towns and provinces, which is why the United Nations and everyone else is having a difficult time trying to partition the country along neat ethnic lines. What about the native-born Latvians whose parents are Russian? They live all over Latvia. Bilbao, the largest city in the Basque portion of Spain, straddles both sides of a river. On one side live predominantly ethnic Basques; on the other, emigrants from various parts of Spain who speak little or no Basque. Are they part of the Basque people? The problem is multiplied all over Eastern Europe and in what used to be the Soviet Union.

Are people willing to relocate into better defined ethnic groups so that democratic nations can be created? Are families with local ties and relatives willing to move out of Bilbao back to Andalusia? What about the Russians who moved to Latvia in the 1950s? If one could do that, then the old Yugoslavia would be three or four neat little areas and one could establish national democracies of the people. But the reality is that nobody is willing to leave home for the sake of racial or ethnic purity. They would rather fight civil wars (as in Yugoslavia), start nationalist wars (as in the old Soviet Union), or exploit technology and effective managerial practices to exterminate whole peoples (as Hitler tried in the 1930s and 1940s with Jews, Gypsies, and various ethnic groups in Eastern Europe).

The solution is to work with existing national governments to democratize them if they are not democracies today, and to reinforce those institutions if already on the path to representative forms of government. It means that these governments should be encouraged to recognize and embrace the existence of multicultural groups within a nation state and give them the ability to participate in decision making through use of democratic institutions. The case of Spain illustrates one of the best examples of that strategy, and that is why we devoted so much attention to it. Carried to its next level of development, what you would want to do is foster development of what Professor Juan Linz has termed, "pluralism of individuals."[4] He and many other political scientists have concluded that the rights of individuals are more important for the health of a democracy than the rights of a nationalist or regional group because groups want to protect their rights at the expense of those of others. In a democracy, that is a formula for disaster.

Is the notion of building democracies by encouraging them through national groups and evolving to a pluralism of the individual difficult to implement? Clearly, the answer is yes, but it is a strategy that is realistic. Complexities come in many forms. For example, if leaders running a national government convert that institution into a democratic form, will those individuals, if they are members of an ethnic majority, allow regional (federated) governments to compromise the rights of members of the majority in a particular part of the nation in order to meet the demands of local voters? Asked another way, using Spain as the example, will the Castilian leadership in Madrid, which brought democracy to Spain, allow a regional government, voted into power by local voters, to force Spanish-speaking Andalusian children who attend school to receive their instruction in the Catalan language?

If democratic institutions can be created through the avenue of modified national governments, then a second step can be taken: reinforcement of democratic values through social policies. Here we believe that there is a profound role to be played by educators and sociologists in influencing what the handed-down values are of the citizens of a democracy. That American and European scholars and political elites understand fully the rules of economic health and political interplay is very clear. What appears to be missing is the incorporation of sociopsychological dimensions into leadership thinking. European sociologists have certainly come into their own in the past two decades and are conducting excellent behavioral studies in each of the major democracies. But their efforts have not been linked to cooperation by political scientists to examine how much further sociological studies must be developed in order to predict prospects for democracy's survival.

Close study of the upbringing of today's children and what they hear in the home, in the street, and in school can arm the political leadership of a nation with insights on what values need to be changed or reinforced. The combined efforts of scholars from various disciplines can lead to a large pool of useful information that would allow them and political elites to speculate on the best way to insure future positive attitudes toward democracy. Unfortunately, to persuade the legislative bodies in Europe and in the United States to take such studies and relevant recommendations seriously is never an easy task. Legislators and many senior officials in democratic governments tend to push aside "egghead" studies. Nevertheless, we should do our best to encourage European governments, universities, and foundations to move in the direction of multidisciplinary studies of handed-down values as they apply to political behavior.

Given the enormous faith Americans, in particular, place in the positive effects of technology, one issue that frequently comes up is the role of television, personal computers, fax machines, and the like. Dissident Chinese students faxing materials back and forth to friends in the United States while protesting government policies at home was a common image in the late 1980s; so too is the wide popularity of video games on both sides of the Atlantic Ocean.

However, the facts would indicate that, if anything, technology provides a mixed influence on the expansion of democracy. The most important technology in this debate is television, because it is the most massively deployed and effective tool for communicating to large audiences. In large part, Italians were persuaded to change political parties in power in the 1990s because of extensive political campaigning via television. When some military officers attempted to topple the young Spanish democracy, King Juan Carlos appeared immediately on national television wearing a Spanish Army uniform to announce that he and the majority of the armed forces did not approve of the attempted coup; his use of television in that situation had an immediate salutary effect on the nation. So it does have a direct influence on people's thinking. On the other hand, no government in Western Europe, and that includes each of the countries studied by us, is willing to give up national control over local television. As the GATT negotiations in 1993–1994 proved, even the suggestion of having a European-wide open access to television, and in particular to allow U.S. television programming wide access, was absolutely unacceptable, even to the point of almost bringing the negotiations to a halt, despite the fact that the treaty had far more important and valuable components in it for the Europeans. The message is clear: Television is a powerful use of technology that can help or hurt the expansion of democracy, but because it is also seen as an important vehicle for preserving local cultures, any thought of making this tool a European-wide medium has a long way to go.

The "information superhighway" that is so much in the press in the mid-1990s is simply a vehicle for transmitting information in new forms and faster, but not yet a tool for fundamentally altering political behavior. Information has been available across borders in the form of virtually unrestricted use of printed materials. The same is true for telephone calls and use of fax technologies, which are not, for all intents and purposes, restricted by any government. In fact, the only restriction is self-imposed because there are tariffs that must paid for telephone calls crossing international borders. Yet, the use of telephones in Europe is not growing. In short, telephonic technology—at the moment the basis of the information superhighway—appears very benign in so far as it affects political attitudes and behavior in Western Europe.

WHAT ROLE FOR THE UNITED STATES?

Since a central theme of U.S. foreign policy for decades has been fostering of democratic forms of government all over the world, no discussion of how to promote democracy would be complete without suggestions on the American role. The first principle to keep in mind is that American and European policy makers should not take for granted that the foundations of democracy in Western Europe are impregnable. Present and future American policy makers, in particular, should be cautious about believing that free elections will ipso facto guarantee the survival of democracy, not only in Europe but elsewhere. In Argentina, Juan Domingo Peron was freely elected by an overwhelming majority, and yet he destroyed democracy under his tutelage. Other cases abound. But the point is that policy makers should not just run out and indiscriminately promote democracy without careful consideration of both positive and negative possible outcomes.

American policy makers may want to be more selective about where they encourage democratic principles. They also will have to recognize that different strategies will have to be applied across the globe, and that results will come at different speeds. Thus, in one nation, the strategy of promoting development of a middle class might be the correct move today, such as in

Central America,[5] while in another it is the promotion of handed-down values through research projects and educational programs.

A useful vehicle for advising governments targeted by the United States for promotion of democracy is more effective use of diplomats. Ambassadors, cultural attaches, and even American academics whose research is supported by U.S. government grants can all study and counsel government leaders on what to do. To facilitate the process, particularly with regard to the role of American diplomats, they should receive intense training in political sociology and cultural anthropology. This is particularly essential for mid-career Foreign Service Officers who specialize in economic and political work because they are the ones who discuss political issues with foreign leaders on a frequent basis and advise the American government on appropriate actions to take. Training can be folded into the normal training period all diplomats go through at the National Foreign Affairs Training Center in Arlington, Virginia. The objective of such training should be to broaden the vision of specialists to the extent that they become more sensitive to sociopsychological aspects in the countries in which they work which may affect the future of democracy.

Another strategy that should be implemented by the United States, concurrent with expanding the capabilities of diplomats, is to take advantage of the extraordinary American academic infrastructure. But rather than simply hand out research grants to university professors as they individually come forward with ideas for projects, a more organized and focused effort to generate scholarship useful to European and American policy makers makes more sense. One effective approach that has been used repeatedly in the United States to study different topics has been the "think tank." A private, nonprofit foundation should be created in the United States to study intensely fundamental issues of democracy. Such an organization should not be political, but rather have as its mission to apply this nation's extensive academic resources and the skills and experiences of this country's people to the following tasks: to study issues related to the transition to democracy, to study and promote strategies that sustain and reinforce democracies, and to advise political leaders on tactical issues.

Since Americans have adopted the strategy of locating centers of scholarship at the homes of presidents (that is to say, the presidential libraries), one could turn to President James Madison, the most prominent architect of the U.S. Constitution, and establish such a research institute at his home in Virginia. Currently there is no presidential library there to dilute focus from this suggested activity.

Such a strategy would be more than just a clever act of symbolism or of convenience (since the center would be near U.S. policy makers in Washington). The fact is that probably one of the first projects to be tackled, and one that would require concentrated study for decades, concerns constitutions. A very tactical problem for European democracies revolves around the concept of constitutions, particularly in nations accustomed to the principles of Roman law that continue to have bodies of law that reflect such a long-standing legal heritage. In nation after nation, not only in Europe but also across all of Latin and Central America, there appears to be confusion between legislation and a basic charter which stresses fundamental principles. Constitutions are frequently changed, and they are often many times longer than, for example, the U.S. document. Given the success of the American Constitution and the high esteem with which it has been held by Europeans, it makes sense that a central task of such a foundation would be to facilitate the effective use of constitutional law in building democracies.

Finally, the extent of the ability of Americans to influence expansion of democratic principles in other countries is dependent on their ability to make their own society work. In the final analysis, it is the United States as a role model that becomes the most persuasive vehicle for promoting democracy. Alexis de Toqueville may have been one of the first Europeans to comment on the success of American democracy, but he certainly was not the last. When, for example, the Spanish politicians sought to write a Constitution in 1869, they were so impressed with the success of American society that they literally copied whole passages from the U.S. Constitution into their own.[6] The American model profoundly influenced the reconstruction of European society after World War II. But while the American experience has undoubtedly served as a beacon to many nations, the long-term influence of the United States will depend on how effective we are in dealing with problems of corruption, unemployment, crime, inadequate public education in major cities, racism, and economic growth. In nations without much awareness of what democracy implies, security and employment under undemocratic regimes will vie with alternatives implicit in an open society. Failure in the United States to cope with the ills of its own society will profoundly and negatively affect democracy's prospects in areas long characterized by behavioral patterns in conflict with democratic values.

Democracy has many faces, and where it takes root the political structure reflects unique characteristics derived from the national cultural mores and handed-down values. That is why any American effort to promote the expansion of democratic forms of government must involve a variety of approaches implemented at the same time.

However, a realistic assessment of the prospects of democracy would have to include the realization that no amount of American and international economic and technical assistance will enable democracy to emerge where fundamental beliefs and attitudes of a nation or area are severely at odds with those essential to political systems and requirements of a democracy. Haiti, vast portions of Africa, and equally vast areas in Asia and the Middle East come to mind very quickly. To the extent that we understand historical forces, handed-down values, and constitutional and legal traditions, the American government can pick where and how to promote democracy.

CONCLUSION

The nurturing, preservation, or initiation of real democracy is some of the most difficult work that any nation's leaders can undertake. Leaving aside rhetoric and nominal or superficial attempts at representative government, it remains a difficult task because of the enormous amount of years involved and the fundamental requirement that the values of a people (a nation) be consistent with what makes democracy work. Because so few individuals can make such a project successful, governments are probably better served if they reinforce national values (handed-down values) and those characteristics so important to the welfare of a successful democracy (e.g., education, thriving middle class). This recommendation is as important for a well-established democracy, such as the United States, as it is for a newly minted one, as in the case of Spain. Britain, France, Italy, and Germany are not immune from the requirement that they keep working on reinforcing key success factors.

Democracy is not guaranteed anywhere. The United States, where, in times of crisis, stress is evident, proves the point. President Abraham Lincoln suspended important personal rights considered crucial to the success of a democracy (e.g., habeas corpus). The United States put Americans of Japanese descent into camps during World War II, a flagrant violation of the civil rights of thousands of U.S. citizens. The point is, nobody is immune from the constant struggle to make democracy work. The European cases illustrate that fragility, but also some excellent success stories. The expansion in women's rights since World War II in all the countries studied is a wonderful example of progress. Expanded franchise and access to political life, made possible in such Mediterranean nations as Spain, Italy, and France, are important and should not be discounted. But, as we have attempted to demonstrate, democracies remain fragile and require additional and constant work to preserve and strengthen.

Chapter 9 offers additional ideas that take the grand strategic perspective we have concerned ourselves with in this chapter to a more detailed level. As in any other human activity, intent must be followed by strategy and then by tactics. So it must be with freedom and its political mirror, democracy.

NOTES

1. Nathan Rosenberg and L. E. Birdzell, Jr., *How the West Grew Rich: The Economic Transformation of the Industrial World* (New York: Basic Books, 1986).

2. Henry Kissinger, *Diplomacy* (New York: Simon and Schuster, 1994), 141, 814–816.

3. Robert Dahl, *Democracy and Its Critics* (New Haven: Yale University Press, 1989), 1–9.

4. Juan Linz, visiting guest lecturer on democracy, University of Wisconsin at Madison, 29 April 1994.

5. James N. Cortada and James W. Cortada, *U.S. Foreign Policy in the Caribbean, Cuba, and Central America* (New York: Praeger, 1985), 2–3, 179–184.

6. Joaquin Oltra, *La influencía norteamericana en la constitución española de 1869* (Madrid: Instituto de Estudios Administrativos, 1972).

—9—

Moving from the Strategic to the Tactical

The genius of good leadership is to leave behind a situation which common sense, even without the grace of genius, can deal with successfully.

—Walter Lippmann

This chapter is devoted to the discussion of how to implement the findings of the previous chapters at a tactical level. A road map for action is described.

The cases from Western Europe demonstrate three realities. First, successful democracies are the result of historically long-standing political and cultural preconditions which are exploited by a national government that chooses to evolve into a democratic form. These are various, but include a society's attitude toward the role of law and government, rights of the individual versus those of the state, sense of national identity (with associated perceived national traits), and specific historical experiences (e.g., rule of great leaders, consequences of wars, and civil wars).

Second, there are several key social and economic circumstances that make it possible to sustain and enhance democratic forms of government. These include relative economic prosperity making it possible to sustain a middle class, and a literate and better-educated population than is required to run an authoritarian state. An expanded role for women that transcends more traditional, even agrarian, forms of lifestyles also appears to be crucial. We see this in women going to school, working, and practicing birth control with significant effects on how children are raised and what values they are taught. Internal migration from the countryside to the city in substantial numbers appears to be a factor as well, since this disrupts more traditional social bonds and patterns of political behaviors, creating new social dynamics and needs.

Third, democracies are not guaranteed to be permanent features in Europe. In fact, Western Europe's experience with democratic forms of government are recent—far less extensive than, for example, monarchies and other forms of personal rule that ranged from the enlightened to the absolute harshness of authoritarianism (i.e., kings, dictators, emperors, manor and war lords). Democracies are fragile, do not have a constancy about them that, for example, a forty-year dictatorship might have, and thus, we must conclude, are always at risk.

Because of the enormous popularity of democracy evident in the Western world at the end of the twentieth century, we can also assume that extraordinary attention will be paid, if necessary, to preserve this form of government. As suggested throughout this book, Europe's democracies have grown up and survived so far because of conditions identified that operate without any conscious guiding hand. To reinforce democracies in the West and to get to the next level of permanence and effectiveness of this form of government requires additional overt efforts by a society. Knocking down communism or exiling a dictator is only a primitive first step. We believe that many tactical actions are also required. These are the same steps one would take to preserve democracy in France or to introduce it into Eastern Europe. Beyond grand strategy—what nations and societies should do in general terms—are less glamorous tactical steps, many of which are linked to an understanding of what needs to happen in specific cases. It is to that level of work we now turn to suggest a tighter framework for action.

UNDERSTANDING EXISTING REALITIES

Essentially, our framework calls for taking the three sets of dynamics and understanding the degree to which they exist and influence political behavior in a nation or ethnic group. Over time, one should be able to develop a set of "success indicators" by which a society can be measured to identify gaps in performance. Figure 9.1 is a simple example of the kind of display of historical realities that must be understood. For each line, one can develop a set of questions to answer and rank the relative performance of a society against those. We created a range from authoritarian to democratic conditions, using that spectrum because the historical reality for all European nations studied by us is that they have defined their options for governance in terms of authoritarian (highly centralized) or more democratic (representative) forms of rule with variations occurring from one extreme to the other.

We suggest that other historical preconditions could be added to the chart. Then, for each line in Figure 9.1, political scientists and sociologists can develop a set of questions whose answers indicate at which end of the spectrum a society sits. For example, take the first line item, "History of strong one-

FIGURE 9.1
Sample Historical Preconditions Assessment

Authoritarian	Democratic
History of strong one-man rule	History of strong regional or legislative rule
Rule of power	Rule of law
Diverse political views	Homogeneous political views
Little value for human life	High value for human life
Little respect for civil and political rights	Tradition of civil and political rights

man rule." One could look at French history and ask to what extent has one-man rule dominated and, for that matter, been perceived as relatively effective in providing economic and political stability? If the answer is "to a great extent," then one would note that fact as being a condition more to the left of the chart than the right. "Rule of power" is the second line. A set of questions needs to be developed that define the extent of the role of the rule of power versus the rule of law in France over many centuries. The answers would allow a political scientist or historian to annotate the chart with a judgment as to which end of the spectrum French society lies.

Figure 9.2 is a fictitious filled-out chart on French preconditions. If one wanted to promote democracy in France, one would quickly be able to go down each line and determine which factors cause France to be at risk and hence need to be worked on, while those conditions that make it possible for France to do well simply need either to be left alone or be protected from erosion. Thus, as we see in this case, strong one-man rule needs to be avoided in the future or legal and constitutional conditions created that channel strong leadership through a more representative and effective political system. Little needs to be done with civil and political rights, since this is a nation with a proud tradition of cherishing such values—a critical success factor for any democracy.

FIGURE 9.2
Sample Historical Preconditions Assessment: France

Authoritarian	Democratic

History of strong   ●   History of strong regional
one man rule   or legislative rule

Rule of power   ●   Rule of law

Diverse political views   ●   Homogeneous political views

Little value for human life   High value for human life
                            ●

Little respect for civil and   Tradition of civil and
political rights   ●   political rights

A similar exercise must then be undertaken for key social, economic, and handed-down value indicators. We believe a gap analysis similar to what we proposed in Figure 9.1 needs to be developed for each of the major topic areas: education of children, rights of women, demographics, and economic health. Figure 9.3 illustrates education. For each line item, a set of measurable questions must be asked that can lead to a similar assessment as demonstrated in Figure 9.1.

Take the first line item, "Low literacy," and think about the kinds of questions we need to ask: What is the aggregate illiteracy? What is the projected illiteracy rate in ten, twenty, and thirty years? What is the literacy rate by generation? Obviously we are interested most in younger generations. We propose that a weighting factor be applied to this topic so that greater emphasis is placed on the circumstances of younger people:

Ages 6–15	45 percent
Ages 16–30	35 percent
Ages 31–60	15 percent
Ages 61+	5 percent

FIGURE 9.3
Sample Education Realities

Authoritarian	Democratic
Low literacy	High literacy
Limited access to public education	Extensive access to public education
Political science not taught	Political science core element of curriculum
Pedagogy emphasizes rote memory	Pedagogy emphasizes debate and questioning
Few university graduates	Expanding number of university graduates
Emphasizes role of rulers	Emphasizes national traditions

The lower the weighted score, the more the assessment in Figure 9.3 would be to the left; the higher the score, the more to the right. A similar analysis could be done by ethnic or social groups; for example, for Italians of southern descent versus Italians of northern descent. That kind of data give you a quick assessment of the nation's literacy component as it affects democracy and, more tactically, tells public officials where to concentrate elementary education programs.

Another line item is political science taught versus not taught. In healthy democracies, children are introduced to concepts of political science, usually in classes devoted to the topic (e.g., in the United States, called civics or government) and through lectures on history at various ages. One can ask questions that establish how frequently in the education of a child civics is taught (e.g., number of classes): When is the child taught civics, and how does the government work? How many classes or teaching hours is this exposure? What is the quality of this training? What is the correlation between children exposed to this education and their fulfillment of civil duties (e.g., voting, serving on juries)?

One other education example illustrates the exercise: emphasis on the role of rulers versus national traditions. Leaving aside the value of teaching children about examples of great leaders who serve as role models (e.g., George Washington, Winston Churchill, King Louis XIV), one should think in terms of cult of personality. Children in China were taught to almost worship Mao as a diety, while in France in the mid-1800s Napoleon Bonaparte and Napoleon III were lionized. We also have how Hitler was presented to German students in the 1930s. At the other extreme are models from the United States and Great Britain, in which emphasis is placed on the role of Congress and Parliament, and on the institutions of government, service to nation, worship of principles of democracy, and law (e.g., First Amendment, Magna Carta).

With questions answered for each line in a more mature version of Figure 9.3, we have a picture of what education's current and anticipated role is in a society. That tells public officials what areas to concentrate on to enhance the probability of democracy working.

Demographics represents an important area that our research indicates must be seen within the context of democracy's viability. Specifically, our analysis of internal migrations in Europe since the end of World War II appears to suggest a profoundly important area worthy of further investigation, because when citizens move away from the community in which they grew up, they invariably do not bring with them all of the social values and rituals of their past; they are modified by new circumstances, many of which are beyond their control. For example, if in early life all relatives lived in the same community as an individual did, chances are that the individual spent some time each week with many relatives, thereby elevating family life and values to a central point in that individual's values and routine. If that person then leaves the community and moves to some city hundreds of miles away where he or she has few or no relatives, the time originally spent with the family is by necessity spent on other activities: work, watching soccer games, hobbies, or whatever, but not with the family because there is no family around. We could, therefore, hypothesize that the role of the family, and the values attached to family rituals and beliefs, would erode to be replaced by others. We need to understand that process in the context of democracy's performance.

Obvious questions that come to mind, therefore, involve both the physical movement of people and what happens to those who have moved. We might even want to validate another assumption: that those who remain behind do not fundamentally change their habits or values. What kinds of questions need to be answered?

For demographics, the following are important:

1. How many and to what extent do people migrate within a nation?
2. Has this internal migration increased, decreased, or stayed constant over the years?
3. What groups or generations within a society have or are participating in this internal migration?

These kinds of questions are very important because, in every case we have looked at, with the exception of Great Britain, there have been profound internal migrations involving millions of people over the past fifty years. Some of that was the consequences of the massive dislocations of refugees as a result of events in World War II, and some was a by-product of fundamental changes in employment patterns. This is as true for Italy as for Spain, Germany, and France.

We need to recognize this reality and understand its implications for democracy. To date, most studies of this migration have focused solely on economic effects. It is time to broaden our understanding of what might, in historical hindsight, be one of the more profound changes that has occurred in the second half of the twentieth century in Europe.

The following questions are important for patterns of behavior:

1. What were the effects of migration on marriage, social relations, and identity with community?

2. What influence did the new surroundings have on religion, education, and family values?

3. What were the results in terms of personal (physical) security, citizen judgment of the effectiveness of government, and, more specifically, police, education, and social services?

4. What role did changing economic conditions and standards of living have on attitudes toward government, politics, and citizenship?

Much of this can be identified through surveys and an actual nose count of what percentage of people vote (men, women, and by generation).

Then there is the issue of women. Our survey of Western European patterns indicates an almost universal expansion of women's rights in the past thirty years, with as yet ill-defined consequences for child rearing, career aspirations, and demographics. In each country, divorce, use of contraceptives, various civil liberties involving voting and management of family assets, and entry into a much broader set of jobs by more highly educated women will come to be seen in the decades to follow as a profound shift in European society. We believe this shift will be judged to have been as significant as the internal migrations that occurred at the same time by the same people. For all intents and purposes, the legal changes profoundly influenced every Western European within one generation. The extent of such social change has not been seen in Europe since perhaps the start of the Industrial Revolution in the eighteenth century, and is more profound than that earlier transformation.

What topics concerning women need to be understood and placed into an assessment tool similar to Figure 9.1? Figure 9.4 suggests some of the key indicators we would want assessed. This illustration has less to do with feminism or women's rights and more to do with what role women play that affects democracy. The change in women's affairs has been so profound and complex that Figure 9.4 does not come close to identifying all the key indicators nations need to assess women's influence on democracy. But it is a start.

The questions that need to be asked are the same as those raised in the previous six chapters. However, Figure 9.4 suggests more consciously the major areas in which these questions must be asked.

FIGURE 9.4
Sample Role of Women

Authoritarian	Democratic
Low investment in education	High investment in education
Limited job opportunities	Extensive job opportunities
Primary child rearer	Shared child rearing with husband and state
Limited legal rights	Legal rights same as men
Few civil liberties	Many civil liberties
Limited political role	Expanding political role
Low internal migration	High internal migration
Predominately rural	Predominately urban

Our suggestions, figures, and questions may seem an unsophisticated gimmick to a political scientist or economist, but make no mistake about the intent—to clearly define issues and variables in terms that are *actionable*. The approach of identifying issues in that form, and then becoming quite specific between realities and aspirations (gaps), is a methodology familiar to business and public-sector managers as sound practices. We are proposing that some approach like this be expanded to include the more academic analyses that are required, not simply to assist public officials.

HANDED-DOWN VALUES

Armed with the kind of data and analysis we are proposing, placed in a frame of reference that, for any given country, key existing attributes support or work against the prospects of democracy, we can then impose on the analysis the question of handed-down values. Once we get past the physical realities of people (e.g., where they live, how old they are, their legal rights, types of jobs they have, and levels of education), one can then ask other questions:

- What do they believe in?
- What are they prepared to act on? To what extent?
- How do they treat each other privately and publicly?
- To what extent do a people display those attributes considered by political scientists to be essential to the success of a democracy?
- How have these values changed over time?

We would submit that handed-down values involve answering these questions concerning the following key themes:

- Give-and-take and compromise in personal behavior.
- Extent to which individual opinions are taken into account in personal, professional, and public decisions.
- Value of civic ethics.
- Value of legal rights for all sexes, ethnic minorities, and age groups.
- Importance of individual versus societal responsibilities.
- Role and importance of family versus the individual or society (the state).
- National characteristics displayed in personal behavior (e.g., individualism in Italy versus authoritarianism in Germany).

These seven variables capture the essence of the questions we raised throughout this book concerning handed-down values. In fact, this list becomes the condensed summary of the attributes of a society required to answer these two questions: What are the prospects of a nation remaining democratic? What areas require additional work to facilitate implementing or sustaining a democracy? All of the other factors—the role of women, education, demographics, and so on—were simply input into our understanding of handed-down values because it is these values that motivate the behavior of people in their public lives.

Imposed on any view of handed-down values are historical realities. We know, for example, that two conditions must exist for democracy's long-term success: A society must be willing to peacefully change its elected officials when circumstances call for that (no revolutions please), and a society must practice democratic principles for at least two generations to increase confidence in the viability of such a form of government.

Those two conditions are a function of national attributes, which are largely a magnification of individual behavior. In other words, handed-down values focus on the activities of individuals—national characteristics on those of a people. Add in specific historical experiences in the formation of national characteristics and you have the makings of a believable assessment of both the prospects of democracy and what areas need work to bolster the process of democracy's success. Obviously, what can complicate this line of thinking is the fact that no population is completely homogeneous; variations exist in each case. Even the British are experiencing this problem—leaving aside the Irish, Scots, or Welsh for the moment—because so many people about which we know little moved to Britain from the ex-colonies beginning in the 1960s. In France, Italy, Germany, and Spain we have long-standing ethnic subcultures of varying definition and intensity, all providing complexity to our picture. In time, these variations will have to be accounted for, as the realities of the Balkans is making so clear.

A ROAD MAP FOR WHAT TO DO NEXT

The challenge facing an academic studying democracy is both to do the kind of useful and relevant analysis required to better understand democracy's attributes and future, and to suggest what should be changed. For the policy maker, the issue is even more narrow, in that the problem is to identify what specific problems need to be addressed and what programs to implement now. Each is dealing with a variation on a theme. The scholar needs a methodology to ask and answer relevant questions leading to a confidence that "he or she got it right." The government official needs to have confidence that he or she is making decisions about the "right issues," and is applying policies and programs that will lead to predictable results. Simply dismissing the need for an analysis with some statement to the effect that, "I will only do what is politically expedient," is to misunderstand how government officials really attempt to operate.

It is a characteristic of our age that specificity is as important to the government official as it is to the scholar. The scientific approach to the study of politics and to the management of nations has long been a given. And yet there are differences between the two constituencies that must be accounted for. The authors have, for example, looked askance at the propensity of political scientists to build models of political behavior because models inherently assume static conditions—convenient for a professor but absolutely unrealistic for a policy maker. On the other hand, a policy maker, who is dealing with constant change and usually is reacting to immediate pressures and conditions, would like to have a methodologically-based approach to broad strategic policy issues that are rooted in the disciplines of the academic. The academic wants to define the issues and document patterns of behavior, while the politico desires the collective wisdom of historians, political scientists, economists, educators, and cultural anthropologists, all rolled into one tidy package.

As the educational experiences of both academics and policy makers have become similar over the past two decades, one can understand how their differences are shrinking. For example, both have increasingly become products of the same university programs. Graduates of leading European universities go into government and faculties. Some even switch back and forth. This is especially the case in democratic societies. President Clinton was once a professor of law, while Dr. Henry Kissinger was both a Secretary of State and a professor of political science. In Europe, professors often staff cabinet-level positions in France, Germany, and Italy. In Franco's Spanish governments in the late 1950s and extending through the post-dictatorship governments, cabinet-level members have occasionally been faculty members, especially in the technical portfolios (e.g., economics, finance, and education). What we do not see happening in Europe to the extent evident in the United States is a policy maker moving back to academia. In the United States, it is not uncommon for an ex-cabinet official or ex-congressional representative to go to work for a think tank or join a faculty. The Kennedy School of Government at Harvard University, for example, is filled with ex-government officials doing real academic work. So the desire to apply scientific methods to the rough-and-tumble world of politics, and particularly democratic politics, remains. The problem is that neither the academic nor the government community has yet developed an effective approach. That has been a major purpose of this book.

Figure 9.5 suggests a start, by providing both communities a road map to suggest how they each get the information they need that will lead to decisions and actions that really influence the prospects for the future of democracy. At first glance, the road map is deceptively simple, but underlying it is the basic assumption that public policy can and should be grounded in multidisciplinary studies (facts) that reflect the "art of the possible." Otherwise, this book and the issues it represents can be characterized as "interesting," but not useful.

The boxes on the far left represent the major components in a society that are important to the fabrication of political behavior influencing the functioning of a democracy. Those are the boxes that scholars from multiple fields have to fill in with the right attributes and the field studies and data required to define them. Since those factors, in turn, profoundly influence the handed-down values in a society, we can then move to the precise definition of those values. We know that handed-down values are also influenced by historical events. Those events, when fused to handed-down values and physical realities (e.g., laws, demographics, educational levels) lead to the development— and definition—of national characteristics. That last addition to our road map provides the political context (or reality) crucial to any policy maker bent on action. The trail of activity, from defining specific attributes of a nation to a clear understanding of national characteristics, makes it possible for both government officials and experts to answer two basic questions raised in this book: What are the prospects for democracy, and, equally important, what needs to get fixed?

We envision this road map operating iteratively. That is to say, for example, as one learns more about demographics, women, education, and the like; since those change, so too does our understanding of handed-down values. And, of

FIGURE 9.5
Road Map for Determining Prospects for Democracy

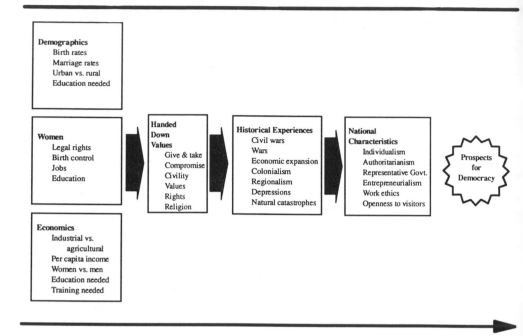

course, every day that comes along brings with it another day's worth of history. The rates of change and the actual content of those changes is greatest to the left of the road map and the least to the right. In other words, the most constant set of conditions upon which to base policy are the national characteristics, while the most volatile are often represented in the boxes to the far left.

Armed with a fact-based, if continuously changing, set of assumptions concerning the prospects for democracy, one can then go back to the individual components represented on the far side of the chart and develop specific policies, programs, and measures of results that give confidence to a society that its form of government is being evolved in a practical and effective manner. Figure 9.6 illustrates the road map extended to incorporate development of national policies, programs, and consensus for action. It takes into account two realities: First, only national governments introduce and sustain democracies and second, the public must be engaged in the process within the context of their daily activities.

Implicit in Figures 9.5 and 9.6 is the assumption that assessments and programs have various timelines and rates of change. We have only just hinted at that feature in this book. For example, if a government wants to encourage internal migration from countryside to city, programs and policies might have

FIGURE 9.6
Road Map for Supporting Democracy's Prospects

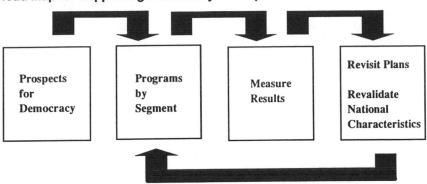

to operate in a five- to twenty-year time frame. Educating a generation in a certain way must function in a time frame closer to twenty years. On the other hand, changing the civil rights of a woman may take less than five years, although we will not see the social consequences for longer periods of time. Some will appear very quickly and others later. For instance, access to the pill will result in an almost immediate change in the pattern of having babies that within two or three years is reflected in official demographic statistics. On the other hand, the increased care and attention given to children, as a result of having fewer and healthier offspring, will not surface until sociologists do studies of these families five, ten, or twenty years later.

This issue of timing is a real problem. It is difficult for academics to know exactly when a change that needs to be studied immediately is occurring in society because most times they are not on the front lines of change, as, for instance, a government official noticing altered patterns of behavior in citizens from programs he or she administers daily would be. The official and, more frequently, national political leaders in a democracy are motivated by the system to respond to immediate concerns in society (e.g., economic conditions, threats of war, etc.) and favor programs that demonstrate results prior to the next elections. In short, long-term policy implementations—which seem to us more appropriate for the creation and survival of democracies—are more difficult to implement in a democratic context.

Ironically, a dictator like Franco, who probably fully expected to spend the rest of his life running Spain, can increase the proportion of long-term policies in government activities more than the president of a country who might not be in office four years later and also has less personal authority. Franco, for instance, could alter the pattern of national politics in favor of constrained rivalries and hence improve the acceptance of give-and-take patterns of behavior, a process that took decades and only became obvious to all involved long after Franco had been in power.

So what is to be done about the problem of timing horizons? Taking a page out of what businesses do suggests a path. Well-run companies face the same problem of timing discontinuities; instead of being one of years versus decades or centuries, it may be months versus years, but the problem is the same. The difference is only one of degree. What they do is to divide all activities into those which are dubbed tactical (e.g., to be done this year or next) and those which are seen as strategic (e.g., an investment for the future and covers two to seven years). Even the world's largest companies, organizations that have as many employees and customers as small nations or states within countries, define long-term strategic directions for the firm. These are hammered out very much the same way a society debates issues. Academics and consultants study issues, they are debated at various levels of the company, and solutions are incrementally implemented and debated again. Eventually, a consensus on direction and the demand for action makes it possible for chief executive officers to articulate a value, policy, or initiative. Senior executives then persuade, normally not mandate, the various constituencies within a company to adhere to their decisions.

In business, a road map for change emerges that is similar to what is represented in Figure 9.5. On the far left of a corporate road map would be issues concerning current and planned products, customers, competition, financing, and infrastructure. Corporate handed-down values are the beliefs of the employees about how to run the business (e.g., role of quality management practices, attitudes toward customers and suppliers), while historical experience is exactly as in a society: events that test and modify values and issues. The same wars, economic variables, and social patterns are added, along with the more specific developments important to a company (e.g., sale of its products to its customers). Substitute corporate culture for national characteristics and the analogy continues. Corporate culture could include such basic beliefs as "employees are treated with respect" (as at IBM), or "the customer is always right" (as at many retail operations). Other attributes could include how behavior occurs: concensus building, fact-based decision making, chain-of-command authority, or sharing of profits with employees. Interestingly, many corporate characteristics are the same or similar to those evident in the society in which the company was created. American companies reflect the values of American society. Japanese companies are very Japanese in their corporate cultures. British and German businesses reflect their local cultures and values. Authoritarian practices, for example, appear most frequently in organizations that were born or operate in societies that reflect authoritarian behavior.

Thus, to draw over to society in general some of the practices evident in business makes sense. If a national leader can channel academic and government resources to identify the current status of democratic practices in the nation and perform a classic gap analysis between what they find out and what the nation aspires to, then national agendas can be set that divide the work to be done into short-term government programs and long-term strategies.

This is very possible to do in government. In the United States, for example, a national aspiration that emerged by the first third of the twentieth century, often called the "American Dream," was the desire of Americans to own their own homes. Over a period of a half century, the U.S. Congress, government agencies, and the banking community collectively and independently developed short and long programs and patterns of behavior that made it possible for Americans to own their own homes. Ask any European visitor to the United States if Americans own their homes more frequently than Europeans and you will hear a resounding yes. Both in Italy and in Spain, the national governments implemented industrialization programs and strategies, transcending two generations, designed to provide employment for the impoverished, agriculturally-based peasantry. In the case of Spain, centers of industrialization were developed both in southern agrarian Iberia and in various parts of the Basque country. In Italy, industrialization in the north was expanded and internal immigration from the south fostered. In the case of Italy, there was the secondary objective of integrating what essentially were two different Italian cultures through the expediency of internal migration. In the case of Spain, especially in the Basque country, the Franco regime wanted to reduce the intensely nationalist Basque attitudes in the north and so flooded the area with job-seeking Andalusians. Over the decades of the Franco regime, the percentage of the population speaking Basque in the home in the northern region declined at the rate of 1 percent per year. (Since his death, that trend has reversed.) In Italy, the percentage of the southern Italian population in the north steadily rose all through the 1960s, 1970s, and into the 1980s. Our point is that strategic national initiatives of long duration are possible to implement: first, if national leaders so choose, and second, if the population is given incentives. And, just as in business, the process of implementing or improving democracy's presence and performance is an interactive process, one that must be under constant review and modification.

For a country that wants to foster democracy outside of its borders—like the United States is trying to do in Latin America, Asia, and in Central and Eastern Europe—it must see itself as democracy's banker, supplier, or customer. Each has a role to play in the success and evolution of a company. The same applies to nations. The United States can provide intellectual capital (e.g., consulting on democracy), provide methodologies for determining what programs are needed on a country-by-country basis to improve the prospects for democracy, and help governments to build the necessary local political, social, and economic infrastructures. Short- and long-term programs can be implemented in a knowing way if both the recipient nation and the U.S. Government understand precisely what is needed. That is the whole point of looking at the kinds of issues addressed in this book.

Can democracy survive in Western Europe? Yes, but it will require continued work. Will democracy spread to Central and Eastern Europe? It is possible for it to spread and stick in the northern part of Central Europe for the same reasons as in the West, but Eastern Europe is problematic. What about the Yugoslavian part of Europe, where the Bosnians and Serbs are battling it out? Since the whole region fought its civil war in the style reminiscent of Spain's conflict of 1936 to 1939, and is also the nearly 1,500-year-old frontier between the Christian and Muslim worlds, the long hand of history presses hard on the shoulders of the area's residents. Democracy as a concept is something even the local school children will not have a chance to read about for a long time. The lesson for Europe is clear: Continue nurturing democracy in the West through sociocultural reinforcement of those patterns of behavior crucial to the successful functioning of democratic forms of government, since it is not a given that it will always thrive. Also, promote the extension of democracy eastward, even though this type of government will be more fragile. Policy makers in the United States, if they are to be more effective in promoting democracy, will have to become more sophisticated students of how that is done.

Selected Bibliography

The bibliography below represents those publications which had the most significant influence on our research. Additional citations can be found in the footnotes.

Adorno, T. W. et al. *The Authoritarian Personality*. New York: Harper, 1950.

Alba, Victor. *Transition in Spain: From Franco to Democracy*. New Brunswick, N.J.: Transaction Books, 1978.

Albornoz., Claudio Sanchez. *La España cristiana de los siglos VIII á XI*. Madrid: Espasa-Calpe, 1980.

Almond, Gabriel A., and Verba, Sidney. *The Civic Culture: Political Attitudes and Democracy in Five Nations*. Princeton, N.J.: Princeton University Press, 1963.

Almond, Gabriel A., and Verba, Sidney. "The Intellectual History of the Civic Culture Concept." In *The Civic Culture Revisited*, ed. Gabriel A. Almond and Sidney Verba, 1–36. Boston: Brown, 1980.

Anderson, Robert D. *France, 1870–1914: Politics and Society*. London: Routledge, 1977.

Arango, E. Ramon. *The Spanish Political System: Franco's Legacy*. Boulder, Colo.: Westwood, 1978.

Arbeloa, Joaquin. *Los Origenes del Reino de Navarra*. 2 vols. San Sebastian: Editorial Aunamendi, 1969.

Ardagh, John. *Germany and the Germans*. London: Penguin, 1991.

Barcellona, Pietro. *La República en transformazione: problemi istutuzionali del caso italiano*. Bari: De Donato, 1978.

Barnes, Samuel H. *Representative in Italy: Institutionalized Tradition and Electoral Choice*. Chicago: University of Chicago Press, 1977.

Barnes, T. D. "Who Were the Nobility in the Roman Empire?" *Phoenix* 28 (1974): 444–449.

Barraclough, Geoffrey. *The Crucible of Europe: The Ninth and Tenth Centuries in European History*. London: Thames and Hudson, 1976.

Bermejo Cabrero, José Luis. *Estudios sobre la administracion central españa (siglos XVI y XVII)*. Madrid: Centrol de Estudios Constitucionales, 1982.

Birch, J. H. S. *Denmark in History*. London: John Murray, 1938.

Birnbaum, Pierre, and Leca, Jean, eds. *Individualism: Theories and Methods*. Oxford: Clarendon Press, 1990.

Bishko, Charles J. *Spanish and Portuguese Monastic History: 600–1300*. London: Valorum, 1984.

Bonjour, E., Offler, H. S., and Potter, G. R. *A Short History of Switzerland*. Oxford: Clarendon Press, 1952.

Bonnassie, Pierre. *La Catalogne*. 2 vols. Toulouse: Publications de l'Universite de Toulouse-Le Marail, 1975.

Bottomore, Tom. *Political Sociology*. Minneapolis: University of Minnesota Press, 1993.

Brandes, Stanley. *Metaphors of Masculinity: Sex and Status in Andalusian Folklore*. Philadelphia: University of Pennsylvania Press, 1990.

Braudel, Fernand. *The Identity of France*. 2 vols. New York: Harper and Row, 1988.

Brown, P. *The Making of Late Antiquity*. Cambridge, Mass.: Harvard University Press, 1978.

Brown, R. Allen. *The Normans and the Norman Conquest*. London: Constable, 1969.

Burns, Michael. *Rural Society and French Politics: Boulangism and the Drefus Affair, 1886–1900*. Princeton, N.J.: Princeton University Press, 1984.

Caine, R. N., and Caine, G. *Making Connections: Teaching and the Human Brain*. Alexandria, Va.: Association for Supervision and Curriculum Development, 1991.

Caroni, Pio. *"Privatrecht": sine sozialhistorische Eifuhrung*. Bassel: Helbing und Lichtenhahn, 1988.

Carr, Raymond. *Spain: 1808–1975*. Oxford: Oxford University Press, 1982.

Carr, Raymond, and Fusi, Juan Pablo. *Spain: Dictatorship to Democracy*. London: Allen and Unwin, 1979.

Churchland, Paul M. *The Engines of Reason, the Seat of the Soul*. Cambridge, Mass.: MIT Press, 1995.

Collingham, H. A. C. *The July Monarchy: A Political History of France, 1830–1848*. London: Longman, 1988.

Collins, Roger. *Early Medieval Spain*. London: Macmillan Press, 1983.

Confessora, Ornella Pellegrino. *Cattolici col papa, leberali con lo Statuto: richerche sci conservatori nazionali (1863–1915)*. Rome: ELIA, 1973.

Connell, R. W. *The Child's Construction of Politics*. Melbourne: Melbourne University Press, 1971.

Connery, Donald S. *The Scandinavians*. London: Eyre & Spottiswoode, 1967.

Corbett, Percy E. *The Roman Law of Marriage*. Oxford: Clarendon Press, 1930.

Cortada, James N., and Cortada, James W. *U.S. Foreign Policy in the Caribbean, Cuba, and Central America*. New York: Praeger, 1985.

Cortada, James W., ed. *Historical Dictionary of the Spanish Civil War, 1936–39*. Westport, Conn.: Greenwood Press, 1982.

Craig, Gordon H. *The Germans*. New York: Meridian, 1991.

Crouch, Colin. "Sharing Public Space: States and Organized Interests in Western Europe." In *States in History*, ed. John A. Hall, 177–210. Oxford: Basil Blackwell, 1986.

Dahl, Robert A. *Democracy and Its Critics*. New Haven: Yale University Press, 1989.

Dahl, Robert A. *Dilemmas of Pluralistic Democracy*. New Haven: Yale University Press, 1982.

Delort, Robert. *Life in the Middle Ages*. New York: Universe Books, 1982.

De Palma, Giuseppe. *Political Syncretism in Italy: History, Coalition Strategies and the Present Crisis*. Berkeley and Los Angeles: University of California Press, 1977.

Donaghy, Peter J., and Newton, Michael T. *Spain: A Guide to Political and Economic Institutions*. Cambridge: Cambridge University Press, 1989.

Donati, Pierpaolo, ed. *Secondo Rapporto Sulla Famiglia en Italia*. Milano: Ediziono Paoline, 1991.

Downing, Brian M. *The Military Revolution and Political Change*. Princeton, N.J.: Princeton University Press, 1992.

Easton, Stewart C. *The Era of Charlemagne: Frankish State and Society*. Princeton, N.J.: Van Nostrand, 1961.

Ehrmann, Henry W. *Politics in France*. Boston: Little, Brown, 1968.

Elliott, John H. *The Revolt of the Catalans: A Study in the Decline of Spain, 1598–1640*. Cambridge: Cambridge University Press, 1963.

Fernandez Conde, Francisco Javier. *La Iglesia de Asturias en la alta edad media*. Oviedo: Deputación de Oviedo, Instituto de Estudios Asturianos, 1972.

Fernandez-Cuesta, Raimundo. *Testimonios, recuerdos y reflexiones*. Madrid: Ediciones Dyrsa, 1985.

Finley, M. I. *Democracy, Ancient and Modern*. New Brunswick, N.J.: Rutgers University Press, 1973.

Finley, M. I., ed. *Studies in Roman Property*. Cambridge: Cambridge University Press, 1976.

Fusi, J. P. *Franco*. London: Unwin, Hyman, 1987.

Gallati, Frieda. *Die Eidgenossenschaft und der Kaiserhof zur Zeit Ferdinands II, und Ferdinands III, 1619–1657*. Zurich: A. G. gebr. Leemann, 1932.

Garnsey, Peter, ed. *Non-Slave Labour in the Greco-Roman World*. Cambridge: Cambridge University Press, 1980.

Garnsey, Peter, and Saller, Richard. *The Roman Empire: Economy, Society and Culture*. London: Duckworth, 1987.

Gillespie, Richard. *The Spanish Socialist Party*. Oxford: Clarendon Press, 1989.

Ginsborg, Paul. *A History of Contemporary Italy, 1943–1988*. London: Penguin, 1990.

Gjerset, Knut. *A History of the Norwegian People*. New York: AMS Press, 1968.

Glick, Thomas F. *Islamic and Christian Spain in the Early Middle Ages*. Princeton, N.J.: Princeton University Press, 1975.

Gordon, Milton M. *The Scope of Sociology*. New York: Oxford University Press, 1988.

Gramont, Sanche de. *The French: Portrait of a People*. New York: G. P. Putnam's Sons, 1969.

Greenstein, Fred I. *Children and Politics*. Rev. ed. New Haven: Yale University Press, 1965.

Gruber, Howard E., and Voneche, J. Jacques, eds. *The Essential Piaget*. New York: Basic Books, 1977.

Hall, Edward T. *An Anthropology of Everyday Life*. New York: Doubleday, 1993.

Hall, John R., and Jarvie, I. C., eds. *Transition to Modernity: Essays on Power, Wealth and Belief*. Cambridge: Cambridge University Press, 1972.

Hammond, M. "Composition of the Senate, AD 68–235." *Journal of Roman Studies* 47 (1957): 74–81.

Hampden-Tanner, Charles. *Radical Man*. Cambridge, Mass.: Schenkman, 1970.

Hancock, M. Donald et al. *Politics in Western Europe*. Chatham, N.J.: Chatham House, 1993.

Hart, L. A. *Human Brain and Human Learning*. New York: Longman, 1983.

Herz, John H., ed. *From Dictatorship to Democracy*. Westport, Conn.: Greenwood Press, 1982.

Hofmann, Paul. *That Fine Italian Hand.* New York: Henry Holt, 1990.

Hooper, John. *The Spaniards.* London: Penguin, 1987.

Hopkins, K. *Death and Renewal.* Cambridge: Cambridge University Press, 1983.

Howe, Neil. *Generations: The History of America's Future, 1584–2069.* New York: William Morrow, 1991.

Huntington, Samuel P. *The Third Wave.* Norman: University of Oklahoma Press, 1993.

Hyde, J. K. *Society and Politics in Medieval Italy: The Evolution of Civil Life, 1000–1350.* New York: St. Martin's Press, 1973.

Inkeles, Alex. "National Character and Modern Political Systems." In *Psychological Anthropology: Approaches to Culture and Personality*, ed. Francis L. K. Hsu, 172–207. Homewood, Ill.: Dorsey, 1961.

Irvine, William D. *The Boulanger Affair Reconsidered: Royalism, Boulangism, and the Origins of the Radical Right in France.* New York: Oxford University Press, 1989.

Johnson, Joe B. "Make Room for Democracy." *Foreign Service Journal* 70 (4; 1993): 16–18.

King, P. D. *Law and Society in the Visigothic Kingdom.* Cambridge: Cambridge University Press, 1972.

Kissinger, Henry. *Diplomacy.* New York: Simon and Schuster, 1994.

Knapton, Ernest John. *France.* New York: Charles Scribner's Sons, 1971.

Lacarra, José María. *Historia del Reino de Navarra en la Edad Media.* Pamplona: Caja de Ahorros de Navarra, 1975.

Lamb, Harold. *Charlemagne: The Legend and the Man.* Garden City, N.Y.: Doubleday, 1954.

Lamsen, J. A. O. *Representative Government in Greek and Roman History.* Berkeley and Los Angeles: University of California Press, 1966.

Lauring, Palle. *A History of Denmark.* Copenhagen: Host & Son, 1981.

Lehmbruch, G. "Consociational Democracy, Class Conflict and the New Corporatism." In *Trends toward Corporatist Intermediation*, ed. P. C. Schmitter and G. Lehmbruch. London: Sage, 1979.

Lewis, Flora. *Europe: Road to Unity.* New York: Simon and Schuster, 1992.

Lieberman, Sima. *The Contemporary Spanish Economy.* London: Allen and Unwin, 1982.

Lijphart, Arend. *Democracies.* New Haven: Yale University Press, 1984.

Lijphart, Arend. *Democracy in Plural Societies.* New Haven: Yale University Press, 1977.

Loyn, Henry R. *Anglo-Saxon England and the Norman Conquest.* Harlow, England: Longman, 1991.

Lukes, Steven. *Individualism.* Oxford: Basil Blackwell, 1973.

Lustick, Ian. *State-Building Failure in British Ireland and French Algeria.* Berkeley: Institute of International Studies, University of California, 1985.

Lynch, John. *Bourbon Spain: 1700–1808.* Oxford: Basil Blackwell, 1989.

MacFarlane, Alan. *The Origins of English Individualism.* Cambridge: Cambridge University Press, 1978.

Madariaga, Salvador de. *Englishmen, Frenchmen, Spaniards.* London: Oxford University Press, 1949.

Madge, John. *The Origins of Scientific Sociology.* New York: Free Press, 1967.

Maxwell, Kenneth, and Spiegel, Steven. *The New Spain.* New York: Council on Foreign Relations Press, 1994.

McDonald, Henry. *The Normative Basis of Culture*. Baton Rouge: Louisiana State University Press, 1986.
McNair, John M. *Education for a Changing Spain*. Manchester, England: Manchester University Press, 1984.
Merida, María. *Entrevista con La Iglesia*. Barcelona: Planeta, 1982.
Moberg, Vilhelm. *A History of the Swedish People*. New York: Pantheon Books, 1972.
Moore, Barrington, Jr. *Political Power and Social Theory*. Cambridge, Mass.: Harvard University Press, 1958.
Moore, Barrington, Jr. *Social Origins of Dictatorship and Democracy*. Boston: Beacon Press, 1966.
Mundos, Equipo. *Los 90 Ministros de Franco*. Barcelona: DOPESA, 1970.
Munoz Alonso, Alejandro. *Las Elecciones del cambio*. Barcelona: Editorial Argos Vergara, 1984.
O'Callaghan, Joseph F. *A History of Medieval Spain*. Ithaca, N.Y.: Cornell University Press, 1975.
Orum, Anthony M., ed. *The Seeds of Politics: Youth and Politics in America*. Englewood Cliffs, N.J.: Prentice-Hall, 1972.
Patrucco, Armand. *The Critics of the Italian Parliamentary System, 1860–1915*. New York: Garland, 1991.
Payne, Stanley G. *Falange*. Stanford: Stanford University Press, 1962.
Payne, Stanley G. *A History of Fascism, 1914–1945*. Madison: University of Wisconsin Press, 1995.
Payne, Stanley G. *Regimen de Franco, 1936–1975*. Madrid: Alianza, 1987.
Payne, Stanley G. *Spain's First Democracy: The Second Republic, 1931–1936*. Madison: University of Wisconsin Press, 1993.
Payne, Stanley G. *Spanish Catholicism: A Historical Overview*. Madison: University of Wisconsin Press, 1984.
Payne, Stanley G. *The Spanish Revolution*. New York: W. W. Norton, 1970.
Pennock, J. Roland. *Democratic Political Theory*. Princeton, N.J.: Princeton University Press, 1979.
Perez-Diaz, Victor M. *The Return of Civil Society: The Emergence of Democratic Spain*. Cambridge, Mass.: Harvard University Press, 1993.
Peristany, J. G., ed. *Honour and Shame: The Values of Mediterranean Society*. Chicago: University of Chicago Press, 1974.
Petras, James. "Spanish Socialism: The Politics of Neoliberalism." In *Mediterranean Paradoxes: Politics and Social Structure in Southern Europe*, ed. James Kurth and James Petras, 95–127. Oxford: Berg, 1993.
Pierce, John C., and Pride, Richard A., eds. *Cross-National Micro-Analysis*. 2 vols. Berkeley Hills, Calif.: Sage, 1972.
Powers, James F. *A Society Organized for War: Iberian Municipal Militias in the Central Middle Ages, 1000–1284*. Berkeley and Los Angeles: University of California Press, 1988.
Preston, Paul. *The Triumph of Democracy in Spain*. London: Methuen, 1986.
Pridham, Geoffrey, ed. *Encouraging Democracy*. New York: St. Martin's Press, 1991.
Prost, Antoine, and Vincent, Gerard, eds. *A History of Private Life*. Vol. 5. Cambridge, Mass.: Harvard University Press, 1991.
Putnam, Robert D. *Making Democracy Work: Civic Tradition in Modern Italy*. Princeton, N.J.: Princeton University Press, 1994.
Ridruejo, Dionisio. *Casi Unas Memorias*. Barcelona: Planeta, 1976.

Rosenberg, Nathan, and Birdzell, L. E., Jr. *How the West Grew Rich: The Economic Transformation of the Industrial World.* New York: Basic Books, 1986.

Rubio Cabeza, Manuel. *Diccionario de la Guerra Civil España.* 2 vols. Barcelona: Planeta, 1987.

Rutkoff, Peter M. *Revanche and Revision: The Ligue des Patriotes and the Origins of the Radical Right in France, 1882–1900.* Athens: Ohio State University Press, 1981.

Safran, William. *The French Polity.* London: Longman, 1991.

Saller, R. P. "Patria Potestas and the Stereotype of the Roman Family." *Continuity and Change* 1 (1986): 7–22.

Saraceno, Chiara. *Il Lavero Mal Diviso.* Bari: De Donato Editore Spa, 1990.

Sartori, Giovanni. *The Theory of Democracy Revised.* Chatham, N.J.: Chatham House, 1987.

Schoffer, Ivo. *A Short History of the Netherlands.* Amsterdam: Albert de Lange, 1973.

Shaw, B. D. "The Divine Economy: Stoicism as Ideology." *Latomus* 44 (1985): 16–54.

Shreir, Sally, ed. *Women's Movements of the World.* London: Longman, 1988.

Shubert, Adrian. *A Social History of Modern Spain.* London: Unwin Hyman, 1990.

Smith, Denis Mack. *Italy.* Ann Arbor: University of Michigan Press, 1959.

Smith, Goldwin. *A Constitutional and Legal History of England.* New York: Charles Scribner's Sons, 1952.

Solsten, Eric, and Meditz, Sandra W., eds. *Spain: A Country Study.* Washington, D.C.: Federal Research Division, Library of Congress, 1990.

Spiegel, Steven. *The New Spain.* New York: Council on Foreign Relations Press, 1994.

Spotts, F., and Weiser, T. *Italy: A Difficult Democracy.* Cambridge: Cambridge University Press, 1968.

Stradling, R. A. *Philip IV and the Government of Spain, 1621–1665.* Cambridge: Cambridge University Press, 1988.

Syme, Ronald. *Tacitus.* 2 vols. Oxford: Oxford University Press, 1958.

Taylor, A. J. P. *The Course of German History.* New York: Capricorn Books, 1962.

Thompson, David. *Democracy in France since 1870.* London: Oxford University Press, 1964.

Thorn, John, Lockyer, Roger, and Smith, David. *A History of England.* New York: Thomas Y. Crowell, 1961.

Treppiari, Susan. *Roman Marriage: Iusti Coniuges from the Time of Cicero to the Time of Ulpian.* Oxford: Clarendon Press, 1991.

Tuñon Lara, Manuel de, ed. *Historia de España,* vol. 9 of *La Crisis del Estado: Dictadura, República, Guerra.* Barcelona: Editorial Labor, 1992.

Valdeavellano, Luis G. de. *Curso de historia de las instituciones españolas.* Madrid: Revista de Occidente, 1968.

Vazquez Gomez, Gonzalo. *Los Valores de los Niños Españoles 1992.* Madrid: CESMA, 1993.

Weber, Eugene J. *Action Française.* Stanford: Stanford University Press, 1962.

Zeldin, Theodore. *The Political System of Napoleon III.* London: Macmillan, 1958.

Index

ABOUT THE AUTHORS

JAMES N. CORTADA is a retired diplomat and former dean of the School of Professional Studies at the Foreign Service Institute. He is the author (with James W. Cortada) of *U.S. Foreign Policy in the Caribbean* (Praeger, 1985).

JAMES W. CORTADA is a historian and author of over 30 books, including *Information Technology as Business History* (Greenwood, 1996). Dr. Cortada is a member of the IBM Consulting Group.

ISBN 0-275-95680-6

90000>

EAN

9 780275 956806

HARDCOVER BAR CODE